☝ Y0-BZL-601

Bishop
Hurricane
Winn SR.

LET'S GO GET THEM!

TAKE HIM
TO THE STREETS

Jonathan Gainsbrugh

HUNTINGTON ⟨H⟩ HOUSE INC.

Shreveport ● Lafayette
Louisiana

Copyright © 1985 by Jonathan Gainsbrugh
Printed in the United States of America
ISBN 0-910311-26-9
Library of Congress Catalog Number 84-062779

Acknowledgements

First of all, I want to thank my helpmeet, Jeanette Grace, for being the best wife in the world. Not only is she the matchless mother of my three pearls, Heaven, Christmas and Christian Israel, but she has been a direct gift from God to help my life shine brighter each day with His Life, His Light and His Love!

I would like to take this opportunity to thank everyone everywhere that has helped me in one way or another to not just get this book written, but edited, and printed as well. My thanks go to:

Rocky and Lynna Akers

Mike and Peggy Wells

Margie Olafson

Tom & Sue Leding

Jim and Darry Anderson

John and Honey Karr

Richard Ventonis

Sarah Duncan

Carl and Sue Kennedy

Helen Hayden Scott

Ivan and Ruth French

Rocky and Barbara Jenkins

All of my Advisory Board, friends, and partners who working together as the Body of Christ have made this book, this reprinting, and this ministry possible!

Foreword

TAKE HIM TO THE STREETS is actually two books in one. The first book or major division, "Stepping Out," includes:

Section I. "Why Reach Out"

Section II. "Outreach"

This material gives comprehensive in-depth teaching that will challenge and inspire EVERY believer who reads it. Every Christian reader will discover scores of ways to increase the extent and effectiveness of his personal evangelism, and the personal soulwinning ministry that Jesus Christ has commanded each of His followers to be engaged in "out in the hedges and highways, compelling the lost to come in" (Luke 14:23).

For example, the material on "How To Write Your Own Personal Testimony Tract," "Tract Evangelism," "The Top 40 Soulwinning Mistakes to Avoid," and the inspirational section on "Turnarounds," will help and encourage any Christian from the newest convert to the most deeply grounded saint.

The second book within TAKE HIM TO THE STREETS, entitled "Street Outreaches," includes detailed information on coffeehouse/street outreaches including:

Section I.   "The Need for Street Outreaches"

Section II. "Inreach
            (The Ministry Inside the Outreach)"

Section III. "Backup (The Business Ministry Behind
            the Scene)"

Section IV. "26 Steps to Opening Night
            (How To Get Started)"

While the second "book" on Outreaches may not appeal to every Christian, it definitely IS intended for every town and area. In the United States alone there are over 3,000 cities with populations of over 5,000 people, as well as over 2,000 colleges and universities. Of these 3,000 towns and 2,000 colleges, how many have Christian coffeehouse/street-outreaches open on weekend nights featuring live music and LIVING Christianity to reach their lost young people with the eternal Gospel? If not, how many need them?

The Author

Jonathan Gainsbrugh, a theology graduate of Oral Roberts University in 1976, met Jesus Christ as his personal Lord and Saviour while hitchhiking in the summer of 1969, because of a young couple involved in reaching out near Sacramento, California.

He grew up the son of a presidential economic advisor on what some might call "easy street." His house had its own private tennis court, pool table, and indoor basketball court. His upbringing included summer camp in the Maine Woods and vacations to the Virgin Islands, Bermuda, Haiti, Puerto Rico, the Bahamas, and Europe. Despite all of this, there was a spiritual emptiness inside him.

Dropping out of college and society in 1966, Jonathan became a professional "flower child," criss-crossing America dozens of times during the next three and a half years, living the "hip" counterculture street-life in crash pads and communes from London to New York. He spent the majority of the time in San Francisco's now famous Haight-Ashbury district. He met a real born-again Christian in the summer of 1969, and consequently was born again.

Since that time he has worked in differing capacities and various ministries, fulfilling God's call of evangelism on his life. The Lord has blessed Jonathan with a beautiful Christian wife, Jeanette Grace, two beautiful daughters, Heaven and Christmas and a son, Christian Israel.

While at Oral Roberts University, Jonathan was led to incorporate his personal ministry under the name of Worldshakers For Christ. After his graduation from ORU in May in 1976, he opened a youth-oriented coffee-house-outreach to minister the Gospel on weekend nights out on Peoria Avenue, Tulsa's "Strip," better known to local residents as "The Restless Ribbon." Here thousands of restless youth seek pleasure and/or answers from drugs, alcohol, immorality and cults. The outreach, **The Ultimate Trip**, now renamed **The Rainbow's End**, has ministered the glorious Gospel to Tulsa's youth through methods described in *TAKE HIM TO THE STREETS*. Having had the privilege of sharing his testimony, ministry, burden and vision on Trinity Broadcasting Network, the PTL Club, and the 700 Club, the author now is eager to help churches and Christians in every city to bridge the gap to their unsaved youth.

Table of Contents

BOOK TWO: STREET OUTREACHES

SECTION I: The Need for Street Outreaches

SECTION II: Inreach (The Ministry Inside)

SECTION III: Backup (The Ministry Behind the Scenes)

BOOK ONE:

STEPPING OUT

I: WHY REACH OUT?

1

Jesus Christ: God's Stepping Stone

"There is one God, and one mediator ("stepping-stone") between God and men, the Man, Christ Jesus" I Timothy 2:5.

God Almighty stepped into human history with an unparalleled invasion of His love, when He sent Jesus Christ (I Tim. 3:16) into this world, to lay down an eternal stepping stone and bridge the gap between an all-holy God and the all-sinful human race.

God loved the world so much that He didn't say "Come to me on your own, save yourselves, leap across the stream of sin by yourselves, either come all the way to me, MEASURE UP TO MY STANDARD OF PERFECTION, or go on, straight to hell!" *No, God didn't say that!*

Instead, He sent down Jesus Christ to be His stepping stone and ours as well!

God understood our weaknesses, and decided to do more than merely invite us to heaven. God so loved us that He built us a bridge to heaven. Now, do we love sinners with that same kind of love? Jesus Christ is God's stepping stone to reach the human race, and to allow mankind to get back to God. Did Jesus meet people half-way or all the way? II Corinthians 5:21 states: "God made Him to be sin for us."

Was Jesus made "sin" or half-sin for us? Again, II Corinthians 8:9 reads, "He became poor for us;" was He made "destitute" or only "half-poor?" Finally, Paul in Galatians 3:13 states, "Christ has redeemed us from the curse of the Law, being made a curse for us." Again, does scripture say "half a curse" or a full curse?

Jesus came to meet people where they were, to bring them where He wanted them to be.

Dare we as Christians do any less? Dare we represent Him in any other manner?

Isaiah wrote, "Behold *I lay* in Zion a stone, a tried stone, *a precious cornerstone,* a sure fountain; he that believeth shall not be put to shame." Jesus Christ was, and is God's "Stepping Stone!"

2

A Stepping Stone Saved Me!

"I looked on my right hand, and beheld but there was no man that would know me: Refuge failed me; no man cared for my soul" Psalm 142:4.

"I could have died and gone to hell . . . and who would have cared?" In the words of King David: "No man cared for my soul" (Psalm 142:4). Who cared for mine?

The highest compliment you can give another person is to care for their eternal soul.

When I was a reject and outcast in high school, coming home after school, crying and pounding the wall with my fists, confused and frustrated, no man cared for my soul.

1967! Hundreds of thousands of runaways and confused young people were seeking "Peace, Joy, Love." They flooded Haight Street in San Francisco, starting the hippie, "flower-power," "drop-out" generation. Yet out of AMERICA'S ONE–QUARTER M-I-L-L-I-O-N CONGRE-GATIONS, (400 CHURCHES IN SAN FRANCISCO ALONE), "No man cared for my soul" and consequently we never found the ideals and the spiritual reality we were seeking!

Crossing America 20 times in those four years, traveling to Europe four times, rubbing shoulders with countless thousands of people, (and God knows how many so-called "Christians") . . . no man showed me that he cared for my soul! While no man cared for my soul, and the souls of millions of other street-oriented youths, the cultists were out recruiting.

No Christians cared for my soul . . . but Satan and his disciples did!

When I walked across Golden Gate Bridge and contemplated suicide by jumping off to end my broken dreams . . . "no man cared for my soul." Finally, in the summer of 1969 while hitchhiking, I ran into a real Christian . . . Finally . . . praise God . . . someone cared for my soul.

Someone cared enough for my soul to bring Jesus out to me where I was. Someone cared enough to support a "stepping stone" ministry outside the Church to help people get to Jesus and to help get Jesus to the people.

Glad Tidings Assembly of God in Sacramento was supporting a young couple who lived 40 miles out in the hills, bringing them groceries and necessities. There, "missionaries" from several churches in town ministered by picking up hitchhikers. They would take them 40 miles from nowhere, offer them a nice place to rest out on the banks of the river, feed them and give them a chance to get it all together . . . with no way out except GETTING SAVED!

Finally, somebody cared for my soul. They showed me the reality of Jesus' Love!

There are thousands in your town tonight saying to themselves, "Does anyone care for my soul?" If you don't . . . who will?

3

The Great Commission: Reach Out!

"If you love me, keep my commandments" John 14:15.

Jesus Christ told His Disciples: "As the Father sends me, even so send I you" John 20:21. Then He commanded them:

In Matthew 28:19, "Go and make disciples of all nations"

In Mark 16:15, "Go and preach the gospel to every creature."

In Luke 24:47, "... preach ... forgivness of sins to every nation."

In Acts 1:8, "Ye shall be my witnesses in both Jerusalem, Samaria, in Judea and to the farthest parts of the earth."

His command was not just to reach all men in the world, but to reach into the world of every man. With over 110 million in the U.S. under 25, take a look any Sunday morning at the great majority of church congregations, you'll see a noticeable lack of those ages 14-25, over 50 million Americans, and many of those this age that *are* present are *really* only "half-there."

With the shift of population toward youth in America, the Great Commission and those striving to fulfill it must shift emphasis as well!

Jesus called His Church to be God's "stepping stones," to be Heaven's fishermen. Fishermen must be taught and enabled either by wading midstream or through using fishing boats, to go fishing... OUT WHERE THE FISH ARE!

4

The Unreached Majority: Young People

"Jesus said unto them ... if you love Me, feed My lambs" John 21:15.

The population of the world is now over four billion, increasing by sixty-five million souls a year. Experts in foreign missions claim that half of the world population, over two billion people, have never even heard the gospel! Over two thousand language groups, over one hundred and seventy million people don't even have scriptures printed in their own languages.

Death statistics on a worldwide scale are frightening. 119,520 die each day; three die every two seconds. Over one soul each second enters eternity, round the clock, year in, year out!

Perhaps this is too vast to relate to. Let's bring it home to just the United States! The U.S. population is now two hundred twenty million. The U.S. Census showed over 50%, or over 110 million Americans are under the age of 25, over 50 million are between 15 and 25. Ther are 3.3 million yearly births in the U.S. each year, over 10,000 each day, while 1.4 million die yearly in the U.S. . . . one dying every twenty seconds . . . round the clock . . . THE MAJORITY OF THESE ARE: YOUNG PEOPLE! LOOK AT THE STATISTICS BELOW AND REALIZE AFRESH WHERE YOUTH MINISTRY MUST BE CONCENTRATED:

Over 1 million U.S. abortions per year . . . *the majority are young people.*

Over 1 million runaways each year . . . *the majority are young people.*

Over 1.5 million suicides each year (the #2 cause of death under 25) . . . *the majority are young people.*

Over 1 million in mental clinics . . . *the majority are young people.*

Over 1 million divorces per year . . . *the majority are young people.*

Over 500,000 junkies (½ million) . . . *the majority are young people.*

Over 500,000 behind bars (over 50% of serious crimes are committed by those under 25) . . . *the majority are young people.*

Over 10 million alcoholics in the U.S. . . . *the majority are young people.*

Sun Yung Moon boasts 500,000 followers . . . *the majority are young people.*

TM (Transcendental Meditation) boasts three million in the U.S. . . . *the majority are young people.*

The homosexuals (gays) boast 10 million in the U.S. . . . *the majority are young people.*

Yoga boasts 5 million adherents . . . *the majority are young people.*

Jesus said: "The broad way leads unto destruction; many (the majority) are entering that way" (Matthew 7:13). Now if the majority of the U.S. citizens (over 110 million) are under 25, then the majority of the souls of those dying, over 50 souls alone since you've read this one chapter, belong to young people (1-25).

Jesus said the majority of those dying, die without Christ. They die and go to hell! The majority of these are young people.

5

Touching the Untouchables

"Be not highminded, but condescend to men of low estate" Romans 12:16

"And when the Pharisees saw it, they said unto His disciples, 'Why does your Master eat and sit with publicans and notorious sinners?'" Matthew 9:11

Addicts
Adulterers
Atheists
Agnostics
Alcoholics
Anarchists
Armed robbers
Astrologers
AWOL's
Backsliders
Barefoots
Bartenders
Beatnicks
Beauty Queens
Beggars
Bigots
Bikers
Billionaires
Bisexuals
Black Muslims
Black Panthers
Buddhists
Bums
Celebrities
Chart readers
Child abusers
"Children of God"
Christian Scientists
Communists
Con-men

Go-Go girls
Gossips
Greasers
Groupies
Grave robbers
Gurus
Hijackers
Hippies
Hitchhikers
Hobos
Homosexuals
Hypnotists
Jet setters
Jews (unsaved)
Jehovah's Witnesses
John Birchers
Judges
Kidnappers
Killers
Ku Klux Klanners
Krishnas
Lepers
Lesbians
Liberals
Mafioso
Marxists
Mary Magdalenes
Masochists
Masseurs
Mediums

Pimps
Playboys
Policemen
Politicians
Pornographers
Prisoners
Prostitutes
Psych. patients
Racists
Radicals
Relatives
Revolutionaries
Rock stars
Runaways
Sadists
"Samaritans"
Satanists
Scientologists
Snobs
Socialists
Socialites
Speed freaks
Spiritualists
Streetwalkers
Strippers
Swamis
Swingers
Telephone operators
Theologians
Throw-aways

Convicts	Millionaires	TM'ers
Cultists	Mohammedans	Tramps
Dealers	Moonies	Transients
Demoniacs	Mormons	Transvestites
Dopers	Movie stars	Unitarians
Drag queens	Nazis	Unsaved ministers
Drop-outs	Neighbors	Unwed mothers
Drug Addicts	Nymphos	Used car dealers
Drunks	Occultists	Warlocks
Eckankars	Outcasts	"White-slavers"
"EST" ers	Palmreaders	"White-robers"
Ex-cons	Parole breakers	Wife-beaters
Flagellists	Parolees	Wife-swappers
Fornicators	Peeping toms	Winos
Fortune tellers	Perverts	Witches
Freaks	Picketers	Yogis

When did you last share Christ with one of the above?

Jesus broke all religious taboos sitting with the Samaritan woman at the well (John 4), in defending the adulteress (John 8), in dining with Jericho's No. 1 tax ripoff, Zaccheus (Luke 19), in touching lepers (Matthew 8:3), healing on the sabbath (Luke 13:14), etc., etc. Do we?

Jesus did most of His soulwinning from the bottom of society's pile: Do we? Jesus was known as a friend of "tax ripoffs," publicans and notorious sinners (Matthew 9:11-12, 11:19). Are we?

Jesus Christ touched the untouchables, loved the unlovables, went after the unretrievables, won the unwinnables . . . are we following Him?

Picture if you can:

1. A young girl of 18, having shot drugs 6 years, ready to commit a double suicide with her drug-dealing boyfriend.

2. Tulsa's Assembly Center with 8,000 kids wildly chanting "Hail Lucifer" to a 30 by 30 foot picture of Satan behind "Black Sabbath."

3. A confused young man who was forced to do homosexual acts with his father from his childhood up . . .

4. A young man leaving a rock concert so drunk that he drives at 30 mph smack into a light pole, emerging with blood streaming down his face.

5. A young lady dancing topless and a soulwinner telling the manager, "What would her mother say if she could see this?" A voice comes out of the club's darkness: "I am the girl's mother, what can I do for you?"

6. A young fellow vomiting and ripping a satanic star and chain from off his

neck.

7. Kids getting up a 4 a.m. to get front row "KISS" tickets to have cow's blood spit on them and see the guitarist make love to a 6-foot snake on a pole.

8. A 13-year old out on his own, both parents alcoholics, letting him do anything and stay gone all night, alone without God or friends .

Who is called to love and touch these people with God's love if not the Church?

Lynette Fromme, the Manson girl who attempted to assassinate Gerald Ford in Sacramento said she was sitting on the curb in Venice, California and Charles Manson came up to her. What if a born-again, Spirit-filled Christian had approached her instead? Why did she follow Manson? In her own words, "A beaten dog will follow anyone who loves it." She did.

Jesus touched the untouchables with God's love and reality wherever He went. He went about doing good. Do we?

"God anointed Jesus Christ of Nazareth with power and with the Holy Spirit, who went about doing good, and healing (touching and loving) all those who were oppressed by ('under the thumb of') the devil . . . for God was with Him" Acts 10:38!

Ask yourself this question: "Who is touching the untouchables in my town? Am I? Is my church?"

6

Asleep At the Wheel

"And when He rose up from praying, and was come to His disciples, he found them sleeping" Luke 22:45.

There is a popular rock group called "Asleep at the Wheel." Is this a valid description of many believers today?

Ask any evangelical church crowd to show by raised hands how many believe there's an eternal hellfire awaiting the lost, and the majority will raise their hands. But, ask them how many are living, praying, witnessing, fasting, preaching, and giving like it, to reach the lost in time, and the majority will this time keep their hands down. Where is the urgency? The situation is desperate . . . but are the saints?

Jesus sat on a hill over Jerusalem (Luke 19:41) and wept, but soon afterwards in Gethsemane once again as He wept, the disciples slept. Asleep at the wheel . . . again! Is there an unspoken attitude of: "They know where we (the Church) are . . . let them come to church or go to hell!

While we criticize the lost for their evilness, and attack true revival as uncontrollable fanaticism, the fact remains true: THOSE WHO PRAY FOR REVIVAL THE LEAST NEED IT THE MOST." A Christian teller in a bank wrote me a note to say she threw out the tracts I always enclosed in my bank deposits, because she was already saved! But what about those around her in the bank? Who cares for their souls? If we don't, who will? Are we our brother's keeper . . . or not?

Christian reader, if everyone had the burden for souls that you have, would there be few or many souls in hell? Did Jesus die and rise again for the quality of Christian life you lived today?

One pastor told us, "We believe in missions, but we do our's overseas, not your kind of thing on the streets." Another church elder confessed: "Before we got fat and rich, we were out on the streets winning souls, just like you're doing now."

Edmund Burke once wrote: "The only thing necessary for evil to reign, is for good men to do nothing." What an expose on the words a believer once told me: "I let the Lord bring my evangelism to me."

God so loved the world, not just the church. Jesus said that a doctor is sent to the sick, not the well. Are we spending more time at doctors' conventions, or are we out making house calls, visiting the sick?

At the time of the Great Chicago Fire, the entire city rose in flames, becoming a literal inferno. The residents fled for shelter in the waters of Lake Michigan. The flames came close to the water's edge, but eventually died out there. D.L. Moody found refuge in the chilly water. Near him was a young lady, sitting at the water's edge, her head in her hands, weeping hysterically, wailing in uncontrollable sorrow. Trying to comfort her, he said: "Young lady . . . YOUNG LADY! Get ahold of yourself, you're safe now, the fire can't reach you here. . . stop weeping, young lady, listen to me, YOU ARE SAVED!"

Through her tears the young lady sobbed out this reply: "Yes, I know I'm saved . . . but I didn't bring anybody with me!

Let's move closer to our day and time. In 1978, the Los Angeles Hillside Strangler took 13 female lives in 5 months.

One of the most publicized victims was a young callgirl. She was heard screaming in the apartment she'd been taken to by "him," heard screaming by neighbors who though they literally "jumped out of their chairs," they never even bothered to call the police or "get involved."

Later on a man at a motel saw another man carrying out over his shoulder a woman's body wrapped in a blanket, placing her in a car and driving off. Did he bother to call the police or tell anyone? Hardly! He chose rather to "mind his own business."

If others were only as concerned about your immortal soul as you are about theirs, would you be saved at this moment? A prisoner in London once told a preacher: "Mister, if I believed this Gospel you say you believe, I'd crawl across England on my knees over broken glass to get the message out."

Fellow Christians and believers; would Y-O-U?

What fireman sees a house on fire, goes up and quietly knocks twice and then, not wanting to disturb the sleeping tenants, drives back to the Fire Station and smugly tells the Fire Chief: "Mission accomplished! I politely knocked twice, didn't disturb the tenants, cause a commotion, act like a fanatic, or otherwise interfere in the lives of the family. What more could I have done?

As Charles Finney put it: "How would you yell S-T-O-P to somebody sleepwalking toward a ledge overlooking Niagara Falls?"

Church: ARE WE ASLEEP AT THE WHEEL . . . ?

II: OUTREACH

7

Come Ye All the World?

"His watchmen are blind: they are all ignorant, they are all dumb dogs, they cannot bark; sleeping, lying down, loving to slumber" Isaiah 56:10.

"When I say unto the wicked, thou shalt surely die, and you give him not warning, nor speak to warn the wicked from his wicked way to save his life; the same wicked man shall die in his iniquity; but his blood shall I require at thine hand" Ezekiel 3:18.

Today many churchgoers consider their full duty of evangelism merely inviting neighbors to church to come hear a celebrity, or to see the world's longest banana split, to view a new movie, or to win a raffle for a new El Dorado. Many believe in paying tithes, attending services and occasional suppers and rummage sales, bingo, raffles, dances, golf, softball, bowling, birdwatching teams, and "sanctified alcohol" but that just won't fill mankind's spiritual void or meet the crying need of the hour.

Only soulwinning will quench that deep spiritual thirst to see the God of gods in action out where the action is!

Was Jesus' Great Commission to the church to tell the world: "Come ye into all the church?" Or is that the Great Omission? One current bumper sticker reads: "Have Jesus, will share!" That doesn't sound like compelling them to come in as Jesus commanded in Luke 14:23.

The prodigal son in the pigpen was not as bad off as the "prodigal" elder brother who never even sent out a search party for his brother, much less rejoice when his brother came home. On the contrary, he became angry. The pigpen in him was his spiritual "prodigality." His lack of concern shows he was more lost than his brother. Which of the two "prodigal" brothers are we closer to?

8

Why Me, Lord?

"Then Peter said to Jesus, 'Lord, and what shall this man do?' And Jesus said to him: 'What is that to you? See that you follow Me!' " John 21:20-22.

"And I sought for a man among them, that should make up the hedge, and stand in the gap before Me for the land that I should not destroy it: but I found none" Ezekiel 22:30.

"And they that turn many to righteousness shall shine as the brightness of the stars forever" Daniel 12:3.

"Be strong and do not lose courage, for there is a reward for your work" II Chronicles 15:17.

"And I heard the voice of the Lord saying, 'Whom shall We send, who will go for Us? . . . Then I said, 'Here am I, Lord . . . send me!' " Isaiah 6:8.

Eric Bonhoeffer wrote: "When Jesus calls a man, He calls him to come and die." But I say, "When Jesus calls a man, it is to come and live, to overflow, and to serve!" "Use-me" Christians will never fail to reap God's best blessings. The Dead Sea and Lake Galilee are classic examples. The Dead Sea is ever receiving fresh water from its source, the Jordan River, but it never gives out at its other end. As a result, it is stagnant; nothing can live in its waters. Contrast the Dead Sea, so appropriately named, with the sparkling blue, fish-producing waters of Lake Galilee, which receives melted snow off of Mt. Hermon from the north and at its southern end gives out its waters to form the lush Jordan River Valley. Which type of Christian are you?

Why does God want to use us? He wants to bless us, to bless others, and in so doing, to bring glory and honor to His Name and Being.

Moses tried every excuse in the book to escape God's call, but God had one specific purpose in mind for this man! God has a unique plan and individual purpose for every member of His born-again family of believers. When men use others for their own private ends, they leave them worse than they started out. Things are different, however, when God uses a person, or even a person's belongings. When Jesus borrowed Peter's empty fishing boat to preach in, He afterwards nearly sunk it with a miracle catch of Galilee's finest fish (Luke 5:3,7)!

God is desperate for men to forsake the "why me?" position and to graduate spiritually to the "use me" privilege.

What if Isaiah had said: "Here am I, Lord . . . send someone else," or "Lord, there he is, send him," or "I've already done my bit for God this week, Lord, don't you remember I interrupted my Sunday morning beauty sleep just to go to church this week?"

God has been calling each of His people into a work of soulwinning and intercession, whoever and wherever they are. "Why me?" may be a stumbling block question in your spirit right now, but give it to God. He will use your willingness and yieldedness to glorify Himself in fulfilling His will for your life!

Remember the words of Jesus in John 12:26 . . . "If any man serve Me, let him follow Me; and where I am, there shall also My servant be: if any man serve Me, him shall My Father honor!"

9

Go Me!

"Go YE therefore, and make disciples of all the nations" Matthew 28:19.

"Go YE into all the world, and preach the Gospel to every creature" Mark 16:15.

Jesus called His people "the salt of the earth, the light of the world, and a city built on a hill for all men to see" (Matthew 5:13-16). It is only when the universal salvation of God is personalized that it becomes effective and meaningful in one's life. Even so it is with Christ's Great Commission! It is only when the "Go ye" command is personalized to "Go ME" that God blesses a believer's obedience and starts moving mountains from out of the path of our little individual faith "tractors."

In Matthew 9:38, Christ said: "Pray to the Lord of the harvest, to *cast out workers into* the harvest." He wants to get the salt of the earth out of the salt-cellars of religion and out into people's lives where it was and is designed to put God's forgiveness and blessing into action! The word for "cast out" in Greek is *ek-ballo* which means to *exorcise, throw out,* or *force out.* It is the same word used to "cast out" demons all through the New Testament. It is, in fact, used in *that* context in the next verse after Matthew 9:38; verse one of Matthew 10.

In Mark 16:17 Christ promised that believers would "cast out devils in My Name." As believers we are also called to cast out soulwinners. The best way to do this is by praying to Christ to cast out the harvesters and obviously, *FOR HIM TO START WITH US!*

Example is the best motivator! Christ is our Example, the pioneer and perfecter of our faith. But Paul the Apostle in I Corinthians 11:1 could say: "Be ye followers of me, even as I am following Christ." The Pharisees "don't practice what they preach" (Matthew 23:4), and they thus earned Jesus' most scathing denunciations! They personalized God's commands to everyone everywhere except themselves. Thank God for Jesus' example!

Let us never be guilty of "keeping the faith," when instead in obedience to Christ's final command, we should always be found diligently occupied in giving it away!!

10

Evangelism Is . . .

"God is NOT willing that ANY perish, but that ALL come to repentance" II Peter 3:9.

Evangelism is God so loving the world that He sent us His Only Son!

Evangelism is Jesus weeping over a doomed, Gospel rejecting Jerusalem.

Evangelism is Moses' prayer: "Lord, forgive them, or blot me from Your Book."

Evangelism is David writing: "The zeal of Thy house has eaten Me up."

Evangelism is Isaiah's surrender to God: "Lord, here am I: send me."

Evangelism is Paul's desire to be damned, that his brethren might be saved.

Evangelism is Luther praying: "God, I won't let You go until You give me Germany.

Evangelism is John Knox interceding: "Give me Scotland, or I die."

Evangelism is the only reason you and I are saved today.

Evangelism is sharing Christ whenever you can, wherever you are, with whomever you're with.

Evangelism is always returning to the question: "But what about Jesus?"

Evangelism is the measure of how great a threat your faith is to Satan's kingdom.

Evangelism is the difference between "life-boat" and "showboat" Christianity.

Evangelism is realizing you may be the first or last Christian between anyone and hellfire!

Evangelism is the executioner of the self-life, the labor room of the new birth, the incubator of the New Creation, and the midwife that births the saints!

Evangelism is seeking out the lost sheep, not expecting them to find the shepherd.

Evangelism is bringing in the sheaves, not expecting them to harvest themselves.

Evangelism is obeying Jesus Christ's commandment to every believer to

"go out into the hedges and highways, and compel lost souls to come in"
(Luke 14:23).

11

Making Fear Afraid!

"God's perfect love casts out all fear, because fear has torment"
I John 4:18.

"God has not given us the spirit of fear, but of power, love, and a disciplined mind" II Timothy 1:7.

"No weapon that is formed against thee shall prosper . . . " Isaiah 54:17.

"Greater is Jesus with you, than the devil that's in the world" I John 4:4.

"The righteous are bold (or feel safe) as a lion . . . The lion is the king of the beasts, and turns not aside for any" Proverbs 30:30.

"Since God is for us (and in us), who can be successful against us?" Roman 8:31.

Fear is generally fear of the unknown. I was afraid to drive, afraid to waterski, afraid to open up a street outreach . . . until I learned how. In each situation, I discovered that fear was the paralyzing enemy trying to keep me from conquering it through faith and action. Satan is the author of fear. Fear, in reality, is faith in reverse — placing more faith in the lies and threats of the devil than in the promise of God! It is said that there are 365 "fear nots" in the Bible, one for each day of the year.

Paul writes in II Timothy 1:7 about a spirit of fear. He writes in II Corinthians 2:15 that "Christ always leads us in His triumphal procession." The triumph of Christ over satan's spiritual kingdom includes a victory over satan's spirit of fear. Take the sword of the Holy Spirit, the Word of God (Ephesians 6:17). Slice up and defeat whatever "fear trip" the author of fear has laid on you concerning sharing the gospel.

As the Lord had His eyes on Peter when he daringly stepped overboard to walk on the water, Jesus will respond to any need you have as you step out for Him!

God's Son will not abandon you as you go out to do battle in His Name and for His glory! He will not let you evaporate, disintegrate, get annihilated, or wiped out. He's the same yesterday, today, and forever (Hebrews 13:8). He took care of and watched over His disciples in Bible days and will do exactly the same for you!

Once in California we were going out to witness at a topless bar one evening, and during the service that morning, I invited others at church to come along with us. At the close of the service, the preacher confessed to the congregation: "I wonder how many of you, like me, are already making up excuses why you won't be able to go out with them tonight?" It was fear eating that man's spirit! If he had come, that fear would have been conquered by five minutes of action!

Jesus has promised to turn our mountains into stepping stones. Our cold feet need to be heated with the fire of the Holy Spirit. Silence that's "yellow" can become golden by acts of faith. It is faith in Christ and obedience through our actions, following the Spirit of the Living God, that will lead us to defeat fear every time in Jesus' Name!

12

Six Soulwinning Plans

"He that winneth souls is wise" Proverbs 11:30.

"He that is wise captures human lives for God" Proverbs 11:30 (Amplified).

"From this time on YOU WILL BE CATCHING MEN" Luke 5:10 (Centenary).

Can you honestly picture Jesus on the shores of Lake Galilee with the crowds of rough fisherman saying: "Every head bowed, and every eye closed now, please . . . no peeking fellows! OK, now, Peter, while no one is watching . . . pssst! Come and follow me. Uh, uh! Hey, you there! . . . shut your eyes. C'mon John, you can follow me now, nobody is watching, no one can see a thing. None of you guys laugh now, and I want you to keep those heads bowed and eyes closed until you count to 1000 by 5's. No cheating either, wait until we at least get over the next hill and out of sight . . . OK, Peter and John, the first thing I want you both to do is to repeat this sinner's prayer after Me . . . Next, I want you to sign these membership cards and fill in your name, address, and social security number for my files . . ."

How does our modern evangelism line up with the Master's? Below are listed a few of the more popular soulwinning plans in current use today. Following this are a number of scriptural examples of soulwinning. Read them and then compare, if you dare!

1) The Romans Road: The basic Romans Road soulwinning plan follows the path of the following scriptures in Paul's letter to the Romans: using verses 3:23, 6:23, 5:8, 10:13, 10:9, 10. The prospect is led along each scripture as a stepping stone toward a final commitment and prayer after reading them all.

2) The Four Spiritual Laws: This plan, put forth by Campus Crusade, runs basically along the same lines. One: All have sinned (Romans 3:23); Two: Sin separates us from God and earns us a penalty (Romans 6:23); Three: God has provided a remedy for sin's penalty (Romans 5:8). Four: This remedy must be personally applied and received (Romans 10:9, 10, 13). Then the prospect is asked if he would like to do that and in prayer, he does!

3) The ABC Plan: This plan consists of getting the prospect to A: Admit he has sinned and fallen short of God's plan (Romans 6:23); B: Believe on the Lord Jesus Christ and he will be saved (Acts 16:31); C: Confess Jesus as his personal Lord both to the soulwinner at that moment, and to others as well (Romans 10:9, 10; Matthew 10:32).

4) The Four Color Wordless Book: This plan is especially good for use with children. It uses a little four-page booklet that has no words and its pages are colored first gold, then the second page black, then the third red, then the fourth white. The symbolism is obvious. God is in a pure, sinless heaven with golden streets (Revelation 21:21). Sin has blackened each of our hearts (Romans 3:23; Revelation 21:27). Jesus Christ's red blood was shed to wash our sins away (Revelation 1:5, 6; Isaiah 53:6). The final white page represents salvation (Isaiah 1:18; Psalm 51:7; II Corinthians 5:17, 21). "The Wordless Book" is published by Good News Publishers, Westchester, Illinois and is inexpensive.

5) Soulwinning Made Easy, by C.S. Lovett. Begin with three approach questions: a) Are you interested in spiritual things; b) have you ever thought about becoming a Christian; c) if someone asked you, "What is a Christian?" how would you answer? From here, Romans 3:23, 6:23, John 1:12 and Revelation 3:20 take the soulwinner and prospect down to the closing prayer.

6) Win or Warn, by C.S. Lovett. This plan utilizes a person's "NO" to the Gospel. As Jesus Himself said, "I would rather have you . . . cold, than luke warm." The plan helps those that are uncommitted to at least admit to themselves they are saying no. They are asked to pray this "No." Then they are lovingly warned of the ways God will try to change their mind.

There are many other excellent soulwinning books but few of them can be summarized in as short a space as those above. I would also recommend **Let's Go Soulwinning** (by Jack Hyles) on door-to-door work, **Evangelism Explosion**, by Dr. James Kennedy and E.W. Kenyon's **Personal Evangelism Course.**

Scriptural Examples of Soulwinning

In the four Gospels, Jesus is never seen leading a crowd in a sinner's prayer, yet the same principles so widely used today are readily seen in His preaching and ministry. While He preached repentance to the crowds in Luke 13, He offered life, love and forgiveness with no mention of repentance to Zaccheus (Luke 19), the Prostitute (Luke 7:47), the ex-thief on the cross (Luke 23:43), the ex-maniac of Gadara (Mark 5:19), and many others. Are we following Him?

Even as Jesus was led by the Holy Spirit and knew when people's pride and sinfulness needed leveling, or when their broken spirits needed uplifting, so we must equally be led by God's Spirit to engage in successful, fruitful soulwinning (Romans 8:16; Matthew 11:19). It was the Holy Spirit that divinely led Philip in Acts 8:30 to approach the Ethiopian eunuch's chariot. Without question, the greatest soulwinning plan, then, must begin and end with total surrender to and dependence on the Holy Spirit to prepare us, lead us, and guide us to share Christ in the supernatural way only He can!

13

Forty Things Salvation is Not

"For by grace are you saved through faith; and that not of yourselves; it is the Gift of God; not of works, lest any man should boast" Ephesians 2:8, 9.

"Not by works of righteousness which we have done, but according to His mercy He saved us" Titus 3:5.

"All our righteousnesses are as filthy rags" Isaiah 64:6.
"The Gift of God is eternal Life in Christ Jesus our Lord" Romans 6:23.

Many today are lost, wandering in circles out in the wilderness of formalized religion, trying to work their way into the family of God. We must be careful in presenting the Gospel not to complicate the grace of God, but rather to show prospects that *salvation is a gift to be received,* not earned, or worked for, *and* that *those who have it, know it!* (I John 5:13; Romans 8:14). Below is a list of forty things erroneously believed to bring or be salvation!

1) Doing your best
2) Saying prayers
3) Submitting to elders
4) Memorizing Scriptures
5) Church attendance
6) Fasting
7) Church membership
8) Working for the minister
9) Tithing
10) Cooking for the preacher
11) Visiting the sick
12) Preaching in jails
13) Traditions
14) Confirmation
15) Catechism
16) Ritual observances
17) Lighting candles
18) Using incense
19) Rosary beads
20) Sunday school teaching
21) Doing good deeds
22) "Moral" living
23) Taking the sacraments
24) Water baptism
25) Infant baptism
26) Shaking the preacher's hand
27) Not smoking
28) Not drinking alcohol
29) Not cursing
30) Not spitting
31) Witnessing
32) Soulwinning
33) Laying hands on the sick
34) Working of miracles
35) Walking up the aisle at every altar call
36) "Mouthing" a sinner's prayer
37) Attending seminars
38) Bringing neighbors to church
39) Being a "good" person
40) All other outward observances omitted in this list

14

Speak "Koine" English

"No man ever spoke like this Man" John 7:46.
"The common people listened to Him gladly" Mark 12:37.
"Wisdom is justified by its results" Matthew 11:19.

The beautiful, Divine simplicity of Jesus' parables is seen in Matthew 11:25: "Father, I thank You that You have hid these things from the wise and prudent, and revealed them unto babes." The simplest, youngest listener could understand, but the conceited "wise men" and intellectuals could only pretend not to!

Christ never drew His crowds or ministered to them by pontificating repetitiously in multitudinous, genealogical eschatologies of the propitiatory mission He had been sent from Heaven to fulfill. Through His crucifixion and resurrection, through His words and actions, He came to declare and make clear the nature of God, not to "cloud it up" any further than religionists already had done.

Koine Greek is the language that the New Testament was written in. It was the language of the people, the common language, the language of the market place. It was not the classical Greek in which Homer and the other great Greek writers had penned their classics several hundred years before.

Many religionists and many sincere believers today insist on using classical English out of the King James translation. They would accomplish a lot more eternal good by giving fewer classical English lessons to the unsaved, and speaking more *KOINE ENGLISH!* Elizabethan "withers" and "thithers" make the unsaved think of Jesus as a Shakespearian character rather than Ruler of the Universe who can fill their life with the Kingdom of Heaven, not just in the "sweet by and by" but in this world, in the "nasty here and now!"

People want God's practical answers to their life questions. They neither want nor need terms like Gabriel's "annunciat," Mary's "magnificat," Zacharias' "Benedictus" or Simeon's "nunc dimittis." The unsaved are secretly thirsting after reality, not external religion. They want real life illustrations and answers, not technical theological abstractions and theories.

When dealing with the lost, we must say what we mean, and avoid religious "jargon." Ken Taylor, the author of the *Living Bible* paraphrase used to read the King James to his daughter daily, He always had to go back and explain the whole thing over again to her! One day he was struck with a "KOINE THUNDERBOLT" when she asked him: "Daddy, why didn't you say that in the first place?" Let's not be guilty of the same error in our sharing the Gospel of Jesus Christ with others!

15

Tract Evangelism

"And He departed, and began to publish in Decapolis what great things Jesus had done for him; and all men did marvel" Mark 5:20. "Behold, the sower went out to sow . . ." Matthew 13:3.

When Jesus delivered and healed the Gadarene maniac, He didn't keep the Good News to himself. I'm sure if he'd had a press, he would have written, printed and distributed countless thousands of tracts in not just the 10 Galilee towns (Decapolis) around the lake, but throughout Israel and the world as well, just as Nicky Cruz, Cookie Rodriguez, Pat Boone and multitudes of others have done in our day.

Why I Like Tracts

1) A tract will never water down its story, blush, or look away.

2) A tract can go where you can't, and stay when you must go.

3) A tract can learn any language, and fly to 150 countries at the same time in 150 directions without the author.

4) A tract costs and weighs so little, takes so little space, looks so insignificant, yet can detonate more spiritual power than a million Hiroshima bombs, affecting souls for eternity!

5) A tract can be crumpled or ripped up, and still do its job.

6) A tract never interrupts you at the wrong time; it can wait!

When distributing tracts and people ask what it is, I say it's:

—an invitation to a feast, party or banquet

—a free paid ticket

—a wedding announcement

—a love letter
—a souvenir
—an eternal road map
—a treasure map
—a reminder
—an eternal life insurance policy
—a trust fund
—one of my business cards
—homework
—some good news for you!
—a recipe for eternal happiness
—a special delivery (at Post Office)

What exactly do tracts accomplish?

Pat Robertson, now host of the "700 Club" Christian Television Network, remembers back to the days before he was saved. His mother *was* saved and sent him tracts in every letter, but even though he ripped them up, they kept his conscience asking: "Is there more to life than this? Will I meet God some day?" Other testimonies of tracts leading people directly to Christ cover the whole spectrum of humanity from professionals to winos.

Where to put tracts:

1) In every bill or letter you send out.
2) In postpaid business reply junk mail envelopes.
3) In phone booths, restrooms, all public places.
4) When out jogging, on neighborhood cars.
5) On cars everywhere (under windshield wipers or door handles).
6) On public bulletin boards at work, supermarkets, laundries, city hall, etc.
7) In the hands of everyone you can, everywhere you go, 'till He comes!
8) In unexpected places, like Playboy centerfolds, beer six-paks, alternately between napkins at a cafe, etc.

Things to avoid with tracts:

1) Always pick up after yourself and team, as much as possible.
2) Avoid giving out wrinkled or dirty, soiled tracts.
3) Make the tracts apply to the individual, (as much as you can).
4) **Never put tracts in private mailboxes!** That's breaking a Federal Law.
5) Be careful not to break new type windshield wipers in lifting them up, (newer cars have lift up door handles, ideal for tracts).

6) Tract passing is always legal on public property but not always on private property. Never get arrested tract passing on private property. In other words, leave private property, *if* asked to!

7) Don't get upset if people refuse your tracts. "STAY IN LOVE" (God's love). Remember: "IF THEY REFUSE TO READ YOUR TRACT, THEY WILL CERTAINLY NOT FAIL TO READ YOU!"

8) Be thorough and extensive, but not fanatical: I heard of someone putting a tract inside a grocery Cool Whip container! That's asking for trouble, and not God-inspired, but carnal zeal.

Tract Possibilities

1) By your front door, install a rack, and keep a varied assortment of tracts for mailmen, "Jehovah's Witnesses," cults, etc.

2) Write a personal testimony tract (see next chapter).

3) Order or print enough tracts to supply and stimulate other tract users.

4) Good News Publishers sells tract racks which can be left (upon request and permission) in many bus stations, doctor's offices, etc. Their address is in the tracts for sale list ending this chapter. They will also send a new tract each month for 14 consecutive months to anyone you designate for a fee of $4.

5) Always stamp or write in your address or phone number for the "awakened" person to contact you or your church.

6) Write prayer tracts: all of it is addressed to God, concerning the salvation, health and prosperity of the person reading it!

7) Put a dozen or more tracts in your pocket each day as you dress; determine to give out that number EVERY day!

8) When you meet Christians in a crowd that commend your tract passing efforts, give 10, 20, 50, 100 tracts to them, challenge them to help harvest the fields (as homework) to help others find their way home to Heaven. I gave some tracts the other day to a Christian who said he had been saved 18 years but had never passed out a single tract to others.

9) At large concerts (or crowds of any type), if people coming out start throwing down tracts, others will too! YOU CAN REVERSE THIS! Have several of your team stand near the doors or gates, reading the tracts, each one very absorbed in the tract message. Exiting people will *CATCH* their interest, and come seeking tracts and read all of theirs as well.

10) If you have no tract at a restaurant, you can write one out briefly with a scripture on a napkin and leave it under your tip. The personal touch works!

11) On airplanes, buses, trains, etc. give tracts to everyone on board from front to back.

12) Be creative — like, **nail tracts:** go out witnessing with a pocketful of nails. Tie it in with Jesus' death for each of us, proving His amazing love and desire for each of us to get to Heaven.

Tract replies to common criticisms and obstacles:

1) When you pass a tract to a Christian who replies: "I'm already saved, I don't need it." Humbly reply: "How many dozens of people around you every day aren't? Are you your brother's keeper? Take it for them. Here's a handful for all your friends!"

2) Some people will say: "Well, the Apostle Paul didn't pass out tracts." You might reply: "You mean to tell me, if the Apostle Paul had a printing press, you really think he wouldn't have used it?

Caution:

Tract passing is addictive and very damaging to the devil's kingdom, for it frees many souls from spiritual blindness and sin's slavery into the glorious liberty of the sons of God. As one brother out tract passing for the very first time told us: "Hey, I didn't know you could get a rush just passing out tracts!" Praise God!

Hints on writing your own tracts:

There is a spiritual pleasure that comes from writing and passing out a tract you have written, which perhaps is only surpassed by the joy of leading a soul to Christ. For in the tract, you can open your heart, and pour out God's love and His reality in your life, into the lives of countless others.

As subject matter, there are four general types of tracts:

1) General purpose year round salvation tracts.

2) Special event tracts (designed for a specific crowd) say a "Fourth of July" tract.

3) Special purpose tracts (on prayer, healing, the Holy Spirit, etc.).

4) Personal testimony tracts (covered in next chapter).

As you write and work on your tract, keep your specific purpose in mind, to keep on the right track! Below are some "do's and don'ts" in basic tract writing:

Do's in Tract-writing

1) DO pray before, during and after you write it.

2) DO plan on revising, rewriting, and improving it several times.

3) DO show it to other Christians (especially elder friends) you respect, asking for constructive criticism and advice (Proverbs 9:8).

4) DO leave space for your name and address (or for another group's rubber stamp imprint at the bottom).

5) DO leave at least 20% of the tract white space, with paragraphs no longer than five or six lines.

6) DO think ahead, empathize, be wise and try to see your tract as the recipient will read it (through unsaved eyes).

Don'ts in Tract writing

1) Don't cramp your tract with too much!

2) Don't use 6 point or smaller type.

3) Don't make it over several minutes' reading length.

4) Don't forget God's Word: Use Scripture, but make it come alive in your own personal life and/or theirs!

5) Don't plan on writing it all in one hour, or even one day. Don't use religious words like justification, sanctification, propitiation, eschatological, etc.

6) Don't ever leave the tract at the printer's without first finalizing the total price, and expected delivery date. Don't expect the printer to typeset it, print it, cut it, and fold it all in one day. Plan on at least three or four days.

REMEMBER:

Tract distributing is a faith ministry like planting seed. Seed never matures and harvests itself in one moment! Yet, God's Word and message of salvation doesn't return void. One Christian lady, challenged by preaching and tracting a football game of 70,000 people with us, went out to witness at a local parade with her two children. She only had one tract left and was on her way home. She crossed the street at the Spirit's leading, and gave it to a lady. Months later at a prayer meeting the lady came up to her, and told her how the tract "burned a hole" in her purse until she read it. She was saved, filled with the Holy Spirit, and healed. All this from just one tract that could have been taken home and shelved!

Below are the names of tract suppliers that sell tracts:

Drop a line to them all or have one of your team do so and ask for samples.

American Tract Society, 66 Kinderkamack Rd., Oradel, NJ 97649, Telephone 601/261-6900

Arthur Blessit Tracts, P.O. Box 69544, Hollywood, CA 90069, Telephone 213/652-7170

Campus Crusade For Christ, Arrowhead Springs, San Bernadino, CA 92414, Telephone 714/979-4422

Body of Christ Ministry, 3657 F. 49th Pl., Tulsa, OK 74135 (excellent)

Chick Tracts, Box 662, Chino, CA 91710 (sample pack $2.50) Telephone 714/622-1333

Christ For The Nations, 3404 Conway, Dallas, TX 75224 Telephone 214/376-1711

Christians in Action, 350 F. Market St., Long Beach, CA Telephone

213/428-2022

Christian Literature Crusade, Ft. Washington, PA 19034 Telephone 215/885-1090

Christian Missionary Society, Box 4097, Phoenix, AZ 85030

Concordia Tract Mission, Box 201, St. Louis, MO 63166 Telephone 314/664-7000

Deliverance Publications, 621 Clinton Ave., Newark, NJ 07108

Ed Human, Box 4806, San Antonio, TX 78285, Telephone 512/ 341-8460

Faith, Prayer, and Tract League, Grand Rapids, MI 49504

Foundation of Praise (Merlin Carothers), Box 2518, Escondido, CA 92925

Full Gospel Businessmen International, P.O. Box 5050, Costa Mesa, CA 92626

Good News Publishers, 9825 W. Roosevelt Rd. Westchester, IL 60134

Gospel Publishing House, Springfield, MO

W.V. Grant Revival Crusades, P.O. Box 353, Dallas, TX 75211

Grason (Billy Graham's materials) Box 1240, Minneapolis, MN 65540

Jesus People USA (JPUSA), 4431 N. Pauline, Chicago, IL 60640

Life Messengers, Box 1967, Seattle, WA 98111

Living Water Productions, 3303 Harbor Blvd., Suite C-9, Costa Mesa, CA 92626

Maranatha Tracts, Box 1468, Costa Mesa, CA 92626

Moody Press, 820 N. LaSalle St., Chicago, IL

Navigators, Box 20, Colorado Springs, CO 80901

New Wave Tracts, Box 66484, Houston, TX 77006
   (full color Spanish & French)

Osborn Foundation, P.O. Box 10, Tulsa, OK 74105

Personal Christianity (C.S. Lovett), Box 157, Baldwin Park, CA 91706

Spiritual Counterfeits Project, Box 4308, Berkeley, CA 94704
   (big on cults)

Sword of the Lord Publications, Murfreesboro, TN 37130

Tribal Tongues Tracts (God's Army), Box 276, Kerman, CA 93630

David Wilkerson Literature, Rt. 1, Box 80, Lindale, TX 75771

Word of Life, Inc., Box 2156, Austin, TX 79767

Worldshakers For Christ, Inc. Box 9664, Tulsa, OK 74157

Free Tract Societies

Christ Rescue Mission, 41 E. Union Blvd., Bethlehem, PA

Free Tract Society, 2408 W. Fifth St., Los Angeles, CA 90057

Gospel Tract and Bible Society, Moundridge, KA 67107

Gospel Tract Society, Box 1118, Independance, MO 64501
Grace and Truth Tracts, 215 Oak, Hillery, Danville, IL 61832
Old Paths Tract Society, Shoals, IN 47581 (over 150 samples)
Pilgrim Tract Society, Inc., Randleman, NC (over 100 free samples)
Tony Wildhaber, Evergreen Christian Center, 1000 Black Lake Blvd.,
    Olympia, WA 98502
Tract Crusade, Box 45801, Tulsa, OK 74145
Witnessing Aids, 117 S. 155th St., Gardena, CA 90248
World Missionary Press, Box 120, New Paris, IN 46553

16

Writing Your Own Personal Testimony Tract

"Jesus said, Go home to your people and tell them the things that the Lord has done for you, and how He showed mercy to you" Mark 5:19.

"And many Samaritans from her city believed in Him because of her testimony" John 4:39

"And they overcame him (satan) by the blood of the Lamb, and by the Word of their testimony . . ." Revelation 12:11.

"The evil spirit answered: Jesus I know, and Paul I know, but who are you?" Acts 19:15.

"Whoever believes in God's Son has a testimony for Him" I John 5:10 Adams.

Why write your personal testimony tract?

Billy Graham once said: "The Greatest need today is for one-on-one personal evangelism and soulwinning." Too many unsaved people can say along with the Ephesian demons (quoted above in Acts 19:15) to most of today's undercover Christians: "BILLY GRAHAM I KNOW, AND ORAL ROBERTS I KNOW . . . BUT WHO ARE YOU?"

Revelation 12:11 reveals the power of the personal testimony of a born-again believer. It was Andrew's testimony that brought his brother Simon (later nicknamed Peter) to the Saviour (John 1:41-42). It was the Samaritan woman's testimony that led to revival in her village (John 4:29-42). In modern days, the success of the Full Gospel Businessmen in winning thousands of businessmen around the world is due more to the *power* of the Holy Spirit using a changed-life testimony than any other factor.

I believe every born-again Christian, by definition, has a testimony contrasting his B.C. (Before Christ) years and his new life in Christ! I believe EVERY changed life testimony has a hidden power similar in potential to the discovery of nuclear fission! This enormous hidden power is still 99% untapped and unused by the Church. I believe personal testimony tracts can be the spiritual nuclear fission process to unleash this unused spiritual SOULWINNING force in every city and country in the world.

This power will smash and destroy unbelief. Theology is easier to argue with than an experience, a life-change, and a personal relationship with God through Jesus. When believers open up their hearts and past lives, bringing their former sins out of the closet, (sins that are now eternally under Christ's blood), sinners are convicted not only of their own unforgiven, unconfessed sins, but of the inferiority of society's advice to "sweep" it all under the rug" when Christ will forgive and forget forever.

How to write you own personal testimony tract

The suggestions below are not hard and fast rules, but are helpful for you to use.

1) **Decide whether you want to cover your whole life** or only part.

2) **Start jotting down, and collecting** in one certain place or book, various interesting bits of your life that would not only interest others as they read, but cause unsaved readers to relate and find their own life in yours, to see themselves in your past actions, thoughts, feelings, dreams, and lifestyle.

3) **Form an outline** of these major and minor life events in proper order.

4) **Write out in longhand a rough script** filling in your life outline. In this script fill in the anecdotes you want the tract to include. Open your heart and life up to the prospective reader of your tract.

5) **Pick the size tract you want to end up with:**

a. "Six-up" (approximately 3"x5")—about the size of an 8"x11" sheet folded in halves, then into thirds, forming six equal parts. This is about the best size for mass distribution, for it not only fits easily into your shirt pocket or purse for carrying, but it also fits well into their shirt pocket or purse for taking home with them! This will hold approximately 250 words per side of eight point type.

b. "Four-up" (approximately 4"x5")—about the size of an 8"x11" sheet folded into straight quarters. It will hold about 300 words per side.

c. "Two-up" size (about 5½"x8½")—this is half the size of an 8"x11" sheet, can hold up to 800 or 1,000 words per side.

d. Full-size brochure folded (8½"x11")—this size, when folded into thirds like a brochure, can hold almost any number of words in different type styles and sizes. Also, it leaves room for more of a cover illustration, or photos before and after Christ. This size can easily hold 1,000 to 1,500 words, per side if needed.

6) Refine your tract script: Edit your script down to your approximate word number allowable in the tract size you desire. Have some friends read it and give you some CONSTRUCTIVE criticism and ideas.

7) Have it typeset. Typesetting should cost $20 or less, even for a full size tract. It will look better and print so much more professionally if you have your tract typeset, instead of merely being typewritten and copied.

8) Plan on having a 20% minimum of white space in your tract: Try to keep your paragraphs no longer than six lines long, then always leave a white space.

9) Include an address and/or phone number where inquirers can contact you or can order more tracts to distribute, whether for free or for a fee.

10) Close the tract with some kind of invitation or challenge. Invite each reader to personally receive Jesus Christ as their Lord, and then to write you and tell you about it so you can share their joy and help them.

11) Print at least 1,000 copies to achieve a reasonable price-per-tract for the whole project.

12) Send and give them to all your relatives, friends, work associates, and daily acquaintances. You'll be pleasantly surprised at what a blessing this will be. It will not just bless your own spirit, but it will feed hungry, curious, lonely, searching hearts of many people around you that would never receive any other kind of a tract!

13) Once it's printed, use your personal testimony tract and soulwinning, God-glorifying incidents that come from its usage, to provoke and challenge other Christians to do the same with the hidden power of their own personal testimonies. Give your interested friends a Xerox copy of this chapter (or get them the entire book).

14) Use these tracts just as you would use any other tracts. (See ideas in the previous chapter.)

Remember, "**They overcame him** (satan) by the blood of the Lamb, and **by the word of their testimonies**" . . . and **praise God** . . . YOU CAN AND WILL TOO!

17

ABC's of Streetwitnessing

"Go out into the hedges and highways, and compel them to come in" Luke 14:23.

"What man of you, having 100 sheep, if he lose one, does not leave the ninety and nine in the wilderness, and go after that which is lost, until he finds it" Luke 15:4.

"A true witness delivereth souls" Proverbs 14:25

The street gives its own teaching courses and rewards its students with its own diplomas! In this section only basic principles will be covered for use in elementary streetwitnessing. These are the ABC's, not the whole alphabet. He Who is the Alpha and the Omega, the "A" and the "Z" will take, teach, train, and thrill you as you learn to do what He dedicated Himself to, and take the Gospel outside the sanctuary to the needs of a hurting humanity needing God's eternal Good News.

1) **Check your motives:** Why are you going out? God's love toward you, and in you toward others, should be your key motivating force. Without God's love you cannot succeed, but with it, you cannot fail (I Corinthians 13:8).

2) **Start out small:** Remember, streetwitnessing is NOT streetpreaching. It is not to crowds or even groups, but to one soul at a time!

3) **Go in "two's":** When Jesus sent out "the seventy" (Luke 10:1) and "the twelve" (Mark 6:7), He sent them out in two's for the obvious reasons.

4) **Pair up novices with those that have more streetwitnessing experience.**

5) **Expect results:** Faith begets faith, expectation produces results!

6) **Pray before you go:** Successful evangelism only comes from a spiritual overflow.

7) **Satan picks off strays: why can't we?** Keep you eyes out for loners, the single soul sitting on a car alone, the fringe character.

8) **Rely on the Holy Spirit:** God's promise is: "Not by might, not by power, but by My Spirit" (Zechariah 4:6). He will not just do the speaking (Matthew 10:20), but the convicting and saving as well!

9) **Have a definite time to meet back at the starting point or the Outreach.**

10) **Ask to pray at the end of each streetwitnessing conversation for and with the prospect.** A one minute prayer can achieve more than a ten minute talk.

11) **Practice at the Outreach witnessing to each other.**

12) **Have a map or chart of different witnessing spots.** Assign teams, get reports, make sure others involved know what God's been doing *out there!!*

Much more, of course, is witten in other chapters in this Outreach section, and in many other books. But one thing is important above all: if you show genuine love and show you care, they'll see Jesus, they'll be touched by God's Holy Spirit, and they'll want His love and reality too! Every witness must be a showcase for the Kingdom of Heaven!

18

The Top Forty Soulwinning Mistakes to Avoid

"He that is wise captures human lives for God (or "winneth souls") Proverbs 11:30.

"Fear not, for I will make you a sharp new threshing instrument" Isaiah 41:15.

Any veteran fisherman can give a first-timer a series of lessons and teach him success secrets that will eliminate a lot of the normal trial and error process of learning. Jesus has called *every* believer to be a successful "fisher of men."

I. PREPARATION

1) **Bring your Bible.** Don't go on the battlefield without your sword! Bring along an extra pocketsize New Testament or two. The prospect can not only read along in it as you explain certain scriptures, but you can give it to him, and write his re-birth date inside when he prays to receive Jesus as Lord!

2) **Go prayed up.** Put prayers on your legs before you put legs on your prayers. Saturate yourself in God's presence through prayer. Prospects

know when you've just left Heaven itself to come out looking for them!

3) Don't wait for a feeling. Set a regular weekly time to go soulwinning. Honor it, and God will honor you with sucess.

4) Don't go alone. Jesus sent them out in "two's" and He still does (Ecclesiastes 4:9).

5) Bring what you'll need! Don't leave without pens, a few 3"x5" cards and a few dollars.

6) Avoid bad breath. Be considerate. Carry mints, certs, etc. with you.

7) Avoid body odor. Satan will use anything to distract prospects.

8) Go well groomed. You're going out as an ambassador for Heaven. Dress to fit the audience you want to reach. Wear a suit at colleges or downtown, but wear blue jeans when out on the street!

9) Go with a plan: Having a basic plan to rely on is handy, especially when the prospect is ready to get saved. If you are a new convert, write the Romans Road plan (Romans 3:23, 6:23, 10:9, 10, 10:13) in the front of your Bible, or use a chain reference. Write Romans 3:23 in front, then 6:23 in the margin and so on through to 10:13!

10) Go in faith expecting: Jesus told many people: "As you believe, it will be done to you."

II. THE APPROACH

11) Don't choose someone too much your senior. There are plenty of "fish" your age or younger; you'll have more credibility with them.

12) Don't wait for the "fish" to make the contact. Fishermen take the initiative, NOT the fish! First you throw the bait, then the fish bites! Start the conversation just as Jesus did at the well (John 4).

13) Hide your hook: Proverbs 1:17 says: "If the bird watches you set your net, forget trying to catch it!" You'll do better with a pocket-size New Testament. Take it out of your pocket at the right moment!

III. THE SOULWINNING CONVERSATION ITSELF

14) Never ask: "Are you a Christian?" Few Americans consider themselves "heathen" or pagan." Too many confuse churchgoing with salvation.

15) Be complementary. Find something good to comment on and relax your prospect!

16) **Use a conversational "runway."** Start on mutual ground, talking about surroundings, weather, etc. and gain the prospect's trust. Fishermen that jerk the hook too hard, too fast, lose both fish and bait!

17) **Don't talk TOO much!** Use questions, if the prospect isn't saying much. Doctors use questions to "locate" their patients; soulwinners must too!

18) **Avoid religious jargon.** Everday religious words like *saved* or *sanctified*, and phrases like *the blood of the Lamb* may be unknown and or shocking to some. Make sure you define these terms when you use them!

19) **Avoid romance.** If the prospect is of the opposite sex, stay in the spiritual realm — don't get too personal. Often it's better to let a sister reach a sister and vice-versa.

20) **Don't concentrate on putting down other's religions.** Jesus promised if we lift Him up, HE would draw all men to Him (John 12:32).

21) **Don't win your argument and lose the convert.** The surgeon who says: "The operation was a success, but we lost the patient," doesn't get much repeat business! Concede anything but Christ!

22) **Don't get sidetracked by little issues.** Always return to "where Cain's wife came from" type questions after a while. Stay on the track, follow your soulwinning plan, return to Christ, and minister the Word of God!

23) **Avoid spiritual snobbery!** Never come on like you are the "holy one" and the prospect is a sinful worm polluting the air you breathe. Be open about your past sins, and **stress God's goodness instead of yours!** Salvation is a wonderful gift you received and you hope he does too!

24) **Don't jump all over the Bible.** Prospects won't be as impressed by vast Bible knowledge as by Godly love and sincerity in caring for and trying to share Christ with them!

25) **Don't accept religious brushoffs.** Many say: "I go to church" or "I was raised . . ." this or that, but if asked where they'd spend eternity if they died this very moment, they confess they don't know. Stress the fact God wants them to know and with one prayer, they will know just like you and millions of others do! (I John 5:13).

26) **Don't pretend to have all the answers.** A prospect will respect your admitting you don't know something much more than your trying to bluff him or change the subject. However, do return to your experience and relationship with Christ. That is one thing every Christian must know and every sinner must learn about.

27) **Don't interrupt the prospect or allow yourself to be.** Let your prospect talk, even if he rambles on. When he's finished, it's only fair that he

listen to you. Remind him of this, and he usually will hear you out!

28) **Don't waste hours on "dogs" or "pigs!"** Jesus mentioned these two spiritual categories of unsaved people in Matthew 7:6. He has ordered us where not to cast our pearls; when spiritual "oinks" and "barks" occur, it's time to move on.

IV. THE CLOSE

29) **Don't go by appearances.** The prospect may not look very "touched," but if the Holy Spirit says "close the deal," your prospect may burst into tears when the Holy Spirit hits his heart with God's love.

30) **Go for their spirit, not just their soul.** Their spirit is the center of their being, their spiritual heart, not just their emotions or intellect. A changed life results from a heart-felt desire to do so.

31) **Swing your sickle.** Even the ripest, golden grain can't harvest itself, and neither do conversion-ready souls. Men are called to be co-workers with God's Holy Spirit. When we do our part, then He does His! ASK THEM: "WOULD YOU LIKE TO HAVE THIS ETERNAL LIFE . . . THIS NEW LIFE IN JESUS . . . RIGHT NOW? WOULDN'T YOU LIKE TO KNOW FOR SURE? LET'S PRAY THIS PRAYER . . ."

32) **Don't hesitate even if they do.** If they balk in answering the above question, offer to pray with them; bow your head first. They'll usually follow you in bowing their head as well.

33) **Avoid being too personal with strangers.** Some people are offended by strangers putting their hands on their shoulder, or holding their hand. Be sensitive to this. Touching isn't necessary for praying. God will touch them regardless; get them into prayer!

34) **Don't be afraid of a "No!"** Even their saying "no" may help them get saved at some future date when they realize what they've refused. **Stay in the Spirit, and remind them they've rejected Christ, not you.**

35) **Don't fail to pray (or offer to) even after a "No!"** Sometimes they'll allow you to pray, even if they won't pray along with you. If they let you "get to first base" go ahead!

36) **Don't force "green fruit."** If they're definitely not ready for Christ, don't try to psychologically pressure them in mouthing a "sinner's prayer." You've done your part, now believe God to do His!

37) **Avoid the "$1.50 vacuum cleaner sales syndrome."** A story tells of a new salesman who sold 50 cleaners his first day out. His boss couldn't believe it and asked: "Did you collect the $150 sale price from each buyer?" The new salesman replied: $150?, I thought they sold for only $1.50

each!" Jesus told us to make disciples, not to get cheap decisions!
38) Never ask: "HOW DO YOU FEEL?" A newly saved person may feel "fireworks" or nothing at all. Right away you must teach them to look to God's Word. God's Word says if they asked Jesus in as Lord, He's come in to stay!

V. FOLLOW-UP

39) Don't just say: "God, you do all the followup!" You need to give them your name, address and phone number, and get the same information from them. *You* need to arrange to see them again, and help them become an integral part of the Body of Christ. See the Inreach chapter on "Follow-up." Where would your Christian life be now if someone hadn't taken a personal interest in you, not just as a soul, but as a person with feelings and needs.
40) Don't see any one night's soulwinning as an end in itself. Don't get too discouraged or too elated when you win a soul, or fail to. Critique your evening's ministry in a book where you can file weekly evaluations of your soulwinning times. Write what you did right, what you did wrong, and how to do better next time out! Edison wasn't discouraged after 1,000 failures in designing the perfect filament for electric light bulbs for he was 1,000 steps closer to finding the right combination to bring light to the world. Each time out you'll be closer too!

19

Sending Out
Witnessing Teams

"Blessed are ye that sow beside all waters" Isaiah 32:20.
"Behold, I send you out . . ." Matthew 10:16.
"Well done, good and faithful servant, you have been dependable with a few (soulwinners), I will make you master over (allow you to send out) many" Matthew 25:21, 23.

You may have a blessed, God-given burden in your heart to reach lost souls, and yet not have others to go out soulwinning or witnessing with: You will!

Developing outreach teams is like anything else. You start a the beginning in this case, one person with a burden for souls. As James 3:5 puts it: "Behold how large a forest one little spark can set on fire." Jesus put it another way in Mark 4:28: "First the blade, then the ear, then the full kernel in the ear." TAKE FIRST THINGS FIRST! Just as in building a (spiritual) bonfire, one faithful spark is all that's needed to start it off. That spark is you, your faith, and Jesus' love in you for souls!

The phrase "sending out teams" necessitates three ingredients, namely: 1) the sender; 2) a place for teams to gather and be sent out from, and; 3) the teams. Let's now look at these three "bonfire" ingredients in detail!

1) The Sender: You must be organized, loving, dependable, inspiring, and have a contagious agape-love for God, Christians and lost souls, to be successful.

2) The Place: If you have an Outreach, the teams will obviously gather there at regular weekly times. **If you have no outreach yet,** pray and see whether God may be leading you to use either your home, a church facility, or a neutral gathering place, like a nearby cafeteria, or apartment complex club room.

3) The Teams: As previously stated, you may have no teams yet, but Matthew 7:7, 8 says you will, so get started.

a. Make a list of Christian friends interested in soulwinning. Call or write them and tell them your plan for regular soulwinning teams.

b. Call friendly pastors in evangelical churches, asking for names and numbers of anyone interested in witnessing.

c. Start small, but be faithful: pick one night a week and it will grow.

d. Make signs for church bulletin boards, sharing your vision and details.

e. Ask pastors to include news of your work in their weekly church bulletin.

4) The Actual Sending Out of the Teams: At our Outreach, we sent out Soulwinning Teams on weekend nights around 9:15 p.m. The doors officially open at 8 p.m. While people arrive and gather in, I usually give a scriptural soulwinning teaching, or review a new book on personal evangelism. About 9:15, ask all those that want to go out with a soulwinning team to go into the back prayer room. Once there, divide the soulwinners up into teams. Use your regular team captains as team leaders. You should be able to count on your captains being there. Thus, when the teaching is over, soulwinners can be gathered in the back, assignments can be made, soul-winners can gather their needed materials (tracts, 3x5 cards for convert addresses, soulwinner report forms, coats, etc.) and get going with a minimum of confusion.

Aircraft carrier jets are quickly and powerfully "catapult-launched" one by one in a tightly knit, organized manner. You will find it works smoother to have one team captain and his team launched before getting the next team "airborne." (Tracts, etc. need to be pregathered by the front door to cut confusion.) Team launching in this manner, one by one, is far superior to trying to launch six team captains with their team members at the same time, all heading for tracts, coats, and the door simultaneously.

Choosing Team Captains:

A street-witnessing team captain should not be a street novice. He should be one who has previously won souls, shown spiritual maturity and dependability, one who loves Christians as well as lost sinners with Christ's own love, and one who has good Bible knowledge and COMMON SENSE!

Team Captain Responsibilities:

1) Take, fill out, and return a soulwinners report sheet each night out.
2) Give a soulwinners report sheet to each team member.
3) Give 3x5 cards (kept by front door or prayer room) to each team-mate.
4) Learn names of team members, and help others do the same.
5) In Christ-like manner, "lord it" under, not over, his flock (John 13:15).
6) Make sure they all know where and what their target is, when the team will be gathering to return, in case anyone gets separated.

Hints on Choosing Teams

1) Each team should have at least 2 or 3, and no more than 6 or 7.
2) Each team should have at least one stronger Christian for each novice.

Things to Remember and Possibilities

1) Have a list of results from the last weekend or the previous night's teams.

Share victory reports to encourage the teams.

2) Sometimes assign the same teams to the same place for a month or more.

3) Continually remind soulwinners that Jesus sent them in "two's," not solo!

4) Get a large chalkboard, or posterboard: Write on such the team captains' names, the destination of each team, and names of those chosen on each.

5) If the target is ten miles or less away, take several cars. Often with only one car and a half dozen people, several are ready to leave, while the driver or another team member has someone ready to get saved. When the fish are biting, no fisherman wants to leave!

6) If people came to go soulwinning together, don't insist they break up.

7) If you have too many first-time novices wanting to go out soulwinning on a weekend night, start a new soulwinner's class on a weekday night, with teachings and practical two-member team lessons just for them. Actually, even Sunday afternoon is a good time to go door-to-door.

8) Lay hands on team members one at a time for individual blessing back in the prayer room. Done occasionally, this gives an added "something extra" to each participant.

9) Use a soulwinner "bulletin-report" to mail and tell soulwinners upcoming events.

Things to Avoid in Sending Out Teams

10) Avoid splitting up husband and wife teams unless they so desire.

11) Avoid "lone-rangers" as team captains; teams need a leader with them.

12) Although we haven't had this problem, avoid a system of team selecting that becomes so mechanical that it gets depersonalized and starts offending your regular soulwinners.

13) Avoid sending out "babes in Christ" into too deep water. New converts inexperienced in street work shouldn't be sent out into your town's "heaviest" bar for their first night's assignment!

14) Avoid confusion especially when more than one team is assigned to the same event. Draw a map on a blackboard or posterboard, and at the minimum have each team captain copy the entire team assignments, so he not only knows where his team belongs, but where the other teams are as well!

20

Sample Soulwinner's Report

"Declare His doings among the people" Psalm 9:11.

A mimeographed 8" x 11" sheet report like the one below given to every soulwinning team will help the director keep abreast of all the Good News going on through the Outreach.

SOULWINNER'S REPORT

FRIDAY AND SATURDAY EVENING: SPECIAL EVENTS

CAPTAIN:
TEAM MEMBERS:
LOCATION:
WHAT HAPPENED:

RECEIVED SALVATION (Get name to follow-up):

21

100 Top Soulwinning Scriptures

"So shall My Word be that goeth forth out of My mouth: it shall not return unto Me void, but it shall accomplish that which I please, and it shall prosper in the thing whereto I sent it" Isaiah 55:11.

SAVED? SAVED FROM WHAT?

John 5:24   from spiritual death

Mark 16:16	from damnation
John 3:17	from condemnation
Luke 7:50	from sickness
Revelation 20:15	from the lake of fire
Hebrews 2:14-15	from fear of death
Colossians 1:13	from satan's kingdom
Galatians 3:13	from the law's curse

WHAT SHOULD WE PREACH ABOUT

John 12:32	lift up Jesus
John 3:16	God so loved
Romans 5:8	while yet sinners
II Corinthians 4:5	we preach Christ

WHY PREACH GOD'S WORD?

I Peter 4:11	say what God says
Jeremiah 23:29	it's a hammer and fire
Isaiah 55:11	it won't return void
Jeremiah 1:12	watches over His words
Psalm 119:130	God's Word brings light
Hebrews 4:12	two-edged Sword
Psalm 138:2	Word above Name
John 6:63	Spirit and Life
Mark 2:2	Jesus did!

ALL MEN HAVE SINNED AND FALLEN

Romans 3:10	none righteous
Romans 3:23	all fall short
Isaiah 53:6	like sheep astray
Ecclesiastes 7:20	not a just man
Matthew 19:17	only One good
Jeremiah 17:9	heart is wicked
Ephesians 2:1	dead in sins

WHAT WILL OUR DECISION BE?

Joel 3:13	valley of decision
Isaiah 1:18	come now and reason
II Corinthians 6:2	now is the day of salvation
Joel 2:32	whosoever calls on
Revelation 3:20	if any man opens
Joshua 24:15	for me and my house

SIN KILLS

Romans 6:23	sin's wage is death
Romans 5:12	death came on all men
Genesis 2:17	ye shall die

WHY BOTHER TO GO SOULWINNING?

Matthew 28:19-20	go ye therefore
Mark 16:15	preach to all
Luke 24:47	to all nations
John 20:21	as God sent Me, so I send you
Acts 1:8	ye shall be witnesses
Luke 14:23	hedges and highways
John 3:16	loved the WORLD!
John 15:8	bear much fruit
Proverbs 11:30	wise men win souls
Matthew 4:19	fishers of men
Genesis 4:9	my brother's keeper
Proverbs 24:11	deliver the doomed

WE CAN'T SAVE OURSELVES

Jeremiah 13:23	leopard and spots
Isaiah 64:6	righteousness/rags
Psalm 49:8	can't redeem self
Galatians 2:16	jusified by faith

CHRIST DIED FOR ALL MEN

I Timothy 2:4	for all men
II Peter 3:9	that none perish
John 3:16	loved the WORLD!
Matthew 20:28	for the multitudes
John 1:29	sin of the WORLD!
Revelation 22:17	whosoever thirsts
John 6:37	him that cometh
Isaiah 53:5	for our iniquities
I Peter 2:24	for our sins
Isaiah 53:10	bruised by God for us
Matthew 18:14	that not one little one perish

GOD SAYS TO ALL: COME!

Matthew 11:28	all heavy laden
John 6:37	not cast out
Revelation 22:17	thirsty come
John 10:10	abundant life
John 7:37	come drink

WHAT ARE WE NOW IN CHRIST JESUS?

II Corinthians 5:17	new creations
Ephesians 2:6	seated in heaven
II Corinthians 2:14-15	always victors
Romans 8:38	more than conquerors
II Corinthians 5:21	God's righteousness
Romans 5:1	justifed by faith
Romans 8:1	no condemnation
I John 3:1-2	God's sons now
Galatians 4:7	heirs of God
Philippians 3:20	heaven's citizens
Matthew 5:13-14	salt and light
Colossians 1:13	transplants into God's Kingdom

HOW ARE WE NOW TO LIVE?

Romans 12:1-2	living sacrifice and holy
I John 3:4	pure
I Peter 1:16	must be holy
I John 5:3	keep His commands
II Timothy 2:15	study God's Word
I Timothy 4:12	be examples
I Peter 2:9	royal priesthood

WHY BOTHER TO BE BAPTIZED?

Matthew 3:16	Jesus was
Mark 16:16	He said we should
Matthew 28:19	part of the Great Commission
Acts 2:38	Peter preached it
Acts 9:18	Paul was!
Acts 8:39	the Ethiopian was

22

Thirty Conversation Openers

"He that has friends must show himself friendly, and there is a friend that sticks closer than a brother" Proverbs 18:24.

Asking questions is the way that doctors find out what's ailing their patients. Similarly, in the spiritual realm, questions are indispensable in personal soulwinning. Below are thirty sample questions you might use as conversation openers:

1. Come here very often?
2. What's happening?
3. Been here long?
4. Got the time?

5. This your car? bench? etc.
6. Can I ask you a question or two?
7. Could you tell me some directions?
8. Hi! My Name is _____ , what's yours?
9. Like some good news?
10. Seen any moonies tonight?
11. Seen any Jesus people?
12. What's going on?
13. Waiting for someone?
14. Why do people come out here?
15. What turns you on? (be ready!)
16. Do you like getting high?
17. Ever been to _____ (use your home church or outreach).
18. Haven't I seen you some place before?
19. Would you like to spend eternity here?
20. Where is everybody?
21. Doing some heavy thinking?
22. What's wrong with this world?
23. Any good stuff going round?
24. Any parties tonight?
25. Anyone told you you're special today?
26. Anything exciting going on?
27. Have you seen me before?
28. Could I tell you about the best thing that ever happened to me?
29. Who's your best friend?
30. Got a friend who loves you enough to die for you?

23

Twenty-Five Ways All Conversations Lead to Jesus

"But when He (the Holy Spirit) is come, He shall glorify Me" John 16:14.

"But when the Comforter is come, Whom I will send unto you from the Father, even the Spirit of truth, which proceeds from the Father, He shall testify of Me" John 15:26.

"For it is not you that speaks, but the Spirit of your Father speaking through you" Matthew 10:20.

Not once in the four Gospels is Jesus recorded as saying to a stranger right off the bat: "Repent or go to hell!" In John 4 with the Samaritan woman, Jesus built a conversational bridge into her world, starting with physical water and then tying it into Living Water!

In most every soulwinning book, there is advice to start a conversation in the natural realm to establish a relationship with the prospect, and then to CROSS OVER CONVERSATIONALLY to the eternal, spiritual realm. Below are twenty-five CROSS-OVER questions to help make that transition.

1. Are you interested in spiritual things?

2. Have you ever thought about becoming a Christian?

3. What would you answer if someone were to ask you: "What is a Christian?"

4. Have you come to the place in your spiritual life where you know if you died tonight where you would spend eternity?

5. If you died and God asked: "Why should I let you into my heaven?" Do you know the right answer?

6. Are you interested in some Eternal Good News?

7. Could you give me some directions? Could you tell me the way to heaven?

8. If I died right now, where would I spend eternity?

9. If you died *RIGHT NOW*, where would *YOU* go: heaven or hell?

10. Do you know where you'll be 100 years from tonight?

11. Have you ever met Jesus Christ personally?

12. Who do you belong to? Spiritually, that is?

13. If Jesus Christ returned tonight, would you be ready?

14. Do you know why Jesus died on that cross 2,000 years ago?

15. Wouldn't it be nice if you could know you're headed for heaven?

16. If God wanted you to know where you're going to spend eternity, would you be interested?

17. If you had a reserved seat in heaven with your name on it, would you be interested in making sure you got to it?

18. How much of Howard Hughes' billions of dollars went with him?

19. Do you know which airline flies to heaven? It's United with . . .

20. Jesus said: "Unless a man is born again from above, he'll never enter into heaven." Can you say that's happened to you?
21. Have you ever seen a real Christian?
22. Are you a follower of Jesus?
23. Do you ever think about eternity?
24. Have you ever wanted to feel close to God?
25. Where do you usually go to church around here?

24

Answering the Top Nineteen Questions

"I will give you a mouth and wisdom that no man will be able to gainsay or resist" Luke 21:15.

"The secret things belong unto the Lord, but those things that are revealed belong unto us and to our children, that we may obey God's Law" Deuteronomy 29:29.

Several questions are repeatedly asked while out streetwitnessing or streetpreaching. Sometimes you'll find it's best to keep on presenting your Gospel soulwinning plan and tell the prospect you'll get back to their question in just a little bit. They may even forget their question when they get wrapped up in God's amazing plan of salvation!

1) **What about all the little children in India that have never heard?** At the Great White Throne Judgment (Revelation 20:11), God won't ask you about the little children in India, but He will ask you what you did with what you heard. What will you say?

2) **Why would a good, loving God let people go to an eternal Hell?** Why would a pure, holy God let sinners into His pure, holy heaven to ruin it as sin ruined the original perfection He created on earth? Really, the amazing thing isn't that some aren't going to heaven, but that so many are. God says in Matthew 25:41, that the "everlasting fire was prepared for the devil and his angels," not for any man, unless they insist!

3) **Why doesn't God just make all men be saved if He's all-powerful?** If God could make all men be saved, He certainly would. But though God is

all-powerful, He can't call sin righteousness, nor can He make a lie the truth. The Bible tells us in Genesis 1:26 that God made man in His own image. God isn't a puppet, and thus neither is man. For God to "pull our strings" as if we were His little marionettes would prove that the Bible isn't true: another impossibility! God has done all He could in sending Christ to die on the cross for me and you. He's done His part, now will you do yours and receive Him as your Lord?

4) Where did Cain get his wife? Cain got his wife the same place I got mine, from the available source of unmarried single women on earth. Notice, he married her, he didn't live in fornication with her. A bunch of people have missed receiving eternal life worrying about Cain's wife. I'd tell you if I was Able . . . Give your heart to Christ and you'll be able . . . to go to heaven . . . someday! "

5) What's wrong with marijuana? Genesis 1:29 says God gave man every herb bearing seed, and marijuana is an herb. Well, that was before Adam and Eve fell; with their sin came a curse on the ground to bring forth thorns and poison plants (Genesis 3:17). In short, there's a snake in the grass: satan! The Bible classifies drugs (consciousness-changers like marijuana) under sorcery (*Pharmakeia*, Greek for drugs) and in both Isaiah 47 and 57 and Revelation 21:8 it is condemned. Drugs are a counterfeit for God's Spirit Who is "the real thing."

6) Do you have to go to church? No, I enjoy going to church, but God doesn't live there. God's house is no longer a building, unless it has two feet on it. God lives in me, and wants to live in you. He wants to put His victory and love into your life. You don't have to get saved in church, but without putting wood on a fire, what happens to it?
(Hebrews 10:25 also applies.)

7) Do you believe in Reincarnation? No, the Bible teaches resurrection, not reincarnation. Jesus said in John 5:28: "All in their graves shall come forth for judgment, the saved and lost." Which will you be? The Bible also teaches in Hebrews 9:27 (and elsewhere) "Once to die, then the judgment."

8) If God has all power, why doesn't He destroy all evil? He wants to and soon will, but if He did it right now, unsaved multitudes would be destroyed along with satan and his imps. Millions are being saved and God wants you to be one of them.

9) Why would a loving God create hell? Because God is love, and His love is so perfect that he won't allow death, shame, sickness or guilt in heaven to ruin the eternal party He's preparing for those that accept His love invitation in Christ to come home.

10) Why did God let Hitler kill 6 million Jews? Hitler wasn't any more

Christian than the devil is or than Karl Marx was Jewish! God didn't let it happen, men did. Don't blame God for the shortcomings of mankind. God made man perfect, and wants to *recreate* all men, Jew and Gentile, perfect in His perfect Son, Jesus.

11) Why should I believe in Jesus as God? I'm Jewish. First of all, Yeshua is Jewish. Secondly, how would you recognize the Jewish Messiah? What did the Jewish prophets write? Do you know the Messianic prophecies in Deuteronmony 18:18, Psalms 22:1, 8, 16, 18; Isaiah 7:14, 9:6, 53:1-12; Micah 5:2; Zechariah 9:9, 12:10, 13:1, 13:6; Psalm 118:22 and others? Did you know the Messiah rejected by Israel was predicted by Israel's own prophets? (Isaiah 8:14).

12) **Why praise the Lord?** It's a command of God, for everything that has breath to praise the Lord (Psalms 149, 150:6). Besides, I believe in giving credit where credit is due.

13) **What's wrong with astrology?** It was an ancient Babylonian art, science, and religion. God condemns it in Deuteronomy 18:10 and Romans 1:25 as an abomination, a type of magical enchantment and sorcery. Stars don't control anything: but the God who made them does and He is worthy of all our worship, love, and obedience (Deuteronomy 6:5).

14) **Which translation? They all say something different. Anyway, the Bible is full of contradictions.** They all say the same thing to me. They all speak of a fallen mankind, and of one Redeemer, the Saviour, Jesus who died in the place of all men, shed the same blood on the same cross, was buried in the same tomb, rose the same third day and ascended to the same Father. He's the same Jesus that has saved millions, including me, and He wants to **translate you now into His Kingdom of love!**

15) **Why did God let my mother die of TB (or cancer, etc.)?** Jesus said: "The thief (the devil) comes to steal, kill and destroy. Did your mother know Jesus personally? Did she believe in divine healing? God's salvation and healing power are available to all, but food or medicine doesn't do anyone any good if not taken. Anyway, I'm sorry about your mother, but there's a worse disease named sin. Jesus cured me, would you like Him to cure you, too.

16) **What's wrong with evolution, anyway?** Evolution is a scientific theory that Charles Darwin thought up. He renounced it on his death bed and called for a Bible. Evolution denies Genesis 1:1 which says, "In the beginning, God created the heaven and earth." Evolution makes man a descendent of the apes, which I think offends every monkey on this planet. The Bible teaches man fell in sin, and didn't evolve up, but devolved down.

17) **What do you mean, saved? Saved from what?** Jesus used the expression "saved" 11 different times in our Bible. In Mark 16:16 He said, "He that believes and is baptized shall be saved: he that believes not shall be damned." So saved means being saved from being damned. Several times Jesus tells people whom He healed that they were saved from their diseases, or delivered from satanic possession. The word *saved* ("sodzo" in Greek) means to "make whole, or sound, to heal, deliver, make free, to prosper, to free, to protect, to preserve, to make or be whole." So to be "saved" means to not only be brought out of satan's death kingdom and sin's curse but to be returned to oneness with God, to share in His nature, blessings, love, healing, and prosperity eternally.

18) **Why do Christians always look and act like losers?** They don't! But there's a lot of "counterfeit money" going around that often passes for Christianity, but it's really Churchianity. God and Jesus are not religion, but a friendship and relationship with God. The Bible is God's jewelbook, not rulebook. Satan has a lot of smoke screens out to keep people from finding the real thing. I've found it; would you like to find it now, too?

19) **Why are PK's (preacher's kids) such "hell raisers?"** Many people expect perfection and higher standards from "PK's" (preacher's kids). Not all PK's are bad! Moses, (Exodus 2:10), Jeremiah (Jeremiah 1:1), Ezekiel (Ezekiel 1:3), and Zechariah (Zechariah 1:1) were all PK's and turned out fine. In fact, they wrote almost half of the Old Testament! If PK's are bad, they've been spoiled either by permissive parents like Eli's kids in the book of I Samuel or they've gone wild because of religious hypocrisy. "God so loved the world," including preachers' kids, bartenders' kids, rich and poor people's kids, and people like you and me. I thank God He forgave me when I asked Him . . . wouldn't you like to ask Jesus to give you Eternal Life now, too?

25

Relating the Gospel

"I am made all things to all men, that I might by all means save some" I Corinthians 9:22.

"Without a parable He didn't even speak to them" Matthew 13:34.

Jesus Christ was always relating the Kingdom of heaven through parables. He would paint a familiar setting, tell a tale, and then point out eternal spiritual truths to His listeners' identifying and relating these common objects with eternal realities and spiritual laws.

To fishermen Jesus spoke of fishing for men. To the woman at the well He spoke of living water. To Pharisees censoring His healing of a blind man, He spoke of spiritual blindness. There are many ways of relating the Gospel; several are discussed below.

Relating through surroundings

At rock concerts, share about the Great Rock that never rolls. At football games, share about the divine quarterback who has never fumbled or been intercepted. At the Fourth of July fireworks, share the fireworks of salvation. At Walks for Mankind, share about Jesus' walk for mankind under the cross! At any event, God's Spirit will give you some tie-in to relate the Gospel!

One way to relate the gospel is through colors. For example, to a woman with a red shirt on, reminder that Jesus spilled His sinless, pure red blood for her salvation. Preach to a man in a white shirt, that Jesus' blood can wash away sin's stains and make his heart whiter than snow. To anyone wearing black, relate the fact that black is worn at funerals, etc.

Another way of relating the Gospel, especially at parades, is through initials. For example, many bands have one or two initials on their uniforms. If it's an "H," for example, share "Does everyone see those 'H's' on their uniforms? Ask youself if that "H" stands for heaven or hell, for happiness or heartbreak, for holiness or hollowness. Are you His today? Let Jesus change your hell to heaven today, and receive Him as Lord of your life." Not only is the band witnessed to, but all the crowd watching and listening are challenged and convicted as well!

Relating through surrounding situations. Even if momentary, this can be very effective. At a red light, preach on a car PA: "Let Jesus give you the green light to heaven today, or "Give Jesus the green light in your heart!" At a yield sign preach: "Yield your life to Jesus today, and He'll take all your sins away!"

There is no limit to relating the Gospel, and you'll find the more you allow God's Spirit to personalize the Gospel to individual situations, the more they'll realize God's love for them as precious individuals!

26

What Are and Why Use Turnarounds?

"So his reply gave them no sort of handle that they could use against him. And in fact they were so taken aback by his answer that they had nothing more to say" Luke 20:46 (Phillips Trans.) Matthew 22:26.

"I will give you a mouth and wisdom which all your adversaries shall not be able to gainsay or resist" Luke 21:15.

"And they were not able to resist the wisdom and the spirit by which he (Stephen) spoke" Acts 6:10.

"For it is not ye that speak but the Spirit of your Father Who speaketh in you" Matthew 10:20.

"The officers answered . . . no man ever spoke like this Man" John 7:46.

What is a Turnaround?

A conversational turnaround is like a move in judo, used to get the opponent off balance, using the opponent's very own momentum to turn the tables, to TURNAROUND the disadvantage to the original antagonist. Cassius Clay could stand all day and turnaround every blow that an amateur boxer might throw at him, because he knows the art of self-defense. Turnarounds are defensive spiritual weapons. If more Christians knew how to defend themselves while out soulwinning, millions more would be out there doing it, unafraid of the devil's darts!

Did Jesus use Turnarounds?

Time after time Jesus' principal opponents, the Pharisees, Sadducees, and Herodians would try to conversationally pin or knock Him down. Time after time Jesus used such turnarounds as those below:

The sabbath was made for man, and not man for the sabbath (Mark 2:27).

I will also ask you a question (Mark 11:29).

Haven't you read what David did, he and his men? (Mark 2:25).

Let him who is without sin cast the first stone (John 8:7).
Even so the last shall be first, and the first shall be last (Matthew 19:30).
Give Caesar, Caesar's things, and God's things to God (Matthew 22:21).

Did Jesus respect Turnarounds in others?

We read in Matthew 15:21-28 of the Syrophoenician woman with the demon-possessed daughter. Jesus told her, "It's not fit to cast children's bread to the dogs until the children are filled" (Mark 7:27). He was testing her faith and spiritual perception, seeing if she would catch it. She DID! She replied, "Yes, Lord, yet the house puppies under the table eat the children's crumbs" (Mark 7:28). Jesus said to her . . . "FOR THIS SAYING (in other words, FOR THIS TURNAROUND), go your way, your daughter is healed" (Mark 7:29). Notice, Peter's turnaround in John 13:9 when he says: "Then Lord, don't just wash my feet only, but wash also my hands and head," (in other words, Lord, THEN GIVE ME A BATH!).

27

100 Common Turnarounds

"A word spoken at the right time is like apples of gold in pictures of silver" Proverbs 25:11.

Actor (you're sure a good) — No, I'm a reactor. I'm reacting to God's love by sharing with you now!

Bank on it (Don't) — Don't worry, I'm banking at the only eternal bank . . . United Bank in heaven. Jesus will open you an account if you deposit your faith tonight.

Believe in God (I) — The Bible says the devil believes in God, too; how come he's not going to heaven? (James 4:19).

Believe in God (I don't) — God believed in you enough to send Jesus to die for you 2,000 years before you were born. Does anyone else you know believe in YOU that much (Romans 5:8).

Believe in heaven or hell (I don't) — Obviously, or you'd already be saved! (or) You will sooner or later (or) Millions who didn't wish they could have a second chance now in hell, but it's too late forever!

Blooming idiot (you're) — I'd rather be a blooming idiot in man's eyes, than a wilting "know-it-all" in God's!

Bothering me (You're) — My guilty conscience did too until one day I asked Jesus to turn it off . . . and He did.

Brainwashed (You've been) — Yeh, it's great! Jesus really did a super job! He's washed away all of the stains and guilt from my sins!

Childish (You're being) — That's right! Jesus said unless we accept God's Kingdom like little children we'll never enter it!

Can't you talk about anything else — Sure I can, but nothing else gives me such supreme joy as talking about my wonderful Lord Jesus!

Christ complex (You have a) — No it's not complex; it's really very simple. It's refusing Christ that gets complex, especially explaining why at Judgment Day!

Con man (You're a real) — You're right. I'm trying to build your confidence in God.

Couldn't care less (I) — God couldn't care more!

Count me out (Why don't you) — God will if you insist, but eternity's a long count to be out for.

Crazy (You're really) — No, serving Jesus isn't half as crazy as refusing to.

Crutch (Jesus is a) — Jesus didn't limp with the cripples; He healed them. Sin cripples everyone spiritually, and only Jesus can heal us from it.

Cut it out! — You can't cut sin out; you've got to "faith it out" by trusting Jesus Christ . . .

Disturbing the peace (you are) — I'd rather disturb your peace and see you saved than see you go to hell in false peace and burn forever. (or) The Bible says there is no peace (to disturb) for the wicked (Isaiah 57:19).

Doesn't make sense (that) — You're right, it's not sense, it's faith.

Doing all right like I am (I'm) — Yes, but from God's standpoint, . . . are you saved or lost?

Do me a favor, leave please — I'm doing you a favor by staying (or) do yourself a favor; give in to Christ now!

Don't discuss religion or politics (I) — Neither do I, praise God! Thank God Jesus is neither, but instead, He's the precious Son of God.

Don't give a damn (I) — God doesn't want to either. He doesn't want to damn anyone at judgment, that's why He sent Christ to suffer our damnation

2,000 years ago.

Don't understand it (I) — I don't either, but it works! I don't understand air conditioning, but it feels good on a hot day.

Don't want to hear it (I) — That's what God will say to all excuses at Judgment.

Do the best I can (I) — God's standard is perfection; only Christ meets that. You can't buy His gift, but it's great to receive His free gift of eternal life.

Dry up, (Why don't you) — I can't, Jesus put a river of living water inside me and it's bubbling stronger every day.

Ecology (I believe in) — The only solution to pollution is the Lord Jesus Christ in men's hearts.

Everybody doesn't have to believe — No, but it's truth or consequences: Jesus said, "If you don't believe that I am the One, you will die in your sins" (John 8:24).

Exhibitionist (You're an) — That's right. I'm showing off Jesus Christ, just like the Bible commands in I Peter 2:9.

Fall for that (I'm not gonna) — Then you'll fall without it; the bottomless pit is an awful long fall.

Fail God (I might) — If you really let God take control of your life, how can He fail Himself?

Fairy tales (I don't believe in) — I don't either, that's why evolution, agnosticism, atheism, went out when Jesus came in . . .

Faith (I just don't have) — The Bible says God has given a measure of faith to every man (Romans 12:3). Use it, don't lose it.

Feel it (I just don't) — Feelings are peelings. Follow God's Word, and your feelings will follow. Feelings change; God's Word is dependable.

Foolishness (That's a lot of) — The Bible says just that! The preaching of the cross is foolishness . . . to them on their way to hell!

For Christ's sake, shut up — For Christ's sake . . . open up . . . receive Christ now!

Fruit (You're a) — Right on! I'm a fruit of eternal life and Jesus is my tree.

Get lost (Why don't you) — I was, but I found getting "found" was a whole lot more fun; why don't you get found too?

Get off my back (Why don't you) — The devils have been saying that to Jesus Christ for 2,000 years. (or) Say that to satan and add "In Jesus Name," and satan will get off your back forever!

Get over it (You'll) — No, the wall to heaven in 200 ft. high, the only way in is through the door; and JESUS is the only door.

Getting carried away (You're) — I wish I was, but I won't be until Jesus comes back. (or) At Judgment everyone will get carried away — to heaven or hell.

Give at the office (I) — Jesus gave at His office on Calvary's cross.

Give the United Way (I) — God gives eternal life, the United way too — only to those united to Jesus by faith . . . are you?

God wouldn't send me to hell — No, you send yourself by refusing heaven (or) that's true, if you let Jesus forgive your sins.

Go home (Why don't you) — That's what I'm trying to help you do forever; to go home to heaven, not to hell.

Go jump in the lake (Why don't you) — That's what the devil wants you to do, to refuse Christ, and go jump in the eternal lake . . . of fire.

Gone overboard (You've) — That's the only way to walk on the water.

Gonna get committed (You're) — I already am. I'm committed to Christ. It's great! How about you?

Gonna get yours (You're) — (Pull out your Bible) I already got mine. It's great. I've got an extra New Testament here; would you like yours?

Good-bye! — No, you can't buy it, it's a gift. It's great to receive it though. Would you like to receive eternal life now?

Good for you! — Not just good for me, it's good for everyone; are you saved?

Go on home — I'd like to, but I can't until the Lord takes me . . .

Go to church (I) — Walking into a stable doesn't make someone a horse and walking into a church doesn't make someone a Christian either.

Gotta go now (I've really) — We all gotta go, but when you go, go to heaven instead of hell — you can arrange that now!

Grow up (Why don't you) — I am, praise God, growing up into the full image of Jesus Christ.

Have a nice day — Have a wonderful eternity; you can, with Jesus.

Hearing things (You're) — That's right, the Bible says, You shall hear a voice behind you, saying, this is the way.

Hopeless case (I'm a) — I was too. Everybody is without Jesus as Lord.

How are you? — I'm saved and mighty glad about it; how about yourself?

If we wanta hear it, we'll go to church — You might have to go to a lot of churches to hear the simple salvation message. Why not save your time and let Christ save you now?

Inferiority complex (You've got an) — You're gonna wish you had one too if you meet God at Judgment without Jesus!

In my own way I believe — Jesus said He is the only way (John 14:6). He also said in Isaiah 55:8, "My ways are not your ways" . . . How about it?

Isn't that asking too much? — It is asking too much to ask God to let you go to hell after He sent Christ to hell to pay the whole bill for you already.

It's for the birds — No, Jesus didn't die for the birds, only for people with eternal souls like you and me. Birds can't go to heaven, but you and I can . . .

Jewish (I'm) — How Jewish are you? Are you one of the people of the book? Are you as Jewish as Abraham (John 8:58), as David (Psalm 22:1), Micah (5:2), Zechariah (12:10), Isaiah (Chapter 53) or Zechariah (9:9)?

Keep it to yourself — I'd hate myself if I did! It's just not right to feel this good and go to heaven alone.

Killing time (I'm just) — Why not let Jesus resurrect it and your life as well?

Lied (I never) — That's at least your second one.

Live up to it (I could never) — Nobody can live up to the ten commandments but Christ. He did, and He'll credit His perfect life to you if you just ask Him to.

Look out (You'd better) — I am on the lookout! Jesus said we'd all better look out, for He's coming at just the moment we think He's not. What if He came now?

Madman (You're a) — No, I'm a gladman.

Making me lose business (You're) — I'd rather you lose business than lose your eternal soul in hell.

Mason (I'm a) — Only Jesus can make you acceptable to the heavenly architect (or) only Jesus can turn your heart into a living stone.

Mind your business (Why don't you) — This is my business, spreading the Gospel . . .

Not interested (I'm) — God doesn't want to say that to anyone at Judgment day when they offer excuses for not receiving Christ.

Nuts (You're) — If I am, at least I'm screwed onto the right bolt.

Outgrow it (You'll) — How can a mortal man ever outgrow the infinite, eternal God.

Pro (You're a real) — I'm not just a real professor, but a real possessor, too!

Prove it — I don't have to; God will if you ask Him; (or) Disprove it!

Recorded announcement (You sound like a) — These words are;

they're recorded in the Bible, and being recorded in heaven right now.

Sap (You're a) — No, Jesus is the sap — of eternal life, I'm just a branch.

See you again — Maybe not 'til Judgment day. Will I see you in heaven?

Shriner (I'm a) — Is your heart a shrine where Jesus is worshiped?

Shrink (You need a) — No, the truth is, both shrinks and patients all need Jesus.

Smart for that (I'm too) — Then you're too educated for your intelligence (or) then you'll just have to be smart forever without it.

Softie (I'm not a) — The Bible says God is the Potter and we are the clay; soft clay gets used but you know what happens to hard clay?

Spare me — That's what God wants to do with you. Why not allow Him to?

That's for losers — That's true! All men have sinned and are losers without Christ. Jesus came and became a Loser on the cross to make us eternal winners.

That's what you say — No, that's what God says — read it right here . . . (Open New Testament and show them verses).

Want a permit (I) — Then get saved cause God doesn't permit sinners in heaven (or) go downtown; they'll give you one!

Whatever turns you on — Jesus isn't a what, He's a Who (or) I've found that whatever turns me and Jesus on, turns the devil off, hallelujah!

Whenever God wants me, He can have me — Do you really mean that? God says in II Corinthians 6:2 that "now is His acceptable time." Let's pray right now . . . I'm sure you're a man of your word and God certainly is!

Where's all this getting you — Closer and closer to heaven every day. How about you . . . where is sin getting you?

Who asked you anyway? — Jesus did! He asked me to share His Gospel and love, and who was I to refuse Him after He died for me and you!

Who's paying you to do this — Jesus paid it all at the cross 2,000 years ago.

Worried about it (I'm not) — Millions now in hell wish they had been . . .

28

Religious Turnarounds

"And no man was able to answer Him a word, neither dared any man from that day forth ask Him any more questions" Matthew 22:46; Mark 12:34.

All things work together — yes, but only to those who are in Christ.

Believe in the Word of God (I) — but have you received God of the Word?

Bible is just a book (The) — No, it's THE Book, God's Book, the Book of Life.

Bless my soul — God will if you let Him.

Bless you! — He has, with every spiritual blessing in heavenly places (Ephesians 1:3).

Bloody religion (I don't believe in) — Good, God doesn't either — doesn't believe in bloody holy wars, crusades, or inquisitions. God shed all the blood necessary for man's salvation (or) that's strange, God does, (read Hebrews 9:22).

Buy that tongues business (I don't) — You can't buy it; it's not for sale.

Can't please God (You) — That's funny, then why did Jesus say, "I always please My Father" and "The things I've done, you shall do" (John 8:29; 14:12).

Church of Christ (I belong to the) — I belong to the Christ of the Church.

Count your blessings — I can't; I've got too many of them.

Delusions of grandeur (You have) — No, Jesus gives me revelations of His glory!

Don't feel led (I) — Lead will be all you feel, if feelings are leading you.

Doubting Thomas (I'm a) — I'd rather be a sprouting promise.

Fanatic (I'm just not a) — Neither am I. I am just a fan of Jesus and won't keep Him in the attic (or) a fanatic is just someone who loves Jesus more than you do!

For heaven's sake — That's what living for Christ is all about!

Found it (I) — Where is it now?

Frozen Chosen (I'm one of the) — No, the frozen are unchosen, it's the unfrozen that are God's chosen — the frigid rigid aren't in God's family.

God controls all things! — How about your life?

God didn't call me to win souls — You mean He calls some to be fishers of men, and others to be spiritual waterskiers?

God doesn't do that anymore — Then He must have changed, and Hebrews 13:8 says He never changes.

God is a good God — He's too good to allow sinners into His perfect heaven.

God loves me just like I am — Yeh, but too much to leave you like you are.

God loves me too much to send me to hell — He loves you too much to force you to accept Christ and come to heaven!

Good person (I'm basically a) — Jesus said, "Only One is good, that is God" Matthew 19:17. Is that who you're saying you are or was He wrong?

Have the Holy Spirit (I already have) — Does the Holy Spirit have you?

Heavenly minded (You're no earthly good, you're so) — On the contrary, all earthly good comes from the extent of heaven in our minds.

Hypocrites (The church is full of) — Better to go to church once a week with some than to go to hell with all of them forever!

I have my own personal religion — Yes, but do you have your own personal Saviour?

Jesus freak (I'm just not a) — There's no such thing, but the closest thing is a religious person that isn't born again.

Jesus saves, but Moses invests — Moses invested his faith in Jesus; have you?

Interpretation (That's your) — No, it's God's Word; read it right here, it says . . .

Karma (I'm paying off my) — Jesus paid it all at the cross; why double-pay the same bill? Do you pay the grocer twice for the same bag of groceries?

Keep the faith — Don't keep it; give it away.

Kill me (You) — No, sin kills but the Gospel brings life.

Know more about God (or the Bible) than you do (I) — That may be true, but what are you doing with it?

Layman (I'm just a) — Did God call you to lay around or lay out the devil?

Lord have mercy — He already has; have you received it?

Many ways (There are) — That's true but only one way ends in heaven: Jesus! Jesus said He was the only Way in John 14:6.

Nobody really knows if they're saved — That's funny, in I John 5:13 it says, "These things are written that you may know that you have eternal life."

Old fashioned (That's) — So is breathing, eating, smiling, living.

Old time religion (I've got) — have you got old time salvation?

Ordained (Are you) — Yes, Jesus ordained and chose me, to go and bear much fruit (John 15:16).

Original sin (I don't believe in) — There are no original sins, just new people sinning the same old sins.

Prayer changes things — What has prayer changed for you lately?

29

Over 100 "Front-Line" Street Turnarounds

"A man has joy by the answer of his mouth; and a word spoken in due season, how good it is" Proverbs 15:23.

"How wonderful it is to be able to say the right thing at the right time" Proverbs 15:23, Living Bible.

"Answer a fool according to his folly, lest he be wise in his own conceit" Proverbs 26:5.

"When arguing with a rebel, prick his conceit with silly replies" Proverb 26:5, Living Bible.

Acapulco gold (Got any) No, I've got something even better, some New Jerusalem Gold (or) I can get you a city made of gold.

Atheist (I'm an) — The Bible talks about you in Psalm 14:1 (or) No, You're just a proud agnostic.

All right (I'm) — No, the Bible says anyone without Christ is all wrong, but you can be "all right," perfect in God's eyes, in Jesus Christ.

All in God's hands (It's) — No, but the devil wants you to think it is.

Angel dust (I take) — Satan is a fallen angel, and he wants to dust you off forever (or) There's no dust up in heaven, only saved souls.

Back off — Jesus promised He wouldn't say that to you if you come to Him now!

Bag (Got a) — No, I found out I could get more from a book — The Bible!

Bar (Where's the nearest) — Only a prayer away! Jesus will quench your thirst forever with His 1,000-proof Living Water!

Be cool — That's what everyone in Hell wishes they were right now (or) I'm trying to help you to be cool forever.

Been saved six times (I've) — Are you living like it?

Beer? (Want a) — No thanks, I don't drink that greasy kid's stuff any more.

Blowing my mind (I like) — The devil likes it more than you do (or) It's like blowing up a bridge; once it's blown, it's gone forever.

Bombed (I like getting) — When the bomb explodes, who's gonna pick up the pieces?

Bottle (I like my) — I found more satisfaction from God's bottle . . . the Bible!

Bottomless dancing (Don't you like) — No, and I don't like the bottomless pit in hell it leads people to either.

Cheers! — That's not cheers, that's tears!

Connection (Got a) — Jesus is my connection; He helps me mainline heaven daily.

Crash (Know where I can) — No, but I know where you can take off!

Crystal (Know where I can get some) — I know where you can find a whole city made of crystal (Revelation 22).

Dealer (I'm a) — So am I. Jesus made me a dealer for His Kingdom of Love.

Degenerate (You're a) — No, I'm a re-generate. Jesus regenerated me. It's great.

Different strokes for different folks — Yes, but only one Saviour for all! (Acts 4:12, John 14:6, I Timothy 2:5)

Dig it (I can) — Only with the shovel of faith in Jesus.

Dime (Got a) — What I got is so good money can't touch it.

Do it! — I did!

Don't take drugs, I just drink (I) — Alcohol's a drug that's killed more people than other drugs ever will.

Do unto others before they do unto you — Is that why Jesus died for us first?

Do you come with the tract? (to a girl) — No, I don't, but Jesus does.

Do your thing — I did, but I found it's more fun doing His thing.

Drag (Want a) — No thanks, I'd rather soar like an eagle with Jesus than drag on the ground without Him.

Drag (You're a real) — Sin is the ultimate drag; it drags people down to Hell.

Drop dead (Why don't you) — I did eight ears ago when I got saved, dead to the devil and sin, and alive to God (or) I am . . . dead to sin and alive to God.

Dropout (I'm a) — I am too. I dropped out of Satan's kingdom when I got saved.

Far out (You're really) or (You're too) — Yeh, too far out of satan's kingdom to ever be dragged back down into it again. How about you?

Free love (I believe in) — How free is it if it costs you your soul?

Gay (I'm) — satan doesn't leave anyone 'gay' when he's finished taking them for a ride.

Get down — That's it. God says if we humble ourselves, He will lift us up.

Get it on! — That's what Jesus wants you to do; to put on His robe of salvation. Get it on tonight!

Get off it! — That's what God's telling you. Get off the road to hell, and get with Jesus back on the road to heaven.

Get the hell out of here — That's what Jesus (and/or I) came to do; to get the hell out of you and me and put heaven back in.

Give me some slack — That's what God's giving you right now. The Bible says "God is not slack concerning His promises, but He is patient, not wanting any to perish," including you!

God (I am) — The God of the Bible knows the number of stars and all their names. Why don't you rattle off a couple hundred real fast (or) God knows everything, so why don't you tell me what I had for lunch yesterday?

G—damn — God's last name isn't damn, but yours will be if you don't get saved (or) God's last name isn't damn, but mine used to be and yours doesn't have to be if you'll let Christ save you (or) Why don't you call on someone you know? (or) God's last name became damn on the cross. Jesus was God, and He took our damnation so we wouldn't have to (or) Do you know Him? 'Who?' "The one you just called on? He's my best friend. He changed my life from hell into heaven. He's really wonderful (or) God damned the devil when Jesus died for my sins, and yours."

Gonna get crowned (You're) — I already am. The Bible says in Ephesians 1:3 "Christ has crowned me with all spiritual blessings in heavenly places."

Go to hell (Why don't you) — Why don't you go to heaven (or) I can't. They don't let real Christians in!

Got plenty of time (I've got) — It's later than you think (or) You're gonna have eternity.

Got your act together (You've really) — No, I cut the act and let Jesus make me real.

Grass (I like smoking) — I'd rather eat steak than Alpo! Grass is spiritual dog food compared to God's Holy Spirit! (or) There's a snake in the grass.

Grass isn't a drug — And beer isn't alcohol either, right?

"H" (I'm strung out on) — So am I, only I'm mainlining heaven with Jesus instead of hell without Him!

Habit (I've got a) — So do I, about five chapters a day.

Handle it (I can't) — I couldn't either. That's the whole point. If we could save ourselves, we wouldn't need Jesus as Saviour. God can handle it though. Let Him.

Happy hour (Don't bother me, it's my) — You can have a happy forever with Jesus!

Head shop (Is this a) — Yes, it's outlet for Jesus, the Head of the Universe (or) No, it's not a head shop, it's a heart shop.

High? (Don't you get) — I don't need to "get" high, Jesus keeps me there? God is called "the Most High" forty-four times in the Bible, and He really is!

I don't believe in the devil — He's got you where he wants you (or) That must make him very happy!

I know where you're coming from — Do you know where you're going to?

I lost it — I did too! I lost my guilty conscience and found eternal life when I gave my heart to Jesus!

I'm gonna join all my friends down in hell — Hell has no friends, (or) They're screaming at you to go to heaven; they don't want you making the same mistake as they did.

I'm not ready yet — That's true! No unsaved person is ready for Judgment (or) God can make you ready in one moment of prayer.

Informer (Are you an) — the only one I inform people about is Jesus Christ.

It's not my time — That's what God says at Judgment Day. It's not my time (or) God's time is now (II Corinthians 6:2) (or) It's later than you think.

Jesus (I'm) — Fine! Let me see the holes in your hands and feet.

Junk (Got some) — I had a heart full, but Jesus made my junk yard into His jewelbox.

Keep moving — That's what's exciting about following Jesus. He keeps moving me closer and closer to heaven every day.

Kicks (What do you do for) — I used to get kicks from drugs, etc, but I was on the receiving end. Now instead of getting my kicks, I give them . . . to the devil.

Knock it off — That's what the devil is trying to do right now with your soul, off the cliff of eternity into hell!

Let me find it on my own — The Bible says the way right to every man ends in death (Proverbs 14:12).

Let me live my own life — By all means, but if you really want to live, only Jesus gives supernatural abundant life, (or) Life without Jesus is just a disguised funeral procession.

Like getting high (I) — I'd rather stay there than go up and down without Christ! Let Jesus put you in orbit (or) Drugs are low compared to Jesus.

LSD (Take) — I don't take LSD; my LSD takes me! Jesus is my LSD, my Lord, my Saviour, and my Deliverer. He's gonna take me all the way to heaven. Where will your trip end?

Mainliner (I'm a) — So is my God. It's all the way or nothing with Him! He gave His all on the cross so we could have His all in our hearts. Let Him mainline you with heaven today!

Moonshine (Drink) — I prefer drinking Sonshine. Let Jesus fill you with His light.

Narc (Are you a) — No, but satan is! He wants to see you busted forever holding onto your sins, and then thrown into hell!

Narrow minded (You're too) — Well, after all Jesus said; "Straight is the gate, and narrow is the way."

On a trip (You're just) — Everyone is! I'm tripping toward heaven with Jesus Christ . . . where are you headed?

Out of it (You're really) — Amen! I'm out of satan's kingdom, and transplanted into God's kingdom of love.

Party (I like to) — So do I, that's why I'm going to God's eternal party in heaven (or) then head for heaven, there are no parties in hell.

Prescription (Know where I can get a) — Yeh, John 3:16 is the ultimate scrip. It'll speed you toward heaven and give you a new life!

Pusher (I'm a) or (I'm not a) — If your best friend was walking over a cliff, would you push him away from the edge?

Putting me on (You're) — Yes, I'm trying to put you on . . . onto the road to heaven and eternal happiness.

Raising hell (I like) — So did Jesus! He came to R-A-Z-E hell, to tear it down.

Read (I can't) — You don't have to read to get saved.

Rebel (I'm too much of a) — You're not enough of a rebel; if you were, you'd be a Christian!

Reds (Got any) — Jesus' red blood took all my downers away!

Revolutionary (I'm a) — I am too! The only way to change the world is to change men's hearts. Christ did it for me!

Right on! — If you're not following Christ, you're walking "right off" — off a cliff into hell.

Score (Know where I can) — You can score every time with Jesus as Lord.

See you in hell (I'll) — No, if you want to see me off this earth, it'll have to be in heaven with Jesus.

Shoot drugs (I don't) — Hitler probably didn't shoot drugs either. One sin evicted Adam from the Garden! Is one all you've done?

Shut up (Why don't you) — The devil's been asking me that ever since I got saved.

Sin is too much fun — Do you call Russian Roulette with a fully loaded 357 Magnum fun?

Sixpack (Got a) — I've got a sixty-six pack that never runs dry (the Bible).

SOB (You're a) — No, I'm a SOG, (a son of God) through Christ.

Spaced out (You're really) — Not spaced out, graced out. God graced me out of my sins and into His kingdom of love.

Spiked? (Is it) (a drink) — No, it's not, but Jesus was spiked on the cross for you (or) Yes, it's spiked . . . spiked with the love of God, and eternal life.

Stuff (Know where I can get some) — There's only one place to get in uncut. There's only one connection for heaven — that won't end up burning you!

Take dope — No, thanks, if I did, I'd come down. (or) I did, but it started taking me.

That guy over there needs it — Well, you receive Christ first so you can help him get saved, OK?

That's what you say — No, read it right here. That's what God says.

THC (Got any) — Give them a tract and say, "Here's some eternal THC. Some Tender Heavenly Care," (or) THC — Take Home Christ!

Trash (Don't give me that) — That's what God says when we offer our self-righteousness instead of faith in Jesus (Isaiah 64:6).

Tried it (I've already) — Where did God let you down?

Turning people off (You're) — I hope I turn them all the way off the road to hell onto the road to heaven (or) Jesus said He would rather turn off lukewarm people and have them cold or hot, but that lukewarm would be spit out of His mouth (Revelation 3:16).

Under the influence (I'm) — So am I; I'm under the influence of Jesus Christ.

User (Are you a) — No, I'm a "use-me." God uses me to reach others with His love, and every time He uses me, He leaves me higher than before.

Wasted (Get) or (I like getting) — I wasted 23 years of my life (or) You're wasting your time if you think you can go to heaven without Jesus.

We are all God's children — All those born-again by faith in Christ Jesus are (or) In John 8:44 Jesus called the Pharisees "children of their father the devil." Is he your god? — he's certainly not mine anymore!

What's happening? — Will you believe me if I tell you? (or) Remember, you asked first (or) The kingdom of God (or) So many beautiful things it'll take me awhile to tell you them all . . . got a few minutes?

When God wants me, He can have me — Do you really mean that? If so, He says: "Come now and let's reason together; I'll make your sins white as snow." Let's pray and let God give you His kingdom now!

Who's paying you to do this? — It was all paid for on the cross.

Worried about it (I'm not) — Millions now in hell wish they had been!

30

Witnessing in Bars

"The Son of Man came eating and drinking, and you complain that I am a glutton and a drinking man, and hang around with the worst sort of sinners" Matthew 11:19.

"And when the Pharisees saw it, they said unto His disciples, 'Why does your Master eat with Publicans and sinner?' " Matthew 9:11.
"The Son of Man came to seek and to save the lost" Luke 19:10.

Witnessing the Gospel at bars, nightclubs, topless joints and dance-halls breaks down into two main divisions: the ministry inside, and the ministry at the door or outside.

MINISTRY INSIDE BARS

One place on earth that reminds me more of hell than any other, even surpassing the cold steel bars in a penitentiary, is the loud, smoke-filled, broken-dreamed interior of a bar. Every minister ought to spend a minimum of an hour a month sitting in a bar, praying, meditating, seeing the "living hell" that slaves of alcohol are caught in! Below are suggestions for inside-bar ministry.

Bring your Bible: Carrying a big Bible can hinder personal witnessing, but inside a bar, the opposite is often the case. Don't go in without your sword (Ephesians 6:17), whether it's in your pocket, or there in your hand.

Bring a partner. The more soulwinning partners you have, the merrier a time you will have seeing the Gospel set sin's prisoners free.

Order something to eat or drink! Bars always have snacks to nibble on. Order a tomato juice or soda to help others relate to you. They don't know whether you're drinking tomato juice straight or a double bloody mary! As you make friends with people in the bar, they may offer to buy you another drink. Take them up on their offer, just qualify it by specifying a juice or 7-up straight or "on the rocks." Usually if you've spent money in the bar, you are "a customer," and once you start witnessing, they won't ask you to leave until you finish your drink (SO DRINK SLOWLY!).

Get the feel of the place: Take a stool or sit at an empty booth, and case the place out spiritually before going into action.

If you are only tract-passing, start at the back of the bar and work toward the door. Show sincere interest in the people: Tell them: "God loves you, and I do too" with your mouth and heart!

Every bar in the world needs a Christian witnessing team once a week. These people are the sick ones, the ones closest to hell, the ones that need Jesus the most! Where are the Christians?

Bind the strongman! (The bartender). In Matthew 12:29 Jesus said "How can one enter into a strong man's house and spoil his goods, except he first bind the strong man? And then he will spoil his house." If you have a team, have the two most experienced go up to the bar and occupy the bartender, the "strong-man," or "pastor" of satan's flock in the bar. If you can keep the bartender busy and get him under conviction, the other team members can infiltrate the rest of the bar unhindered.

Share your testimony with him/her. Tell him that the reason why you're there is that something wonderful happened to you on your way to hell, and you want to share it with other people. Tell him you've come to share some really good news, and to share God's love. Ask him if he'd give you five minutes to say something encouraging to the whole bar by shutting off the jukebox. If you've brought a guitar and tambourine, ask him if you can play a song or two to the whole crowd! Sinners do respect "guts" and "sincerity" and you'll often be very surprised at the respect they'll show a servant of God who cares enough about their eternal souls to come out and share the Gospel on their own turf.

Look for loners; pick off stragglers. Satan picks off "stray lambs" and we can do the same. Someone sitting alone in a booth or at a bar stool away from the others is often easier to share Jesus with.

Take out your Bible and read it silently. You can do this without saying a word to anyone. People will come up and start asking you what you're reading. If you jot down notes, or start writing a letter, they'll beat a path to your table.

MINISTRY OUTSIDE THE BAR

Some bars have signs that read: "Private club, admission $1 or $3, etc. Sometimes there's really no need to go in, although the Moonies and Krishna devotees push their way on in without a second thought. Still, anyone that goes into a bar has to eventually come out. Below are some suggestions for ministering outside of bars.

Don't block the doorway. At a bar on a public street with a public sidewalk in front of it, public easement makes the sidewalk First Amendment territory, BUT the bar owner can have you removed if you are "blocking the sidewalk." To prevent this, stay four feet from the door, and have your team arranged down the sidewalk in either direction, so every passerby can be witnessed to and given a tract without clogging up the bar's doorway. There is no legal basis for a bar owner's claim that witnessing Christians are making him lose business. The First Amendment doesn't guarantee his business! It does guarantee the right of citizens to exercise religious and speech freedoms on public land!

Be careful about sitting on cars, especially those directly in front of the bar. Some people are touchy about *who* sits on their car!

Putting tracts on every car in the parking lot of the bar is a good thing to do outside while the rest of the team works inside the bar.

When singing out in front of a bar, be careful that the sidewalk is not blocked. That charge is the only one a bar owner has to legally have your witnessing team removed from public sidewalks.

If the owner or bartender physically threatens to remove you, humbly remind him of your First Amendment rights, and why you're there in the first place. If he persists, tell him to remove you legally by calling the police. Nine times out of ten, they'll avoid this. If threats persist and they refuse to call the police, tell them if they won't call the police, then you will, or one of your team already may have done so.

Don't be discouraged or misled by appearances. Every lost soul inside the bar very quickly knows Christians are outside, and why they're there! The Holy Spirit is convicting people, and often those who laugh the loudest are being dealt with the deepest. Billy Sunday, one of America's great evangelists, was out drinking with his buddies in Chicago. A street team came singing "old time" hymns outside the bar. His buddies started laughing and mocking the Church and cursing God, but Billy Sunday got under conviction and came to Christ that very night. A light shines brighter the darker it surroundings become.

THINGS TO AVOID IN BAR WORK

Don't bring "baby Christians" out to learn to "swim" in dangerous, deep water. Witnessing should start in one-on-one street work, not bars.

"Becoming all things to all men" doesn't mean drinking alcohol with the drunken, etc. Don't compromise your spiritual position by accepting a beer, smoking cigarettes, smiling at dirty jokes, etc.!

If ladies are on your "bar team," don't pair two ladies together and do make sure they are dressed modestly. Have the ladies witness to females, not males, in the bar.

If asked to leave the inside of a bar, do so! Don't force yourself to get thrown out. Remember, you *are* on private property inside the bar.

Don't antagonize sinners by condemning the bar or alcohol. Rather, lift up Jesus as life's answer. He will draw men to Himself (John 12:32).

31

Evangelizing Rock Concerts

"The Spirit of the Lord is upon me; He has anointed me to preach the Gospel to the poor; to heal the brokenhearted and to announce that captives shall be released, the blind shall see, and that God is ready to give blessing to all who come to him" Luke 4:18.

"Go ye out into the hedges and highways and compel them to come in, that My house may be filled" Luke 14:23.

Every year in hundreds of cities at thousands of rock concerts, millions of American young people gather at large concerts halls to "worship" the rock stars themselves, drugs, alcohol, and sex! There is no greater opportunity to reach more unsaved young people in one place at one time than through evangelization of these rock concerts.

Many Christians feel out of place bringing Christ to one of these events. Dope dealers recognize the tremendous opportunity to "push" their products: why don't more Christians? A young man told me he didn't even like Tulsa's Assembly Center, commenting: "That's the devil's territory!" I replied, "That's why I love it!" The devil was defeated two thousand years ago at Calvary, according to Colossians 2:14-15. It's time for Christians to come out of their closets. When Christians do come out in the power of the Holy Spirit, the devil will go back into his! Jesus came to "destroy the works of the devil" (I John 3:8); and John 20:21 says He's sent us to finish the job!

As in bar evangelism, there are two main areas in evangelizing rock concerts: inside and outside. There are two major divisions that apply to each of these areas, namely presenting the Gospel through tracts, and/or verbal efforts. These two areas and ministry divisons will now be covered.

Evangelizing inside

Although the building is private property, there are ways the Gospel can be preached inside the concert itself. Most every young person smuggles something into the concert, such as drugs, alcohol, or pills.

Why not smuggle in some tracts? It is well worth the price of several tickets to send two or three-man Gospel teams into the concert itself, to work behind enemy lines. Go in pairs; don't go alone!

Using materials inside

Tracts — Tracts, written for "counter-culture" use, can be left in rest-rooms, on refreshment counters and tables, window ledges, steps, etc. Putting the "zig-zag" man's face on a tract guarantees the kids will read it!

Stickers can be stuck in similar places unobtrusively, as you walk around the walkways and aisles. Jesus papers could also be passed out (if allowed in).

Be creative: Rolling papers with scriptures typed or written on them will also be picked up by the concert-goers.

T-shirt messages: Just walking around the concert for two hours with a T-shirt that has a message like "Ask me" or "Only Jesus satisfies" or "The end of the age is at hand" can spread a lot of Gospel salt. The right "come-on" printed on a T-shirt can draw the spiritually hungry to come up to you and ask for more of whatever you've got!

Using vocals inside

From the stage: Once concert dates are scheduled, go to the promoter and politely ask for five minutes to speak from the stage to the crowd either giving a "heavy" changed-life testimony (e.g. suicide, or ex-junkie) or singing an original song or two.

Backstage: Sometimes a saved ex-musician, a pretty sister, or someone having a "personal gift" for one of the performers can open the door to the backstage area, either before or after the concert. It's usually easier *after* the concert.

One-on-one witnessing: During breaks or quieter songs, this can be effective.

Pick off the strays: Keep your eyes peeled for those over-dosing, or who have drunk too much, etc. sitting alone weeping, head in their hands, having a bad acid trip, or having just lost their boy or girlfriend. They may be extremely open to some Good News!

Preach from the stands. Because of the building being private property, and the frisking by ticket-takers, this is done without a PA. As soon as the lights are turned on, preach the Gospel to the exiting crowds. If you climb to the top rows, those below you headed out won't climb up to try to stop you.

Using materials outside the concert

The area just outside the doors is usually public property, therefore First Amendment preaching and tract passing territory as well.

Tracts: Tracts can be systematically put under the passenger side windshield wiper of every car in nearby parking lots before the crowd lets out. They should also be handed out at the doors to the exiting people.

Banners and poster-board signs: Kids not only read these type of Gospel devices, but banners especially get photographed and put into newspapers, reaching thousands, even millions more souls with God's message!

Stickers, bumper stickers, Jesus papers, and other materials can be given out.

Using vocals outside

Witnessing: Whether picking off "strays," walking with and sharing with groups of young people as they go to their cars in the parking lot, or saying a short scripture or message to each person leaving the auditoriums outside the doors, this is something even the youngest Christian can do to share God's love with these multitudes "dying to meet" Jesus!

Preaching without a PA: Young people are looking for reality and something to believe in. Preaching barethroated, if done in God's love and His Spirit, will touch many lives. There is a natural, organic element to this preaching style that compensates for the lack of volume that a P.A. loudspeaker would give.

Preaching with a PA system: When working with a team, point your PA system away from the doors catching the exiting crowds as they head out into the parking lots. Going out even fifty or a hundred feet into the parking lots keeps the PA from interfering with the tract passing at the doors, turning the people off to the tracts before they take them.

Using music: Whether pre-recorded or live, acoustic or on a flat-bed truck with a full-scale electric band running off of a portable generator, music establishes common ground with young people. They WILL gather around to listen in if the sound is right!

One final word

If nothing is being done to spread the Gospel at rock concerts in your area, it should be! Give Jesus your "bread and fishes" and let Him amaze you with what He can accomplish!

32

Choosing and Using a Portable PA

"Faith comes by hearing God's Word" Romans 10:17.
"Cry aloud, spare not, lift up your voice like a trumpet" Isaiah 58:1.
"How then shall they call on Him in Whom they have not believed? And how shall they believe in Him of Whom they have not heard? And how shall they hear without a preacher?" Romans 10:14.

I: CHOOSING A PORTABLE PA

George Whitefield was reported clearly heard preaching over half a mile away. I wish I had that type of a natural voice, but I don't. When I preach out-of-doors to large crowds, I use a portable PA (a battery-operated loudspeaker system).

There are two types of portable (Public Address Systems) (PA's). The first is a bullhorn allowing one hand operation, with a trigger-microphone built into the PA's handle. Below are several advantages of this type:

1) It leaves one hand free to hold (and/or) read from a Bible.
2) It leaves a hand free to pass out tracts.

3) It leaves no cords or wires dangling loose for someone in the crowd to pull on, yank out or cut with a knife.

4) It has no separate expensive microphone that can be separated from the unit, thus incapacitating the PA as a whole.

5) In essence, the whole unit is an integral extension of your mouth and body, eliminating many interference problems that PA type number two allows.

Fanon, Inc., 15300 San Fernando Mission Blvd., Mission Hills, CA 91345 (213/365-2531) produces several 1-piece bullhorns.

Model #	Watt Power	Max. Range	Retail
MV5	5 watts	300 yards	$ 99.95
MV10S	10 watts	500 yards	$101.50

Prices - 4/20/80

If you check around with ministers and electronics stores in your area, you may find one that gives a 10% - 30% discount to religious organizations. God provided us with a contact here in Tulsa. If you can't find one, buy yours through us, and save many dollars. The savings are substantial! Our contact gives us the wholesale price, which oftens amounts to over 40% discount savings. You could almost buy two for the price of one!

Don't be fooled by the maximum range statistics promised by **any** portable PA units. The estimated range is **always** more than you'll get out of your PA system out of doors, fighting the wind, and other hidden, background noises!

The second type of Portable PA system has a separate microphone attached to the main unit by a cord. For three years I have used my 'Half-mile Hailer' PA unit. It is produced by Permapower Electronics, 5615 W. Howard Ave., Chicago, IL 60648 (312/647-9414). This unit has excellent range, sharpness, and carrying power to spare. I recommend it to the street-preaching enthusiast as the ultimate portable PA system! Its specifications are:

Model # S-610, 16 watts, Range: 880 yards, retail $240, wholesale $193. Another fine long distance "type-two" portable PA unit with external mike is Fannon's Model MV20S, 20 watts, 1000 yard estimated range, retail $212.50, wholesale price $127.50.

Perma Power now offers a clip-on cordless microphone that includes a small belt-clip transmitter and a FM receiver that allows the unit to work up to 200 feet away from the microphone and the speaker. The price is **ONLY** $500. This also requires a special FCC license.

II: USING A PORTABLE PA

"Though I speak with the tongues of men and of angels, and have not God's love, I am a clanging brass or tinkling cymbal" I Corinthians 13:1.

"My sword shall be bathed in heaven" Isaiah 34:5.

"Not by might, not by power (or wattage), but by My Spirit, says the Lord" Zechariah 4:6.

"He that blesses anyone with a loud voice early in the morning, it shall be counted as a curse to him" Proverbs 27:14.

Streetwitnessing and/or streetpreaching will produce only trouble, unless the words spoken come from a heart conquered by God's amazing love. A streetpreacher's motives must always be to please the Lord Jesus Christ, or Holy Spirit results will never manifest. One should never spend more time out preaching than he has spent on his knees interceding and weeping for their lost souls.

William Booth, founder of the Salvation Army, was a streetpreacher consumed with God's burden for lost souls. He said that he wished his evangelists could spend five minutes in hell's flames! He said THAT WOULD BE THE CHIEF PART OF THEIR TRAINING!

The inevitable question in using a portable PA is: How loud? I say you should preach loud enough to be heard, by those you are trying to reach, and no louder. Fisherman cannot catch fish by gunning their motors at one end of the lake. Fish must be attracted to be caught, and catching fish is what "fishing" is all about!

33

A Car PA?
Here's why and how!

"Go ye out into the hedges and HIGHWAYS and compel them to come in" Luke 14:23.

"Redeem the time (Make the most of every opportunity)" Ephesians 5:16.

Why use a car PA?

The Great Commission is a large order to fill. Everyone . . . it's over-whelming. Still, each day thousands of Christian people spend thirty minutes to an hour or more in their cars driving to and back from work, or shopping. A car P.A. system is the best way I know to fill the hedges and highways with the Word of God!

My personal experience with a car PA

I've used a car PA loudspeaker for four years, and it has been a nonstop blessing. You can reach people with the Gospel while you're driving down the street. One man actually spun around and looked toward heaven as though he thought God was speaking to him. In a way, He was! God can take people by surprise and catch them at some of their most vulnerable, un-guarded moments. Using a car PA is not just profitable to the LOST but supercharging to the car PA preacher as well! Preaching by car PA doesn't reap too many immediate results, but as Jesus Himself said, "The sower and the reaper will rejoice together." People that hear you may come to Christ, and you may not find out how your words affected them for a month, a year, or perhaps not until you meet in heaven!

What to buy?

Deluxe systems can be acquired, but to start out inexpensively you'll need three elements: a microphone, an amplifier or power source, and a speaker.

As far as a microphone goes, any CB mike will work fine, as long as it only picks up sound right on it. As far as the amplifier or power source you'll need, every car cassette, eight track or car radio has an amplifier in it that can be tapped as a power source usable in car PA preaching. This power is usually limited, though, so if you have the money, below are several amplifier models specifically produced for car PA's!

Philmore #PA 250 - list price $93 (wholesale $67), 15 watts power.

Philmore #PA 260 - list price $65 (wholesale $45), 10 watts power.

Avoid Philmore's #PAK 4 and PAK 3. The speaker horns included are 6 inches and not effective. You'll want 8 inch horns (see below). Philmore, Inc.'s address is 40 Inip Drive, Inwood, New York 11616, (239) 516-6161. Radio Shack also makes car PA amplifiers for about $50.

The third initial car PA element is the speaker or "horn." Do NOT buy a 6 inch horn, no matter what the salesman tells you. Anything smaller than an 8 inch speaker horn will fail! The best 8 inch speaker horns are made by:

Fannon: 8 inch horn, model MDA, 6-8 (retail $39.00, wholesale $24.50).

Radio Shack also carries 8 inch horns for $35.00.

Installation of your car PA system

You can get the whole job done professionally for around $30 at a car hi-fi shop, or do it yourself.

1) Mount the speaker horn by its bracket as far front under the hood up against the front grill as possible. If there is not room there, mount it beneath the car facing forward. The more invisible the horn is, the better.

2) Mount the amplifier inside the car, under the dash, near the driver's seat.

3) Connect the speaker-horn by the speaker wire to the amplifier.

4) Connect the amplifier to your car battery (or on some models, plug it into your car cigarette lighter).

5) Insert the mike "jack" into PA amplifier mike input, press the "on" button.

6) Preach! (II Timothy 4:2).

Things to remember while using:

1) The faster the car speed, the shorter sermon lines should be.

2) When preaching in a stationary position, keep windows and doors rolled up and locked, not only to cut "feedback" but to eliminate any interference by the crowd.

3) Don't use a loud P.A. in hospital areas, or in residential areas form 10 p.m. to 8 a.m..

4) Always minister in humility and love, never in pride or arrogance.

Over 50 one–line car PA sermons

"A witness who tells the truth saves men from being sentenced to death" Proverbs 14:25, Living Bible.

"A true witness delivers souls" Proverbs 14:25, KJV.

Are you one step from heaven or from hell? (to someone walking)

Are you ready if Jesus came back today?

Are you too good for heaven? Too good for Jesus Christ? Too good to be saved?

Believe on the Lord Jesus Christ and you shall be saved. (Acts 16:31)

Black cars remind me of how sin made my heart until Jesus gave me a new one. (to driver of a black car)

Boycott hell; give your heart and life to Jesus right now!

Christians get more out of life . . . especially at the finish line!

Don't be caught dead without Jesus. (outside a funeral parlor or cemetery)

Don't bogie at judgment day. Let Jesus help you hit an eternal hole-in-one. (golfers).

Don't miss heaven because of the hypocrites. (to people gardening on Sunday morning)

Don't miss heaven; it's out of this world.

Don't strike out at judgement, let Christ hit you a home run today! (baseball)

Following satan can be breathtaking . . . permanently!

Get saved now; avoid the rush later! (to people in a line outside a movie)

God has your number . . . do you have His? (to telephone repair crew)

God's not dead . . . I just talked to Him this morning!

God sent Jesus to hell for you . . . will you go to heaven for Him?

Have you thought about your eternal destination today; where are you headed? (outside bus or train station, or bus stops)

How much will you take with you when you die? (outside bank drive-in window)

If 50,000 watts hit you right now, where would you spend eternity? (to lineman on pole)

If religion were a crutch, it's better to limp into heaven than run into hell (man in wheel chair or on crutches)

If you died with a taco in your mouth where would you spend eternity?

If you don't believe in the devil, he's got you where he wants you.

If you're not as close to God as you used to be, guess who moved?

If you're tired of coming down, let Jesus put you into orbit!

If you're too good for heaven, you won't be too bad for hell.

I'm a fool for Jesus Christ; whose fool are you?

I'm having more fun going to heaven than you are going to hell! (amusement park)

It is given to every man once to die, but after this comes the Judgment!

I was a manhole until I let Jesus Christ make me a whole man! (man hole workers)

Jesus Christ was crucified personally for your sins!

Jesus wants to put the garden of Eden back in your heart. (gardening crews)

Let Dr. Jesus heal your heart of sin today. (outside hospital)

Let Jesus buy you out of the devil's pawnshop today. (outside pawnshop)

Let Jesus fill your tank with eternal life today. (driving by gas station)

Let Jesus give you a one way ticket today. (airport)

Let Jesus take the hell out of you and put heaven back in!

Let Jesus write you an Eternal Life insurance policy today. (insurance company)

Millers doesn't have the real high life . . . only Jesus Christ does! (outside a liquor store or bar)

Only one airline can fly you to heaven; fly UNITED . . . with JESUS CHRIST! (at airport)

Pull your car over now and ask Jesus Christ to save your soul. (at red light)

Red cars remind me of the red blood Jesus spilled on the cross for your sins!

Satan is banking on your never asking Christ to save you. (bank drive-ins)

Sin may be breathtaking . . . but only Jesus Christ is deathtaking. (amusement park)

Stop refusing Christ before He starts refusing you (at a stop sign)

The best thing that ever happened to me was asking Jesus to save my soul.

The only people in hell are those who refused Jesus Christ on earth.

The only safe way to be is to live for Jesus Christ. (in Safeway parking lot)

There are no fire departments in hell. (fire station)

The solution to pollution is Jesus Christ in every heart. (to nuclear demonstrators)

Think eternity before your time on earth runs out. (clock store)

This is your conscience calling you to turn from sin and turn to Christ! (crowds exiting an x-rated movie)

We're all naked before God (outside a "topless joint").

What if your heart were to stop beating right now? (to a jogger)

What shall it profit a man to gain the whole world, and to lose his soul?
(downtown to business men)

Where will you be five-hundred years from now?

Where would you be if you had died yesterday? (funeral procession)

White cars remind me of the color Jesus made my sin-stained soul.

34

Streetpreaching ABC's

"How beautiful upon the mountains are the feet of him that brings good tidings, that publishes peace; that brings good tidings of good, that publishes salvation" Isaiah 52:7.

"And they went forth and preached the Word everywhere" Mark 16:20.

"Wisdom cries without; she utters her voice in the streets" Proverbs 1:21.

Who shall we elect as history's greatest street, field, seashore and out-of-doors preacher? Who else but our wonderful Lord Jesus Christ! Who then will be number two? Let's nominate Peter, the former coward, and Paul, the former Christian killer as a tie for second place. Then of course, there's Savanarola of the 16th century Florence, who preached sermons so "red-hot" that crooked bankers literally threw their gold into the streets. There is George Whitefield, who could be clearly heard a half-mile away without a microphone and John Wesley who rode over 100,000 miles on horseback to preach out doors from such pulpits as his father's tombstone, docks, warehouse steps, coal mine entrances, and occasionally even in church sanctuaries. In our days there's been Berkeley's Holy Hubert, and the unparalleled Arthur Blessit, who has nearly carried his cross around the world, preaching on the streets of five continents!

Is there room or need for more streetpreachers? Amen! There's a whole world full of street corner pulpits, 99% empty! The hedges and highways are still full of sinners with hungry hearts.

Below are some streetpreaching suggestions for beginners.

1) **Grow into it:** A car PA will help you grow in boldness, as will passing out tracts and learning to witness at every possible opportunity. Go out with other streetpreachers and while helping them, watch and learn.

2) **Expect the unexpected:** I've had crowds pat me on the back, or punch me on the back as well, throw rocks, bottles, and even money in mockery, as well as come up and stuff $20 in my pockets. I've had them congratulate me, threaten me, call me Hitler or a saint, roll up their windows and roll them back down again, bless God, curse God and me as well, laugh or weep, respect or despise me! There's never a boring moment out on the streets with Jesus!

3) **What will you need?**

   A) **People:** My attitude towards crowds on the street is, "the more, the merrier?" I've been privileged the last four years to preach five mile sermons to America's largest street crowd of one and a half million people at Pasadena's annual Tournament of Roses parade, using a loudspeaker and following after the last float before the grandstand crowds dispersed. When you go streetpreaching, either find a crowd, or bring one with you!

   B) **You need to be heard:** "Faith comes by hearing the Word of God" (Romans 10:17). Faith doesn't come from guessing at mumbled noises in the distance. You either need perfect silence (rare on today's motorized streets), a strong anointed voice like George Whitefield's, or a portable Public Address system!

   C) **You need to preach God's Word:** They'll never believe it if they don't hear it, and they'll never hear it if you don't know it. Skip Elizabethan English and speak Koine English! You need to be spiritual, scriptural, but non-religious out on the street to draw and attract the people that don't feel any need for God, Jesus and the Bible!

4) **Lift up Jesus, don't tear others down:** John 12:32 says it all so well: The Holy Spirit was sent to testify of, and glorify Jesus (John 16:14). Let Him do His job through you.

5) **Be cheerful and positive:** Some streetpreachers look like dill pickles! The Bible says God's Spirit produces love, joy, peace, gentleness, goodness. Be a good advertisement for the Kingdom of God and the fruit of His Spirit.

6) **Relate to your listeners:** See "Relating the Gospel."

7) **Don't preach too loud.**

8) **Don't go alone:** Jesus still sends them out in "two's;"

9) **Don't let your outreach exceed your upreach:** Pray two hours for every hour you preach on the streets.

10) **Don't let visible results, or lack of them, discourage you:** God's Word never returns void, if we faithfully do our part and send it out!

11) Don't preach in private structures: See Outreach chapter on "Street Legalities."

12) Don't eat before streetpreaching: You'll enjoy your ministry and food more, if your pray beforehand, and eat afterwards!

13) Don't lose the crowd for "dogs" or "swine": Jesus referred to "dogs" and "swine" in Matthew 7:6 . . . read it! Often if you ignore a heckler, he fades away into the night. Find someone in the crowd that either is interested or at least neutral. Preach toward them, not giving any energy to a troublemaker.

14) Keep an eye out for advertisements of large crowds to preach to:

   a) Rock concerts nearby or within two hundred miles are good "targets."

   b) Race tracks, sporting events, football, basketball, baseball, draw crowds.

   c) Exiting movie crowds are often unreached. Find the "exit" times, preach a half hour to several exiting movie crowds in one evening.

15) Write several key preaching ideas and scriptures down before you go out: Either use stick-on labels to place on your P.A. unit, Bible, or microphone, or use several 3"x5" cards in your pocket that you can pull out and preach from.

16) Preach your personal testimony: Tell the people what Jesus means to you and has done for you in your life! Weave the Word of God into your testimony. People relate to "people" stories; use the hidden power of your testimony to tell them "the greatest story ever told." **"Revelation 12:11 works; use it!"**

17) Pray-preach! Preach to the crowd in the form of a prayer to God. This is an effective technique to throw a spiritual "prayer-net" over the whole crowd. For example, preach: "Father, I ask you to convict that lady in the red shirt over there of her sins. Show her her need for a Saviour. Lord, touch each person here, don't let one die and go to hell by refusing Jesus Your Son."

18) "Prophecy-preach." You may prophesy God's Word barethroated or by PA to a crowd. For example: "How long will you run from Me, children of men. I know your hurts, your sins, your shames, but I love you, I want to heal you. Come to Me, let Me set your spirits free. Come to Jesus My Son. He will give you eternal life today."

35

Streetpreaching Possibilities

"Multitudes, multitudes in the valley of decision: for the day of the Lord is near . . . in the valley of decision" Joel 3:13.

"And seeing the multitudes, He was moved with compassion on them, because they fainted, and were scattered abroad, as sheep having no shepherd" Matthew 9:36.

"And they went forth, and preached the Word everywhere" Mark 16:20.

Possibilities in streetpreaching are infinite. Below are a number of ideas.

1) **Contact each local assembly center and concert hall in your area** and get on their monthly mailing list. Also get local sports calendars in their proper seasons.

2) **Take advantage of the large crowds at professional sporting events:** Last year there were 224 National Football league games each averaging over 57,000 precious souls in attendance, totalling 12 million in yearly attendance. There were also hundreds of professional baseball, and hockey games across the country. WAS ANYONE THERE FOR JESUS CHRIST? WAS ANYONE THERE PREACHING, WITNESSING, OR TRACT PASSING?

3) **Plan ahead on attending international crowd events,** like the Summer and Winter Olympics, Soccer Championships, large religious pilgrimmages, the yearly Festival in Rio de Janeiro, etc. One group that sends teams to some of these events is Youth With A Mission. Their address is: Box YWAM, Solvang, CA 93463.

4) **Take communion before going out to preach.** John Wesley took communion every morning, and instead of it being or becoming a dry ritual to him, it helped him shake his world with God's love, and power!

5) **Preach over CB unit:** Be a "Good News-good buddy." Ask: "This is Good News Buddy #47. Anyone out there love the Lord? You'll find someone to talk with about Jesus, while hundreds of other precious souls listen in.

6) **Draw responses from the crowds.** Once I drew a crowd by having a conversation with a young street guy about which was better: marijuana or

Jesus! While preaching to crowds, you can get them to raise their hands, to stand up, to follow you in a J-E-S-U-S cheer, to give the one way sign, to sing a chorus with you, intrigue them, interview them, challenge them, somehow get them involved!

7) **Put a pulpit into the back of a pickup truck,** use it to hold street meetings with a crowd of outreach regulars coming along with you (or without). You can do this outside rock concerts, popular clubs, or in parking lots where young people hang out.

8) **Preach to parade crowds,** not just following the end float, but before the first float as well.

9) **Have every car that has a built-in car PA system drive up and down the strip** at least once each night.

10) **"Plant" a strong Christian in the audience or crowd** to ask pertinent questions thus involving the crowd around him.

11) **Hook up a cassette player to the car PA system,** so the unit can preach even while all hands are busy passing out tracts nearby.

12) **Have two streetpreachers at a distance preaching alternately to the crowds** while at the same time holding a soulwinning "dialogue." Sometimes you can plug 2 'mikes' into one PA.

13) **"Pray" preach and "Prophecy" preach.** See "Streetpreaching ABC's."

14) **Use a foreign language gospel cassette on a tape player** at noon on college campuses. It can be hooked up to a portable PA system for more volume, if desired. Curiosity makes everyone ask what it's saying, plus passers-by who speak that language hear God's Word preached directly to them in their own language. Gospel tapes in over 100 languages are available free by writing to the Osborn Foundation, Box 10, Tulsa, OK 74102.

15) **Use creative ideas:** It's the unusual that grabs people's attention. One time we dressed one brother up in a red devil outfit in black chains and another as the Lord Jesus. We had the devil testifying over a PA to large crowds, giving the one way sign, and confessing that Jesus really did defeat him and that only Jesus Christ can save people from eternal hell. People in the crowd paid attention!

16) **Sometimes a visual idea will grab people's attention** even without a word being said. For example, at noon hour in a busy spot, hold up a copy of the Bible in one hand and a copy of *Playboy* in the other. Conviction will fall on everyone passing by. Streetpreaching will only add to the effectiveness. We also use a large red styrofoam cross, which is lightweight but carries a heavy visual message in public places.

36

Streetpreaching Trouble:
What To Do If . . .

"A wise man stays cool, even when he is insulted" Proverbs 12:16.
"Call upon Me in the day of trouble: I will deliver you" Psalm 50:15.
"The lips of the wise protect them" Proverbs 14:3.
"A kind answer turns away anger, but harsh words stir it up" Proverbs 15:1.
"The Name of the Lord is a strong tower; The righteous run into it and are safe" Proverbs 18:10.

The Book of Acts, the ultimate textbook on streetpreaching, reveals the healthiest, most powerful Church this world has ever seen.

It relates not just the miracles and glory, but the suffering that early saints went through in serving their Lord. "They rejoiced that God had counted them worthy to suffer dishonor for His (Jesus') Name" (Acts 5:40).

There is a reason beginners should not go streetpreaching alone. You will learn many things and face many situations in "Streetpreacher Seminary" on the streets that are not and cannot be taught in any off-the-street type classroom. Ministry outside the sanctuary is the greatest crucible for one's faith. You'll learn a confidence in God's Spirit, His power and His protection, an inner confidence that laughs at threats, jail, and even at death itself (see I Corinthians 15:55-56).

Jesus said: "Behold I send you out as lambs in the midst of wolves; therefore be wise as serpents and harmless as doves" (Matthew 10:16). There is a "street-wisdom" you will gain through street-ministry experiences. Our Lord's promise in Luke 21:15: "I will give you a mouth and wisdom that no one can gainsay or resist" was not only fulfilled in Stephen's life (Acts 6:8), but will be in your life and ministry as well, as you step out and speak up, in love, for our Lord.

What to do with threats

If satan could have killed me, he would have long ago. But he can't, because "greater is Jesus within me, than the devil in the world" (I John 4:4). There is, however, a right way, and a wrong way, to handle threats. Though I've been threatened scores of times, I've never been hurt. If I had acted in my flesh, however, I would have been. LOVE IS THE ULTIMATE WEAPON: LOVE IS THE ULTIMATE DEFENSE. As God's Word says: "Love is as strong as death . . . Many waters cannot quench love, neither can the floods drown it" (Song of Solomon 8:6-7). God's love never fails! (I Corinthians 13:8).

Below are some replies to answer different "standard threats" encountered on the street:

1) You better shut up or I'll cut you up:

When former New York gang leader Nicky Cruz told David Wilkerson many years ago the above line . . . JESUS' LOVE WON!! Brother Wilkerson replied: "If you cut me into a thousand pieces, every piece will still be crying out: 'Nicky, JESUS LOVES YOU!" As Proverbs 15:4 puts it: "A soft answer turns away wrath."

2) Shut up or I'm going to flatten you all over the sidewalk:

a) Before you do, let me tell you that I really love you, and so does Jesus Christ my Lord. Plenty of folks don't care whether you die and go to hell or not, but I do, because Jesus cared so much He died . . .

b) Go right ahead and hit me, if that will help you see how much you need to get saved.

c) God says what anyone does to the least of His brothers, they're doing to Him. Would you say that to Jesus Christ if He was standing right here in the flesh. He is here, with nailholes in His hands which He suffered on the cross for you and me . . .

d) God says in Psalm 17:8 that I am the apple or center of His eye, and God doesn't like people sticking their fingers into His eyes. Pick on someone more your own size!

e) If you hit me tonight, next week there may be thirty or forty Christians here.

3) I'm gonna kill you (or) I'm gonna blow your brains out!:

a) You can't kill a dead man. You'd be wasting your time and ammunition.

b) I'm already dead. I died eight years ago (. . . whenever you got saved). I died to satan, died to sin, died to hell, and came alive to God's love.

c) Before you do, let me tell you one short story (share your testimony, relating your own past frustration and search for reality in a phony world).

d) I'd rather lose my life for you than have you lose your soul forever!

e) Jesus Christ in me is greater than the devil that's in you. He loves you
. . .

f) Satan! I bind your spirit of murder right now in the Name of Jesus Christ your Master! You will not rip this man off for Eternal Life and the heavenly life God has prepared for him (When you bind the devil in Jesus' Name in a situation like this, always make it clear by your words that you are speaking to the demon murder spirit, and not calling the man himself "satan").

g) You don't have to take my life, I've already given it to help share Jesus' love with others. If killing me will help you get saved and find the beautiful plan Jesus has for you, then go ahead!

h) Would you kill someone that loves you? I love you and Jesus Christ does too!

i) Mention of or pointing out of police often helps. You can use a reply like: "That's a good way to throw away ten or twenty years of your life in prison; why not let the Lord give you a beautiful new heavenly life tonight instead and ask Him into your heart."

What to do with one heckler in a group or in a listening crowd:

Obeying Jesus' injunction not to "cast your pearls before swine," (Matthew 7:6) is easier defined in a one-on-one situation than with a mixed crowd. It's one thing to stop trying to convert a "barker" or "oinker," and it's another thing abandoning potential sheep because of one big mouth! There is a proper time to leave, but not necessarily the moment the first spark starts flying. Several options are:

a) Ignore the heckler! (Where there's no wood, the fire goes out" Proverbs 26:20).

b) If the crowd is favorable, ask them how many want you to continue. The heckler will be outvoted and silenced.

c) Have everybody, or at least the Christians there, pray aloud for the heckler to be saved and filled with the love of God.

d) Have everyone sing a chorus, like "Oh, the Blood of Jesus," to bring spiritual unity and to drown out the heckler's words.

e) You might offer him several words on your PA mike; he'll usually make a fool of himself quickly and leave to save face! Keep the mike in your hand.

If people come up to you and quite heatedly say:

1) **You're doing it all wrong,** say back to them: "Well, I'm willing to learn, come show me how." Ninety-nine percent of the time they'll disappear like

snow in August.

2) **You're turning people off,** you might reply: "Jesus said cold is better than lukewarm;" or, "What are you doing to turn them on to Jesus Christ?"

3) **It's too loud:** You might reply: "It's not the mike, but your conscience. Jesus will turn it down or off right now if you ask Him to. It really works! He did it for me, and He's ready right now to . . ."

Dealing with Actual Violence

Suppose, despite all precautions, that violence actually does erupt. Arthur Blessit's classic street manual, **Tell The World** gives some great practical insight on how to handle this on page 87.

1) Keep your Bible between you and your attacker; make them hit God's Word!

2) If knocked down, calmly get on your knees, placing your face down between your legs with shoulders up, so that your arms cover your ears and sides of your head. THIS IS A PROTECTIVE POSITION OF PRAYER, making your attacker think you're merely praying, while at the same time your most sensitive body parts are protected.

3) **PRAY OUT LOUD** for your attacker, for God to deal with him, letting him know you love him, until he relents . . .

4) **If another person is attacked, throw yourself between them,** if there are several Christians, throw in fresh bodies, each will be protecting the other by rotation and also confusing and dividing the attackers' focus!

5) **If girls are being handled, have them say:** "Here, if you want to hold something, hold the Bible!!

I may add that one of the team should quietly go to a private phone and call the police to come restore order. Very often, a sister stepping in between the attacker can shame the rowdy person for using such a crude method of declaring his so-called "manhood." This can also help. One cardinal rule is: NEVER MEET VIOLENCE WITH VIOLENCE. Obey Romans 12:20-21, and conquer evil with good, and satan's hatred with God's Love!

Handling Trouble with the Police

Never forget that the police are public guardians, and are paid to, on the one hand, enforce the laws, and on the other hand, to protect life and property, including yours! **Never** react emotionally or violently, using abuse, to deal with anyone, especially officers of the law, no matter how you may be mistreated. The same Apostle Peter replied: "We must obey God rather than men" (Acts 4:19, 5:29) also wrote in I Peter 2:13 "Submit to every ordinance of man for the Lord's sake."

Things to remember to avoid street trouble

1) Never go streetpreaching alone.

2) Bring a spare mike and cord unless using a cordless bullhorn!

3) Never let hecklers hold your mike. Keep control of it!

4) If a crowd closes in momentarily stop preaching; let them cool off.

5) If you're in a super-controversial emotional crowd such as the time I preached on Yom Kippur outside a conservative synagogue, you can always hire an off-duty policeman to stand near you in his uniform. THERE ARE CHRISTIAN POLICEMAN AVAILABLE! The crowd won't know the officer is with you, keeping things peaceful by his presence, and telling them to file charges legally if they want to!

6) One of your group can get a special deputy's license which allows him to wear a uniform. Remember Matthew 11:12, 19. If it works, use it. If it can help get the Word to the unreached and save them from hell, use it. Paul used his Roman citizenship to survive the Jews to get to Rome!

7) If you've preached to a hot, heavy crowd, you can circle the block going home!

8) If an officer asks your name and address before an angry crowd, either give him a Post Office number, whisper it in his ear, write it on a piece of paper, show him you driver's license, or ask him to step over to the side, to prevent the crowd from dropping by your house later on!

9) If your Outreach is highly controversial and well known, you may want to keep valuable office machines and records in another office location. We found this necessary as threats came in to burn us down, or break in and wipe us out. If you have adequate insurance, that still only covers part of this threat situation. Valuable papers and IRREPLACEABLE tax records, etc. may be safer in a non-public, unpublicized "off-the-strip" location.

37

Streetpreaching Materials

"Go ye OUT into the hedges and highways, and COMPEL them to come in" Luke 14:23.
"My people are silent and perish for lack of knowledge" Hosea 4:6.

There are few books written on streetpreaching. If you can add to the list below, I would very much appreciate hearing by letter your additional suggestions to the following list.

Bless Your Dirty Heart, by Hubert Lindsey (University of Berkeley's streetpreacher), Logos $1.95
Books by Arthur Blessit: Box 69544, Hollywood, CA 90069
    Tell the World, Turn On to Jesus
    Arthur Blessit's Street University
(available both in book and cassette)
    A Walk with the Cross
Foxe's Book of Martyre, Marie Gentert King, Editor, Spire Books, Fleming H. Revell Co.
Dick Handly materials, free tapes on streetwork, tracts, supplies, write Box A, Downey, CA 90142, 213/861-1444
Revivals of Religion, Charles Finney, Fleming Revell
Soul Patrol, by Bob Bartlett (adventures of a street ministry), Logos $3.95
Soulwinning, Join This Chariot, by T.L. Osborn, Box 10, Tulsa, OK 74102

Any materials you can find on Guillermo Savanarola, 15th century streetpreacher in Florence, or George Whitefield, the prince of streetpreachers, will both be well worth your effort.

38

Thank God for Police

"Let every soul be subject to the higher powers, for the powers that are, are ordained of God. For rulers are not a terror to good words, but to the evil. Do that which is good, and you will have praise from the same For he is the minister of God to you for good" Romans 13:1-4.

"The policeman does not frighten people who are doing right, but those doing evil fear him . . . the policeman is sent by God to help you" Romans 13:3-4, TLB.

"We know that the law is good, if a man use it lawfully" I Timothy 1:8-10.

"I exhort that first of all supplications, prayers, intercession, and thanksgiving be made for all men, for kings, and for all that are in authority" I Timothy 2:1-2.

As a dropout, and rebel, police represented authority and the establishment to me! I hated them because of my rebellious carnal nature. Now I know that many police officers are wonderful Christians and all of them, whether Christian or not, have a God appointed job ot do. They often have a very thankless job, and yet they help keep all "hell" from breaking loose here on earth, restraining "the lawless, and disobedient, the ungodly and sinners, the unholy, profane, murderers of fathers and of mothers," etc. (I Timothy 1:8-10).

Police help a street minister in many ways. I've often thanked God for the privilege of having police around while out in tighter situations ministering outside the sanctuary. Here's a few ways in specific:

1) While street preaching with a loudspeaker at a rock concert, or to a drunken mob exiting a football game, a policeman or two is always a good steadying influence on a wild crowd.

2) The mere possibility or mention of police in the area or even of patrol cars passing by, very often "cools down" a potentially explosive person or crowd.

I can truly now say with all of my heart: THANK GOD FOR POLICE!

39

Street Ligalities:
Know Your Rights and Wrongs

"As much as is possible within you, live at peace with all men"
Romans 12:18.

"Submit yourself to every ordinance of man, for the Lord's sake" I
Peter 2:13.

"Then Peter and the other apostles answered and said: We ought to
obey God rather than men" Acts 5:29.

"If I am innocent, neither you nor anyone else has a right to turn me
over to these men to kill me. I appeal to Caesar's court" Acts 25:11.

As Christians we are to obey all the laws of the land EXCEPT where they
contradict the commands of God. In the Bible example quoted above (Acts
5:29) Peter placed God's command to "Go and preach the Gospel" (Mark
16:15) as a superior command to the Jerusalem Sanhedrin's citywide
"disturbing the peace" ordinance and ban on streetpreaching.

Ignorance of the law is no excuse for disobeying it. Check downtown in
your home city, or when traveling, to find out local ordinances that deal with
streetpreaching, tract-passing, parades, concerts, etc. Do this, but also
memorize the basic elements of the First and Fourteenth amendments of the
U.S. Constitution below:

The First Amendment of the U.S. Constitution Bill of Rights reads:

"Congress shall make no law respecting an establishment of religion, nor
progibiting the free exercise thereof: or abridging the freedom of speech, or of
the press; or of the right of people to peaceably assemble . . .!"

The 14th Amendment to the U.S. Constitution Bill of Rights reads:

"No state shall make or enforce any law which shall abridge the privileges
or immunities of citizens of the United States, nor shall any state deprive any
person of life, liberty, or property without due process of law **nor deny any
person** within its jurisdiction **the actual protection** of the laws."

The right to free exercise of speech and religion as guaranteed by the First
Amendment applies in every place that is specifically **not** private property.
These are three main areas of legalities that every Gospel street-worker will
touch upon at different times. These three areas are: 1) streetpreaching, 2)

tract-passing, and 3) street-witnessing.

I: STREETPREACHING LEGALITIES

Call your city hall and find out how your local "disturbing the peace" statute reads. In Oklahoma, a policeman cannot have "his" peace disturbed. Only a private citizen can, and he must press charges by going downtown to the police station. Local ordinances will always have loopholes large enough to let a street-preacher through, even if it means losing the first-round local court case, taking it into the Federal Court System by appeal, and winning a Civil Rights suit there for violation of First Amendment rights.

Tulsa's "Disturbing the Peace" ordinances are typed in below.

Section 401: "Noises" City Code, Tulsa, Oklahoma

"It shall be an offense for any person at any time to willfully or maliciously disturb the public peace or quietude, life, health, or safety of any individual in any manner by creating any noise of such character or duration so as to be loud, disturbing, and or unnecessary, including, but not limited to the following:

A) A sounding of a horn or danger signal device on any vehicle except as a danger signal.

B) The playing of any radio, phonograph or any musical instrument in any manner or at such volume particularly between the hours of 11 pm and 7 am so as to annoy, or disturb the quiet, comfort, or repose of any person in any dwelling, hotel, or other type of residence.

C) The allowing of a habitual howling, barking, or other annoyance by the possessor of any dog or animal.

D) The discharge of the exhaust of any motor vehicle except through a muffler or other device which will prevent loud or explosive noises therefrom."

It's obvious that Tulsa's statute does not specifically ban loudspeakers. The reason it doesn't specifically cover loudspeakers and streetpreachers: The First Amendment! The next chapter covers in depth how I was arrested for loudspeaker streetpreaching and acquitted by a local court.

As a courtesy, you'll usually be asked, then warned once or twice by an officer that a citizen has made a complaint about your loudspeaker "disturbing the peace." To have an official complaint filed however, at least in Tulsa, the citizen must go downtown in person, and fill out a form. Only then can an officer officially arrest you! By the time they return you'll usually have covered the crowd and can be gone. Or, you can "just be leaving" as they return.

Where do local statutes meet the First Amendment?

In the fall of 1978 we visited with Tulsa's Police Chief for several hours to share our vision of having a streetpreacher's training center right here in Tulsa. We shared with him that we wanted to exercise our First Amendment rights. We told him that we desired all street-preaching/disturbing the peace situations to be handled legally and constitutionally, not emotionally or physically, which had happened to us several weeks beforehand.

We had been reaching on a public sidewalk on the corner outside a synagogue on Yom Kippur and one police officer had insulted us, physically manhandled us, threatened us, and turned a deaf ear to our request for help as a $40 microphone was destroyed.

The Chief agreed with us to write out a memo summarizing proper procedure in such cases, and to send it down to the entire police force. He told us this memo would include 1) our rights, 2) police rights and duties to all parties involved, 3) the rights of private citizens to file a complaint legally, 4) proper procedure for all three of these areas.

Four major deterrents to arrest while streetpreaching on public property

Mentioning either individually or combined, the following four items will often either make the annoyed person leave, or delay and reconsider his prosecuting action:

1) Claim your First Amendment rights and predict victory in a local courtroom. If you are withing your constitutional rights, you very well may win, even in a first round local court case.

2) False arrest suit: One reason "disturbing the peace" isn't filed every time a neighbor's dog barks and annoys someone is that if the legal complaint is overturned in court, the prosecuting party is then legally liable in a false arrest suit, to financially cover damages such as lost time, reputation, and court costs.

3) A civil rights suit: Mentioning the possibility of this shakes up local policemen and brings in the spectre of "Big Brother," (the federal government) stepping in "spanking" the local court for trespassing in civil rights areas *guaranteed* by the First Amendment and the Bill of Rights!

A Civil Rights suit often reverses a local court decision, particularly in these areas. To qualify, however, you must first have been arrested to get into the Federal Courts. To file a civil rights suit, call the local Federal District Attorney and talk to him. It is his job to use the Federal Courts to balance out local laws and enforcement agencies, keeping them in proper relationship with the overriding Federal Laws, such as the U.S. Constitution and Bill of Rights.

4) A citizens compaint on an officer: If an officer, who is a public servant, treats you insultingly (with cursing and/or violence), it is important that you get his badge number and/or name. You'll need it if you later have to file a formal complaint to keep streetpreaching in your city handled in a rational, legal, civilized manner! Carrying an official police department complaint form folded in your wallet (or a xerox) might be of some help when brought out at the right moment. Sometimes officers do get emotional and antagonistic.

If you are arrested:

You should seek out a good Christian attorney sympathetic to street-preaching. Find one before you start hitting the streets. Talk over local laws, and eventualities with him beforehand. If you are allowed two calls at the stationhouse, call a friend, then call the newspaper.

Never resist arrest, get emotional, or abusive either physically or verbally even if you are abused yourself, even by law enforcement officers. If there is a local ordianace that unconstitutionally forbids streetpreaching and loud-speakers, don't get arrested alone. Bring a few good Christian friends as witnesses that can show the positive side of what you were doing, when the case reaches the court room.

II: TRACT PASSING— RIGHTS AND WRONGS

You will see from the following tract that the U.S. Supreme Court decided in 1938 that Freedom of Religion and Press not only includes printing, but distributing religious tracts as well. Tract passing to people in a crowd is not littering, even if every single person you give one to, after taking it, throws it down to the ground. Legally, the litter offense is theirs, not yours. Xerox off a copy of the Supreme Court tract-passing decision below and keep it in your wallet. Enclose it in plastic sheets available at "5¢ and 10¢" stores; you'll use it sooner or later.

Though you don't legally have to, it leaves a good impression for your team afterwards to pick up discarded tracts.

A sample case illustrating tractpassing legalities

You've just finished putting 1000 tracts on every car in a large parking lot, when the security officer tells you what you've done is illegal, there's a sign over "somewhere!" and you not only have to stop "soliciting," but must take every tract off every car or go to jail. What do you do? Here are some ideas.

Solution:

1) Tell him you haven't seen the sign (unless you have). They're usually inside larger malls, on a small plaque, and not really visible unless you stumble upon them inside!
2) Tell him you're finished for the day and just on your way home; start packing up!
3) Offer a tract to him, ask him about his soul, and eternal destination.
4) If it comes down to arrest, mention that you are a Christian, and that most of the center's business probably comes from church-going Christian people. Then add on that your arrest would be terrible publicity for the shopping center.

Usually some combination of the above suggestions will convince the security officer to let you go. If, however, they fail **YOU** must make the decision whether the issue is worth going to jail over or not. Your bail will be less than $60, and the fine would probably be $26 or less. Even if you lost the local court case, the decision may be overturned in local Federal court as well.

Supreme Court Decision 1938: Freedom of Press includes Distribution

Third Edition — Total 120,000 Copies
The Right to Distribute Tracts

Gospel tract distributors are sometimes hindered in their work by Town and City Officials. Sometimes they are forbidden to give out Christian literature from home to home. Many Towns and Cities have passed ordinances against such distribution. In the light of a U.S. SUPREME COURT decision such ordinances are wrong, unlawful and ANY LOCAL OFFICIAL WHO STOPS GOSPEL TRACT DISTRIBUTION HAS NOT ONLY GONE BEYOND HIS POWER, BUT HAS INTERFER-ED WITH THE CONSTITUTIONAL LIBERTY OF THE DISTRI-BUTOR.

In an opinion rendered by CHIEF JUSTICE, THE HONORABLE CHARLES E. HUGHES, on March 28, 1938, in the case of Lovell versus the City of Griffin, Ga. (see Volume 58, No. 12, April 15, 1938), the following was said:

"The LIBERTY of the press in NOT confined to newspapers and periodicals. It necessarily embraces pamphlets and leaflets. LIBERTY of circulation is as essential to that FREEDOM as LIBERTY of publishing. Indeed, without the circulation, the publication would be of little value."

Early in 1943 the rights of tract distributors were again contested and two members of a certain religious group were convicted; however, the SUPREME COURT of the U.S. again upheld its original decision in the following opinion by JUSTICE BLACK:

"We thing the JUDGMENT must be REVERSED because the Dallas ORDINANCE denies to the apprellant the FREEDOM of the press and of RELIGION guaranteed to her by the FIRST and FOURTEENTH AMENDMENTS OF THE FEDERAL CONSTITUTION . . . one who is rightfully on a Street which the State has left open to the public, carries with him there as elsewhere the CONSTITUTIONAL RIGHT to express his views in an orderly fashion. This right extends to the communication of ideas by handbills and literature, as well as by the spoken word."

III: STREETWITNESSING LEGALITIES

The major legality streetwitnessing deals with is private versus public (city, country, state, federal) property.

Public property is First Amendment territory, perfect for streetpreaching, tract-passing, and/or streetwitnessing! As one brother put it so well after his first time out tract-passing, "We have just as much right to be out here telling people about Jesus as they do out here to be drinking, cursing God, smoking dope, and raising hell!" Amen to that!

Private property is not public property, and must not be treated the same. NEVER get arrested for refusing to leave private property. Everyone that lives on private property (their home, apartments, etc.) has to at one time or another usually at least once a day) come out driving down public streets and walking on public sidewalks. You can wait for any crowd at the door or curb, for example, at a football game. City streets are public property, but if you were arrested for preaching inside the stadium, you would lose in court, for trespassing on private property without permission.

Public Easement is the legal engineering term which means the curb, the sidewalk, and up to a certain distance from the center of the street that legally belongs to the city, and is public property. Even where no official sidewalk exists, there is still a public easement. For example, if you want to picket or witness, preach, tract-pass outside a porno movie theatre that has no sidewalk, call downtown, ask the City Engineer what the public easement is at such-and-such an address. The theatre manager will back off when you start mentioning "public easement," and officers likewise won't arrest you if you're exercising your First Amendment rights on "public easement" (public) property.

40

My First Arrest, Acquittal and Lawyer's Letter

"If the world hate you, you know that it hated Me before it hated you" John 16:18.

"And they laid hands on them (Peter and John) and put them in prison until the next day" Acts 4:3.

"And they laid hands on the Apostles (again), and put them into prison" Acts 6:18.

"As they tied down Paul to flog him, Paul said to the officer: Is it legal for you to whip a Roman citizen who hasn't even been tried?" Acts 22:26.

When I started preaching out on Tulsa's "strip," there were no ripples downtown. But when I started preaching downtown at the Assembly Center, Tulsa's largest public meeting place holding 9,000, at rodeos, circuses, rock concerts, etc., eyebrows began to raise. I kept preaching.

At a regional Jehovah's Witness convention here in Tulsa, some brothers and I went to preach outside their final Sunday meeting. I studied a book by Charles Trombley, a converted "Witness", and the Lord showed me some loopholes in their beliefs to point out to the exiting crowds.

After putting special tracts on each car, the meeting let out, and they knew immediately that I'd studied their doctrine and found loopholes. Some of their elders began following me as I preached in my van, honking their horns trying to drown me out, then trying with their cars to keep me from turning and completing my preaching circuit for the next go-round circling the building. Realizing they couldn't silence me, they had me arrested. I submitted and went to jail!

Friends bailed me out within an hour and a trial date was set two months away. I knew I was on public property and well within my constitutional rights. We won the case, the judge threw out the charges, and my lawyer wrote a letter that helped many other streetpreachers. Keep such a letter in mind if you can get a local lawyer to write one up for you either before or after any arrest or hassle. I also found out afterwards that the Tulsa DA (District Attorney) had tried to make a deal with my Christian lawyer, saying: We'll drop all charges against Jonathan if he'll just promise TO BE A GOOD BOY for six months. He then went on to explain a "good boy" meant no preaching on the streets and at the Assembly Center. God had a better deal and a better plan! Hallelujah! Below is a copy of the letter my lawyer wrote me:

Brian Reeves
Attorney-At-Law
December 5, 1975

Dear Jonathan:

I discussed your question regarding your right to preach at the Tulsa Assembly Center and Municipal Theatre with a couple of City Attorneys.

Their concensus is that you are within your First Amendment rights of Speech and Religion in preaching to people on any of the sidewalks, streets, parking areas, etc., which surround these buildings, as long as you do it in a peaceful way and do not physically block traffic.

There are some questions, however, as to your right to actually enter these buildings for the purpose of either preaching orally or passing out materials.

If you are approached by any policeman who requests that you leave the area because he feels you are either on private property or because he feels you are creating an illegal disturbance, remember that he is only trying to do his job. He has no way of knowing that the land is public property and that you have been found by Judge Herbert to have a right to preach using your loudspeaker in these areas.

I am certain when you explain these things to the officer, he will be happy to cooperate with you.

Sincerely yours,

Brian Reeves

You will find in an area where streetpreaching is an entirely new phenomenon, that you will have to "win" your territory much as Joshua going into Canaan had to possess the land. At first they wouldn't concede me the right to preach outside the Assembly Center. Finally through a court case, they had to, and now anyone preaching to the crowds there is rarely even questioned by police.

The same process took place over the issue of preaching with a loud-speaker on Tulsa's new million-dollar downtown mall. The preacher was arrested, but acquitted at his trial under First Amendment guaranteed freedoms. This paved the way making it easier for other preachers to preach to the thousands of businessmen that stroll the mall during lunch hour.

One last progression along this theme. Recently some new street-preaching territiory here had to be won, and was. The County Fairgrounds had long hidden behind a "mystical" clause, with its security personnel stating that it was a public trust, and that they had a county law prohibiting preaching and tract-passing. Time came for this unconstitutional barrier to go. First, the County DA was contacted and chatted with concerning the unconstitutionality of such a law covering public property, whose upkeep comes from public funds. Then a registered letter was sent to the head of the County Fairgrounds, telling him that First Amendment protected religious activities were going to be engaged in, also advising him of the DA's opinion. The night of the concert there was no trouble with the authorities. This same principle can be successfully used in your area too!

Finally in closing I would like to include some comments of the trial judge on First Amendment grounds.

"It seems to me that the main thrust of the prosecutions objection was what he (the defendant) was saying. But, if the subject content of what Mr. Gainsbrugh was saying is important, it is in that he was attempting

to express what he felt was a religious doctrine which, if anything, would give him at least some increased right to speak and perhaps to incur the wrath or at least the annoyance of listeners or passers-by.

"Now, on the other hand I do not mean to indicate that the defendant can take his sound truck and when and where he will turn the volume up and interrupt or disrupt the Jehovah's Witnesses meetings indoors, then we would have a definite violation."

41

Starting a Local School Drug Abuse Program

"When the enemy comes in like a flood, then shall the Spirit of the Lord raise up a standard against him" Isaiah 59:19.

The drug scene I first encountered in 1964 as a university freshman is now in every Junior High School in the country, and most grammar schools as well. Below are some ideas to help develop a school drug-abuse program utilizing ex-users to present school assemblies. The satanic flood of drugs can be fought, and at the same time born-again Christians can powerfully present the Lord Jesus Christ as their personal answer to their former drug problems!

Choosing the people for the program:

A good "track record" is necessary for any participant. He or she should not be a new believer, to prevent their falling through pride. Participants should have had experience in drugs, dope dealing, crime, teen-alcoholism, immorality, etc., and now clearly be rooted and growing in Jesus Christ and His Word.

Preparing the testimonies

A director or coordinator of the drug abuse program is essential to see it become a reality. Meetings should be scheduled weekly, for two hours per night. Start out with each one of the half dozen or so members sharing their testimonies. Use a cassette recorder to record the whole evening. The more invisible it is, the better. At the second meeting, have the director write down the chief events in each testimony, forming an outline, eventually aiming for a seven-minute testimony. Include how and why each speaker was drawn in the drug scene, and a few "adventures" on the way to the bottom. After five minutes or so, bring the testimony around toward Jesus and salvation. The third week have each speaker work from and with outlines. The fourth week record each testimony on a separate cassette, then let each participant take his or her tape home to listen to and improve upon. Ask each member to write out their testimony from the tape, to form seven minutes of typewritten copy. They should be firming up exactly which "adventures" to include. "Ad-libbing" should be excluded. The testimonies will, in this way, eventually become a smooth, power-packed, Holy Spirit anointed series of mini-sermons.

Start in the churches

When you have four or five good testimonies ready, with one or two lively songs to start with and/or in between, seek opportunities to present the program in local churches, whether to whole congregations or youth groups. At each church, after the service, ask each minister for constructive criticism. Also ask for a recommendation letter to help open the doors of the local Board of Education and public school system for the program.

Getting public school acceptance

One evening have the program presented to a gathering of Christian lawyers, psychiatrists, doctors, policemen, and other professional people, particularly Christian teachers. Afterwards ask those who would like to be on an advisory board, and/or who have their name used to help this program be accepted and be presented on a county-wide basis in all the Junior and Senior High Schools, to sign up on certain lists or cards. Also have them write down their comments (both positive and negative).

Add a Christian doctor and psychiatrist to the program to discuss the physical and psychological aspects and proven side-effects of drugs. They might be included on a question and answer panel at the end of the program, with kids in the audience being allowed to ask the panel, including "ex-users," any question they wish. Some kids will respect "ex-users" more, while others will be more impressed by a respected doctor/or psychiatrist.

Ask your pastor and others if they know of any members of the Board of Education or other influential people in town, like the mayor, police chief, etc. that might be able to help get the door opened for the program, especially if any of the above are Christians or at least churchgoers.

Once you have gotten the testimonies and the entire program "homogenized," it may be best to turn the entire thing over to a local Christian doctor or other professional. If the program is headed by them, their professional status will give the program much more respect in the eyes of the School Board than if it comes sponsored by a street Outreach or local streetpreacher. Use recommendation letters gathered from each presentation to help open future doors. Send Xerox copies ahead of the program to school superintendents and principals.

Call the local police departments, and get statistics on local drug abuse problems. Use things like local newspaper articles and statistics to help open doors. Breaking inertia is the hardest part. Once the "ball gets rolling," and the program has its first couple of school assemblies, future contacts will come easier.

Some educators and school superintendents will play "ostrich-with-the-head-in-the-sand," and can only be made to admit the "need" by verified statements, from surveys of kids, newspaper articles, police statistics, and other FACTS! You should find out what the schools are doing in the way of drug abuse programs themselves. They usually have lectures by police, movies, and slide-shows, but it is mainly "peer-pressure" that brings kids into drugs, and "peer-pressure" can be powerfully used to either keep or bring kids out of the drug scene as well.

At some point put part or all of the presentation down on an audio or video cassette to be sent ahead to open doors for the program, and get an open invitation into all the schools of a certain district. It also may be easier to start your program in a nearby smaller town's school-system. You can then use recommendations from the smaller schools as stepping stones into the larger city school systems.

Drug Abuse Program Ideas

1) You should write and/or visit the nearest Teen Challenge center in your area.

2) Use a local Christian Jesus-rock band to spark interest in the assembly.

3) If you are refused a schoolwide assembly time-slot, ask for a lunch hour or "after-school" time slot in the gym, or outdoors in warmer weather.

4) Have a question-answer period afterwards. This helps get the students involved.

5) In churches (particularly), a parents "question-answer period" with no kids allowed may be very beneficial in helping parents to understand and to deal in the best way with the problem, or in preventing it in their own families.

6) Offer free paperback books to help get the message across or draw kids. If you offer Susan Atkin's *Child of Satan, Child of God* book, or Ted Watson's *Will You Die for Me,* spread the word that a free book on one of the Manson girls or guys (the Helter-Skelter crowd) will be given away free to everyone at the assembly, lunch hour or afterschool program, this will help draw a crowd. You can ask local churches and businessmen, even civic clubs to help sponsor the distribution of these books and to foot the bill. Also contact the publishers and/or authors of these books themselves, sharing your vision and asking them to donate 100, 600, or 1000 of these books for this specific purpose!

7) Contact the director of "Hotline," Box 1000, Anaheim, California 92806, and ask him to send you any material and ideas for Drug Abuse programs that he may have.

Books useful in this type of work

Jesus Factor, published by Logos, $1.95 paperback. This documents an actual government funded report that verifies 10% methadone cure for junkies vs. an 80% plus Jesus factor drug rehabilitation success rate by the Teen Challenge ministries over the years.

Drugs and You, published by Simon Schusters Pocket Book Divison.

Nicky Cruz Gives Facts on Drugs, by Nicky Cruz, Logos, $.50

Once a Junkie, by Sonny Arguinzoni, cassette, Logos, $4.95.

42

Thirty Outreach Possibilities

"All things are possible to him that believes" Mark 9:23.

Why reach out in America?

Jesus was born in Bethlehem, which in Hebrew means "House of Bread." America today is the world's storehouse of spiritual bread. Over 85% of the world's missionaries are supported through American finances, America's Christian Institutions, and Churches! Even though unsaved Americans do have and need access to the Gospel, the potential this country has for fulfilling the Great Commission worldwide has only barely been scratched.

As we keep feeding the Word of God into all parts, especially the unreached parts, of the American system and American society, God's Word will keep coming out at the other end in greater measure and in greater power, bringing eternal souls into our Heavenly Father's kingdom!

1) **Start a testimony file and testimony library** at the Outreach, both on cassettes and written down. Having someone share their testimony while being recorded by cassette will help get it into written form!

2) **Rent or acquire a "drug-abuse" pro-Jesus billboard** through a public service approach at some local advertising company.

3) **Start a Jesus discipleship live-in house** for converts and training.

4) **Start a 24 hour emergency hotline telephone** counseling service.

5) **Write tracts in the form of a prayer.** "Father, I thank you that the person reading this right now is being touched by your Spirit, and . . .

6) **Take copies of this book and help other Christians** and churches in nearby towns and military bases to open the Outreach they need.

7) **Have monthly baptism-picnic-fellowships** at nearby lakes in the middle of whatever crowds you can find during the warmer months in your area.

8) **Hold Jesus parades:** Christmas, Easter-Resurrection, etc.

9) **Hold Jesus music festivals** or outdoor Gospel concerts as weather allows.

10) **Present this book to your Seminary or Bible School professor of Missions or Evangelism:** start a local youth Outreach as an ongoing part of

the field-training in your church, or Bible School.

11) Develop and pioneer an after-midnight youth-oriented television testimony and music program, to follow Midnight Special or Saturday Night Live. Ask a local station manager to give you public service time!

12) Send ministry teams into nearby prisons, jails, detention centers, orphanages, rest homes, girls homes, Methadone and V.D. clinics, etc.

13) Start and maintain Christian paperback book racks in such places as bus stations, airports, train stations, doctors' offices, etc.

14) Start a weekly meeting in a movie theatre, perhaps featuring a Jesus band. If it's a time they don't use the theatre (like Sunday morning) you should get it very inexpensively.

15) Enter floats, banners, etc. in local parades, talent contests, etc.

16) Use poster-distributing services to distribute your Jesus posters or tracts in places that you yourself might never go into.

17) Develop a street music group with guitars and tambourines that can play in the back of a pickup or in a poolhall parking lot, playing uptempo songs that can relate to the lost, adventure seeking youth.

18) Have street witnessing teams give out free donuts, fruit etc. as they walk and witness down the street. People will listen to you if they're eating your food.

19) Start "fishermen's clubs" and clock in hours of the fishermen. Have a monthly award for the "Fisherman of the month" with a extra-special prize that people will strive after to win. It might be a super Bible, a meal out for two at a steak-house, a fishing pole, several albums, etc.

20) Post a list of unsaved prisoners to write to on your Outreach Evangelism bulletin board. You can find such lists in secular magazines like Rolling Stone, and other hip media publications on sale at places like headshops.

21) Develop a ministry of picking up hitchhikers, especially on rainy or snowy days. These people will listen to every word you say, because your deeds have already proven your words!

22) Start, and encourage your friends to begin a mailing list of all your old, unsaved friends. Dig out their addresses and send them all a tract or personal note regularly.

23) Hire a skywriter to write short evangelistic Christian messages or scriptures over large crowds of people, such as NFL games, large parades, rock concerts, etc.

24) Witness cross-country and worldwide by telephone for free. Dial the area code, ask for a name, whatever name comes to you, then witness to the operator and share the marvellous plan of salvation from God with them!

25) **Start a gospel sing in a park** where kids hang out, during warm weather.

26) **Call up and arrange for the director to be on local call-in talk shows.**

27) **Whenever local festivals are announced** for several months ahead, have several good local Gospel-rock or folk groups get in on the schedule.

28) **Start a program of brothers picking up hitchhikers at dusk.** This will work well if you have a live-in house with 24 hour surveillance and staffing, as well as bedding and meals available.

29) **Run ads in the weekend entertainment section** of your city's newspapers. Use the ad as bait, utilizing a "come-on" that arouses the reader's curiosity. For example, the ad might read: "Tired of coming down? Call 749-3733!" Hours can be specified, or a phone mate answering device can be hooked up to give a **short super-positive** Gospel message.

30) **Reach out by telephone locally without leaving your house.**

a) Call systematically by profession through the yellow pages, or alphabetically starting with page one of the 'A's' in the white pages. Identify yourself right away and what you're calling for. You will find people ready to receive Christ, or at least polite, the great majority of the time. Have materials ready to mail them. Perhaps you can divide up the entire phone book and train telephone soulwinning teams at different churches in your area, once you get the system running successfully yourself.

b) You might call every bar in town, using the above approach, or just saying a quick "Jesus wants to give you a new life," or reading a Scripture portion before hanging up. God's Word will never return void! If you start off immediately reading Scripture over these phone calls, and they keep listening, keep on reading. If they hang up, it will still convict them, because they're not just hanging up on you, but on God's Word.

BOOK TWO:

STREET OUTREACHES

I: THE NEED FOR STREET OUTREACHES

43

The Need for this Book: A Dozen Cries for Help

"And a vision appeared to Paul in the night: There stood a man of Macedonia, and prayed him, saying, COME OVER INTO MACEDONIA, AND HELP US" Acts 16:9.

Below are excerpts from some of the letters and calls we receive.

1) "There are five times the number of kids cruising on Van Nuys Boulevard as your Peoria, and nothing going on at night for Jesus." *Van Nuys, Calif.*

2) "Kindly send information on how to open a place like yours. We are beginning to have trouble with roaming gangs of youth. A Christian coffeehouse is what this town needs to bring our children to Christ." *C.M.M., Hamlin, New York*

3) "Please send help to our small town of 3,000. My 17 year old daughter smokes "POT" and "everyone" in High School does also. Son-in-law is in a

mental hospital for drug-abuse." *Texas*.

4) "Here in New Orleans the counter-culture is thriving in the French Quarter. I DON'T KNOW WHERE TO START TO OPEN A PLACE ... CAN YOU H-E-L-P? I KNOW JESUS WANTS SOMETHING LIKE YOUR ULTIMATE TRIP HERE!" *J.R.M., New Orleans, La.*

5) "I spent a week in Georgia at Hunter AFB, where my daughter is stationed. I met many young people who smoke marijuana, and drink so much. I left with a heavy heart. Someone must reach these young people. DO YOU HAVE TRAINING SESSIONS TO PREPARE OTHERS TO DO WHAT YOU ALL ARE DOING?" *M.C., Gettysburg, Pa.*

6) "I am praying earnestly for an Ultimate Trip, or similar place in Joplin, Mo. There has been a running battle between the Main Street merchants, and the young people who park their cars at night. THERE IS NO SUCH PLACE FOR KIDS HERE! YET I KNOW THERE IS A NEED!" *J.P., Joplin, Mo.*

7) "Our daughter was in the drug culture, but she has decided to follow Jesus. Her friends are all street people. A coffeehouse ministry is what they need. **NONE OF US KNOW HOW TO GET IT GOING!**" *R.E., Ephrata, Pa.*

8) "Our rural town of 5,000 has big drug problems ... what can we do to reach these young people for Jesus?" *Leyton, N.Y.*

9) "I would appreciate information on operating an outreach-coffeeshop. Our area is in terrific need of such a place. So many young people with no place to go." *M.D.C., Manlius, New York*

10) "We wish to begin a work in Salinas, California. There are a lot of drugs and witchcraft in this area. *S.B., Salinas, Calif.*

11) "I believe the Lord would have His people where the needs are. I am interested in information on the Ultimate Trip; how was it started?" *Glendale, Ariz.*

12) "I have a friend interested in starting something similar here in Kingston, Ontario. Please send information. With Queens University, the prisons, the military, etc., the NEED IS TREMENDOUS." *Ontario, Canada*

These letters are just the tip of the iceberg of need among this country's unsaved young people to be reached out to, where they are. The *Need* is in *every* city, *every* weekend night. If we, as Christians, do not offer a Christian alternative to the attractions the world offers, we are throwing young people to the devil!

Come to think of it, your city does need a stepping stone youth outreach (or several), doesn't it?

44

Our Vision:
Thousands of Outreaches!

"And other seed fell into the good soil, and bore fruit, and reproduced, some an hundred-fold, and some sixty, and some thirty-fold" Matthew 13:8.

There are thousands of cities in America and abroad that have hundreds of thousands of churches dealing with hundreds of millions of people.

Now, of these thousands of cities, how many have a "night life" for sinners: concerts, "strips," nightclubs, hangouts, etc.?

And of these hundreds of thousands of churches (250,000 churches in America alone), how many have any kind of an Outreach, outside the four walls of the church, **out where the action is?** Who will reach the millions of young people under thirty out seeking pleasure and fulfillment Friday and Saturday night?

Almost everyone reading this has had to cross a stream or brook at one time or another. The choice of crossing was simply either find a bridge, get your shoes and feet soaking, possibly getting swept away, or use a stepping stone to cross.

The Church is God's bridge between Himself and mankind, His stepping stone between Jesus Christ and the human race. It is sad but true, that shaky bridges built of the rotten lumber of cold traditionalism and eaten by the termites of ritualistic religion, have discouraged many from crossing over. These, of course, do not negate the transcendent, personal reality of Jesus to those who already know Him, but to those who don't, as Paul writes: "The god of this world has blinded their minds" II Corinthians 4:4. If sinners know that some bridges are rotten, they won't venture across.

Since they don't trust the bridge, and the racing stream is ready to sweep them away, many are pacing up and down the riverbank, knowing they need to get across.

To remedy this, the true Church must place stepping stone ministries in midstream, outside the sanctuaries, out where the people are. It must send guides out to escort the lost across into God's spiritual promised land, flowing with milk and honey; Eternal Life in Jesus.

A stepping stone ministry is a bridge between two places, one full of wall-to-wall Christians, the other, full of wall-to-wall sinners.

45

The Great Omission: Outreaches!

"For the Son of Man is come to seek and to save that which was lost"
Luke 19:10.

". . . about three years ago when I came to Tulsa, I saw the young people out on Peoria. I didn't know what to do, only to put them all on my prayer list. Now God has sent you to be the one to help, I'm going to do everything I can to help you."

Ten years ago the hippies and counter-culture of free sex, dope smoking, drug dealing, rock music and eastern cults, was mainly in New York's lower East Side and Greenwich Village, L.A.'s Venice, and Haight Ashbury in San Francisco. Now the counter-culture is in every city in America, including Plessis, New York, population 214, and Weedpatch, Arkansas. The counter-culture has its "stepping stone" hangouts: teen bars, foozball and pool halls, gamerooms, parking lots, rendezvous, etc. Does the Church?

Every U.S. town over 50,000 has its "skid row mission" for bowery bums, the older wino's . . . but there is a new mission field in America . . . "The strips," in hundreds of our cities.

Young people cruise their towns, driving or hitchhiking back and forth, looking for the "action." Are the Christians, who know Jesus has the real "ACTION," out looking for them? Are we putting God's love into **action out** where the action is? These are respectable business neighborhoods that turn into "spiritual ghettos" after dark. Here teens score or deal dope, pick-up girls, race their cars, drink booze, and locate parties. These new TEEN-AGE "SPIRITUAL SKID ROWS" NEED NEW EVANGELISTIC TACTICS . . . NEW MISSIONS . . . TO REACH THESE MILLIONS OF UNCHURCHED YOUNG PEOPLE!

Teen Challenge's 100 outreaches are doing much, but is it enough? What about your city or one nearby?

Our greatest national resource is not Fort Knox's gold, Texas' oil fields, California's Redwoods, or Hawaii's beaches; it is our youth. As lifeguards, we must get into the water and rescue the perishing.

Every sizeable city has dozens of places for the younger population to spend time on weekend nights. Remember, more people attend "church" with the devil's crowd Friday and Saturday nights combined than any Sunday morning at church. They have movies, bars, parties, races, pool halls, rock concerts, etc. What does the Church offer?

Are we unconsciously saying to the devil: "You can have them on Friday and Saturday nights . . . just as long as they make it to church on Sunday morning," or "if they really want to measure up to our standards . . . let them come to us?" We must go to them on their nights, and on their territory! What good fisherman dares console himself by saying: "Those fish know where I am if they want me?"

46

Laymen Don't Have to Lay Around

"And He gave some apostles, and some prophets and some evangelists, and some pastors and teachers . . ." Ephesians 4:11.

"Provoke one another unto love and unto good works" Hebrews 10:24.

An army made up of five generals wouldn't be much of an army. Yet millions today think there are two classes of Christians, the "super-dupers" (Apostles, Prophets, Evangelists, Pastors and Teachers) and the remaining supposedly "ordinary" Christians, "laymen" not in the aforementioned five-fold categories. NOTHING PLEASES satan MORE THAN THIS TYPE OF UNSCRIPTURAL THEOLOGY . . . FOR HE KNOWS THAT GENERALS WILL NEVER WIN THE BATTLES WITH THEIR ARMIES SITTING AT HOME WAITING FOR THEM TO SEND BACK THE VICTORY REPORTS!

A literal translation of Ephesians 4:12, the next verse after that quoted at the start of this chapter is:

"For the perfecting (maturing, growing up of the saints — God's people) . . . for the work of the ministry . . . for the edifying of the Body of Christ."

"For the training of the saints as servants in the Church in order to get His Holy People ready to serve."

God has called none of His "eagles" to sit around the barnyard. Instead He is calling forth His Church today, His special people, to grow up into Christ's fulness. Laymen today are tired of laying around.

David Wilkerson, Nicky Cruz, Brother Andrew, Billy Graham, Pat Robertson, Jim Bakker, Oral Roberts, Rex Humbard, Jimmy Swaggart, T.L. Osborn, and dozens of other great men of God are not called to do it all. GENERALS CANNOT WIN THE WAR.

Daniel 11:32 reads: "And the people that know their God shall be strong and do exploits." The "laos" . . . the laymen THAT KNOW THEIR GOD SHALL BE STRONG AND THEY SHALL DO EXPLOITS!

A stepping stone Outreach is a layman's training center, and as God's army steps into action, stepping stone Outreaches will spring up here and abroad with increasing effectiveness till Jesus comes!

47

Getting Started

"In the beginning . . . God created . . . the heavens and the earth" Genesis 1:1.

God has planted His dream in each believers heart. Every born-again believer has received the Lord Jesus Christ on his life throne. God's love-dream for humanity has come in as well.

This dream is unique and individual in each heart, yet all of these dreams collectively make up God's entire plan for mankind. This dream is a supernatural yearning to please and serve God.

In the words of another letter we received:

"How I long for God's Spirit and His servants to unite in such an effort to save the perishing. We seem to spend so much time witnessing to Christians, as you say." Ohio

Who will start the needed Outreach in your town or nearby? Shall we say with so many others: "There he is Lord, send him," or shall we unite with Isaiah in saying: "Here am I, Lord, send me!" (Isaiah 6:8).

II: INREACH
(The Ministry Inside)

48

What Is Inreach?

"I will feed My flock, and I will cause them to lie down, says the Lord God. I will seek that which was lost, and bring again that which was driven away, and will bind up that which was broken, and will strengthen that which was sick ... Therefore will I save my flock ... I will make with them a covenant of peace ... and they shall dwell safely in the wilderness" Ezekiel 34:15-26.

Inreach is the ministry within the stepping stone Outreach itself. It includes any ministry within the Outreach building structure during open nights, including preaching, teaching, counselling, music, testimony, worship, sharing, Bible studies, staff training, coordinating volunteers, refreshments, followup, ride giving, housing, door-greeting, and more.

Inreach is the launching pad for the outreach teams. Teamwork is its number one priority. It must always be kept neat as it represents Jesus to all visitors. Inreach is the foundation of the entire Outreach operation.

49

Setting the
Spiritual Thermostat

"For our God is a consuming fire" Hebrews 12:29.

"I know your works, that you are neither cold nor hot. I wish you were cold or hot. So then, because you are lukewarm, and neither cold nor hot, I will spew you out of my mouth" Revelation 3:15-16.

"He that comes after me is mightier than I . . . He shall baptize you with the Holy Ghost and with fire" Matthew 3:11.

Young people today aren't looking for "Glad tidings of great joy," but "the most wonderful news ever announced!" That rings a different bell! The two translate the same verse, (Luke 2:10), but only the second one brings the Gospel into the "now!" In Tulsa we named our Outreach "The Ultimate Trip." We could have named it "The mediocre trip," or "The pretty good trip," but to us the Good News of the Gospel is not just plain ole good news!

Young people today are looking not for "an" answer, but for "the" answer. Jesus compared His Kingdom to a wedding feast, not a funeral. He described Himself as the Resurrection, not the "rigamortis!" Many young people are out to change their world. Their idealism and dreams are God-given and the TRUE Gospel can harness these ideals to glorify God.

When you ask many Christians what they've been doing, many reply: "Oh, nothing much,"; and when asked, how they are, many reply: "Not bad," or "Allright, I guess." I feel like shouting: "False advertising!"

What gauge should be used to determine the proper spiritual "temperature" of the Outreach, if not the words of the Lord Himself! He said: "I am come that they might have Life super-abundantly." He offers Life, not religion! Love, not lectures! An example, not a signpost! He came to give us REALITY not bells, candles and beads!

Millions of young people will end up in hell's flames unless somewhere between here and there, they run into REAL Christians, living their faith, loving one another, overwhelmed by "The Most Wonderful News Ever Announced!"

50

It's a Team Dream!

"The locusts have no king, yet go they forth all of them by bands" Proverbs 30:27.

"Behold, how good and how pleasant it is for brethren to dwell together in unity" Psalms 133.

"By this shall all men know that you are my disciples, if you have love one to another" John 13:35.

The goals of the Outreach should be written down. Every staff member must fully agree with these goals.

All potential workers on the team must:

1) Have their BA (born-again) degree! (John 3:3,5,7)
2) Know and study their Bibles. (II Timothy 2:15)
3) Accept and respect the leadership. (Hebrews 13:17)
4) Be loving. (I Corinthians 13:1-13)
5) Be teachable. (Acts 20:32)
6) Be dependable. (Luke 16:10, Matthew 25:21,23)
7) They must respect ALL parts of the ministry: Inreach, Outreach, and Backup.

The different functions of Inreach working together are like a well-trained football team, or symphony orchestra. A coffeehouse Outreach is a war canoe that needs a minimum of six to a dozen paddlers to reach maximum speed.

I Corinthians 12:28 mentions the ministry of "helps." It is "helps" that makes the ministry a reality. Thank God for the "use-me's" that have left behind the religious slums of "bless-me" Christianity. It is the workers, not the shirkers, that receive God's best.

The "family" feeling will develop as the team works together making the Outreach dream come true.

51

Miscellaneous Inreach Personnel Needs

"Let us speak the truth in love; so shall we all fully grow up into Christ. He is the Head, and on Him the whole body depends. Bonded and knit together by every joint, the whole frame grows through the due activity of each part, and builds itself up in love" Ephesian 4:15-16. NEB

"In each of us the Spirit is manifested in one particular way, for some useful purpose" I Corinthians 12:5.

In Jesus Christ's own personal ministry on earth, He was the "One," then there were the three (James, Peter, and John), the twelve (the disciples), the seventy (Luke 10), the one hundred and twenty in the Upper Room (Acts 1:15), the five hundred (I Corinthians 15:6), then the four and five thousand He taught and ended up feeding (Matthew 14-15). In Inreach, many different talents and types of people can each find a very useful, vital role to fulfill. Below are a number of basic positions. Each position has a brief sketch of the qualifications and/or functions required for that specific position.

1) **The Director:** Must be a spiritual conductor to the entire Outreach "orchestra!"

2) **The Board of Directors:** See the "Backup" Incorporation chapter.

3) **Preachers and teachers:** These should definitely **NOT** be new converts. They should be established in "the WORD" and practice what they preach.

4) **Door greeters:** A warm welcome, friendly smile, and open heart overflowing with God's love. This should be the first impression any newcomer, whether saved or not, receives. This is vital!

"A man (and Outreach) that has friends must show himself (itself) friendly" Proverbs 18:24.

5) **Counselors:** See the Counseling chapter later in this section.

6) **Musicians:** See the Inreach chapter on music.

7) **Drivers:** Each open night at least one committed brother should be on hand to pick up those without cars, especially new converts. Reimburse car

expenses. Never send a single brother out after a girl-rider, or vice-versa. Instead, mix and match.

8) Phone answerer: It will eliminate a lot of confusion if you assign one person on each "open" night to take phone calls. Having them write and distribute messages on 3x5 cards avoids verbal interruptions during Bible studies, in the prayer room, or counseling. Limiting calls to three minutes is a good rule.

9) Worship leaders: A worship leader should be an Outreach regular, someone who is spiritual, enthusiastic, a good strong singer, and has a likeable personality.

10) Intercessory prayer warriors: See the Prayer room chapter.

11) Refreshments: See the Inreach chapter under this same heading.

12) Literature deacon: You'll eventually need one person in charge of this.

God's scriptural principle of blessing and responsibility requires that we show ourselves faithful over a few things (Matthew 25:21,23), before He puts us in charge of greater things. Let this be the rule of thumb when filling positions on your Inreach personnel team.

52

Overview of a
Typical Inreach Evening

"To every thing there is a season, and a time to every purpose under the heavens... He hath made everything beautiful in its season (to suit its time)" Ecclesiastes 3:1, 11.

If you officially open at 8:00 p.m. on weekend nights, your evening schedule might include many of the features below.

6-7 p.m.   If a band is coming in, have them get there early to set up, balance their sound levels, etc.

Cleanup (vacuuming, trash emptying, etc.), can be done at this time.

Staff meeting on Saturday night (usually a bigger night crowd-wise than Friday's)

7-7:30 p.m.   All staff should arrive (even on Fridays) by now at the latest.

7-8 p.m.   Nightly intercession on weekends (we called it "Happy Hour!")

8 p.m.   Door greeter in position inside the front door.

                Head counselor and helpers ready to lovingly minister to all that drop in.

8-8:15 p.m.   Time for fellowship, many arrivals, visiting, etc.

8:30 p.m.   Call the main group into the main room for a short worship time and 20 minute Word teaching or Bible study.

9 p.m.   Teaching is over, welcome and recognize all visitors and first-timers. Take collection or mention needs and the offering box.

                Band starts playing and ministers most of the time until closing, except for their breaks. During breaks short, lively testimonies are excellent, especially for young people sharing how Jesus has changed their lives. Have them cover not just what they're out of, but what they've come into as well!

9:15 p.m.   If you're sending out Outreach teams, stop the band after a few numbers, and assemble all the ones going out for the evening back in the prayer room for brief instructions and dividing into teams.

9:30 p.m.   By this time, all the Outreach teams should already be out the door.

The band is playing 30-45 minute sets, intercessors perhaps are praying back in the prayer room, the door greeter is greeting, counselors are counseling, etc.

During slow nights, or "lull" spots, extra Inreach people can always stay busy, "redeeming" theirs (and God's) time by going in the back prayer room and praying on half-hour shifts. They also can write short notes each week to recent converts, missing regulars, or guest book names.

53

Teaching or Preaching?

"And Jesus went about all Galilee, teaching in their synagogues, preaching the gospel of the Kingdom . . ." Matthew 4:23.
"Go ye into all the world, and preach the Gospel to every creature" Mark 16:15.
"Go ye therefore, and teach all nations . . ." Matthew 28:19.

From the above Scriptures it is obvious that the Great Commission includes both teaching and preaching. Jesus is repeatedly found in the Gospels doing both. Which one is more important? What are the differences?

Both have one supreme element in common: The Word of God. Both involve upbuilding, and correcting both saints and sinners. But there are several important, distinctive differences that need to be understood and taken advantage of, especially in a street-Outreach setting!

Preaching

Inreach preaching should never be done to a group of less than half a dozen. Sitting in a circle and sharing the Word informally is more effective with smaller groups. A microphone isn't needed to talk across a spool table! Unless the microphone is called for by a sufficient number of people, avoid it; it looks "churchy!" Perhaps Jeremiah 23:29 best describes preaching: "Is not My Word like a fire, . . . and like a hammer that breaks the rock in pieces."

One Bible teacher described the difference between teaching and preaching in this way. "The difference is in: 1) what is assumed, and 2) what is emphasized. In preaching, you emphasize the "why," the inspirational aspect, and assume the "how," or informational is available from other sources. And with teaching the reverse holds true."

Teaching

"My doctrine shall drop like the rain, my speech shall distill as the dew" Deuteronomy 32:2.

The above scripture from Deuteronomy, describes the ministry of teaching. In teaching, the listener is trained, guided, instructed, informed, and enlightened. Teaching should be used more inside a street-Outreach ministry, while preaching should be happening more on the outside, at rock concerts, on the street, etc. Like a hammer and a saw in a master craftsman's tool box, neither preaching nor teaching outweigh each other. The important thing is fulfilling Proverbs 10:21 which states: "The lips of the righteous . . . feed many."

Teaching and/or Preaching Possibilities:

1) Before teachings are given, distribute note paper and pencils.
2) Invite respected neighborhood ministers in to teach, especially those from the churches that have been supportive of the Outreach.
3) Buy a blackboard to use as a visual aid during teaching times.

54

Counseling

"And His Name shall be called Wonderful, Counselor . . . The Prince of Peace" Isaiah 9:6.

"The Lord has given me the tongue of the learned, that I may speak a word in due season to them that are weary" Isaiah 50:4.

"And now, brethren, I commend you to God, and to the Word of His grace, which is able to build you up" Acts 20:32.

"All scripture is breathed out by God, and is useful for teaching the faith and correcting error, for re-setting the direction of a man's life, and training him in good living" II Timothy 3:16.

"The advice of a wise man refreshes like water from a mountain spring, and satisfies like a good meal" Proverbs 13:14, 18:20.

The Good Samaritan in Jesus' parable (Luke 10:30-37) found a wounded man on the roadside too messed up for the preacher or Levite (Sunday School Teacher) to get involved with! But the good Samaritan cared for him. Our Lord, the Great Physician, has sent us on a similar mission, to pour "oil and wine" and God's Word into the hearts and lives of our spiritually wounded world.

Counseling is "binding up the broken-hearted . . . giving beauty for ashes, joy for mourning, and the heavenly garment of praise for sin's heaviness." Counseling is like a spiritual Intensive Care Unit, using a "scriptural oxygen tent." It is God's personal touch to the personal needs of both saints and sinners. Even regular Outreach staff members will from time to time need counseling. Counseling is like giving a spiritual "tune up," lifting the hood and changing the "spark plugs, filter, and the oil itself."

Jesus named the Holy Spirit "The Comforter" (or Helper) from the Greek word *Paracletos* (one called alongside to help). A counselor is called to be a paraclete as well.

Choosing a counseling director

Counseling is a ministry gift from God, and those given this ministry by Him will surface as soon as opportunities for counseling do. The counseling director should be mature as a Christian (a minimum of five years), and one who sees only an opportunity to love and minister God's grace to people, and bring glory to God!

Things to avoid in counseling

1) Watch the boy-girl attraction. (Keep hands off of opposites, and have women counsel women, and men counsel men, when possible).

2) Avoid condemning the counselee or his wrong ideas. "Love covers (not condemns) a multitude of sins." Proverbs 10:12.

3) Avoid talking more than listening. (If they don't open up, use questions).

4) Avoid interrupting the counselee!! "He that answers a matter before he hears it out, it is a shame and a folly unto him." Proverbs 18:13

5) Avoid passing on secrets you are entrusted with. "A talebearer reveals secrets, but he that is of a faithful spirit conceals the matter." Proverbs 11:13

6) Avoid phrases like "I think," "I believe," "I feel;" speak God's Word. "If any man speak, let him speak as the oracle of God (let him say what God says)." I Peter 4:11. God watches over HIS Word, not ours!

Jesus preached repentance!

"Repent" is the first word of Jesus recorded in the New Testament (Matthew 4:17). Jesus told the crowds twice in Luke 13: "Unless you repent, you shall all perish." If sin is the problem, the cure is true Biblical repentance, not just sorrow of the heart, not a change of heart, but both!

Counseling materials

There is much material in Christian bookstores on counseling. Second to the Bible, however, in street-Outreach work, I recommend Dave Wilkerson's books, *The Untapped Generation,* and *Jesus People Maturity Manual.*

55

The Prayer Room

"... And He (Jesus) went out into a mountain to pray, and continued all night in prayer to God" Luke 6:12.

"My house shall be called a house of prayer for all nations" Isaiah 56:7.

"They that wait upon the Lord shall renew their strength; they shall mount up with wings as eagles" Isaiah 40:31.

"Call unto Me and I will shew you great and mighty things which you know not" Jeremiah 33:3.

As the engine room is to any great oceanliner, so the prayer room is to any ministry, especially a "front-line" street-Outreach! Jesus commanded His disciples to "fast and pray," not pray fast! Prayer is the most important thing we do! Never let your outreach exceed your upreach. When the vertical becomes shorter than the horizontal beam, a cross ceases to be a cross.

Why a separate prayer room?

At our first and second locations, we tried using our one separate room for intercession, counseling, phone answering, sermon and communion preparation, tract storage, and "you-name-it." It became (spiritually) like having a combination foreign car garage, gourmet kitchen, woodworking shop, and oil-painting studio all in the same room. AVOID THIS! Use sheetrock and partition off a separate area for a prayer room!

Prayer Room Possibilities

1) **Nightly Intercession:** We had a spiritual "Happy hour" 60 minute prayer before opening each night.

2) **A Prayer Book:** Start a 8" x 11" three-hole binder with sections for: a) salvation, b) healing, c) marriages, d) finances, e) a record of answered prayers.

3) **Continuous intercession during open hours:** Have a half-hour sign-up sheet on the prayer room door.

4) **A 24 hour prayer chain:** One phone call can be relayed by others to reach dozens of people.

5) **Occasional all night or half-night prayer meetings:** Jesus did it. Do we?

Keeping the prayer room in action on open nights can help more than words can tell. It will influence the soulwinning teams out on the streets.

"As we neared the end of the witnessing route, there seemed to be a draining of our strength. WE OBSERVED HOW TERRIBLE IS THE STUBBORN, SULLEN, ARROGANT, IRRESPONSIBLE BEHAVIOR! WHAT WILL PENETRATE SUCH CONTEMPT AND DISREGARD?" (the above an excerpt from one soulwinner's report).

THE ANSWER IS OBVIOUS: ... ONLY PRAYER!

56

Followup, Not Swallowup

"He shall feed His flock like a shepherd: he shall gather the lambs with His arm, and carry them in His bosom, and shall gently lead those that are with young" Isaiah 40:11.

"By this shall My Father be glorified (and praised), that you bear much fruit, and that your fruit remain" John 15:8.

"Go therefore into all the world, and make disciples of all nations" Matthew 28:19.

Our Lord's Great Commission was not to get "decisions," but to "make disciples." The news media carries stories of newborn babies abandoned on doorsteps, etc. Since it is a crime in the natural, how much worse is it in the spiritual realm? What sane grown-up would leave a newborn babe at home and tell it:

"Now I'm going off for a two month trip. The icebox is here if you're hungry, the checkbook is in the desk if you need money, there's the thermostat if you're too hot, there are diapers in the hall closet, and if you REALLY need me, the phone number where I'm vacationing is by the phone."

Followup is helping newborn Christians to learn to follow and trust God in every part of their lives. Babies mainly do four things 1) cry 2) wet 3) sleep and 4) eat. Babies use a lot of pampers and spiritually, newborn Christians do the same. They must be pampered spiritually, changed, fed, comforted, and, most of all . . . LOVED! Surveys reveal that being "loved" is a baby's number one need!

Four way followup

An easy plan to use in followup after someone has received Jesus is to explain four ways of talking: "Up . . . Down . . . In . . . and Out!"
1) Talking Up: Talking up to God, your Heavenly Father through prayer.
2) Talking Down: God talks down from heaven to us in His Word.
3) Talking In: Let others talk (in) to you through fellowship.
4) Talking Out: Talk out about God to others, with others!

Followup is a process

The world-famous snow-white dancing Lipizan stallions are born JET BLACK!   They lighten up shade-by-shade on the outside as they mature day-by-day on the inside, but all the while, whether full-grown snow-white in color, or jet-black at birth, they are Lipizans!

God has many spiritual "Lipizans" and some take more time to change "color" than others. Some need more spiritual "brainwashing" than others (Romans 12:2). I did!

Integrate them into a church

Ortiz writes in his book *Call To Discipleship* that many converts are left like a pile of bricks, which any thief (satan) can carry off one at a time. But, he continues, if they are built into a wall (into Christ's Body, the Church), to steal the brick, the thief must first carry off the wall!

The morning after syndrome

The devil pounces on many new converts the next morning and shouts: "You don't feel saved, do you? You don't look saved; you must not be saved." Give converts something immediately to take home with them, to read, and to memorize, a printed scripture card or a 3" x 5" card with a victory verse handwritten on it. Several good verses to start with are II Corinthians 5:17, I John 4:4, Hebrews 13:5, Matthew 28:20 and Revelation 12:11! Ephesians 6:17 tells us that God's Word is the Holy Spirit's Sword, so don't allow newborn "lambs" to leave your presence without something to send satan packing with his tail between his legs in defeat!

Conversion: true and false!

D. L. Moody was once approached by a drunk saying: "Mr. Moody, don't you remember me . . . urp! . . . I'm one of your converts!" Moody replied: "You must be one of mine, because Jesus' converts just don't turn out that way."

Billy Graham estimated 90% of his "decisions" eventually forget what they decided. BUT THANK GOD FOR THE 10%! Jesus Himself said: "Have not I picked you twelve, and one of you is a devil?" In Jesus' parable of the Sower in Matthew 13, three of the four soil-types never reached maturity, but the good soil bringing forth 30, 60, and 100 fold made up for the rest!

Followup mistakes to avoid

1) Don't depend on someone else to do it (Proverbs 12:27).
2) Don't have too many or too few people contacting the same convert at once.
3) Don't force converts to confront their old sinning buddies right away. Let them gain confidence, and strength!
4) Don't cross sex lines, especially in visitation followup.
5) Don't let the converts' fire grow cold. Do "followup" while the coals are hot!
6) Don't let converts go out with no place to go. Extend Christian love to them. If you can't put them up for a night, find them a place.
7) Don't show-off new converts! Doing this depersonalizes them, can deeply trouble them, and make them question their conversion.

Followup materials

At the Outreach, keep materials on hand that you use for followup. Below are some materials we have used.
1) *The Next Step*, by Chick Publications, price $1, Box 622, Chino, CA 91710
2) *The Basic Five*, a set of five 15 minute Bible studies. TCF, 3657 E. 49th Place, Tulsa, OK 74135
3) *What's Next*, Harrison House Publishers, Box 35035, Tulsa, OK 74135
4) The Navigators have a complete series: Box 20, Colorado Springs, CO

80901

5) Also send for samples of the materials the larger ministries like Billy Graham, Rex Humbard, PTL Club, 700 Club, Jimmy Swaggart, etc. are using.

6) *Grow Up Spiritually* is an excellent $2 paperback by Kenneth E. Hagin. Also his mini-book *The New Birth*, $.50 each, ideal for new converts. Write Box 5012, Tulsa, OK 74150.

Followup possibilities

1) Start a spiritual Big Brother and Sister program, assigning one strong believer to each new convert as their special "Lamb" to feed and love.

2) Begin a weekly new converts night class (Mondays are good), particularly if they are "spooked" by the established churches.

3) Call, visit, write, and take them out to meals.

4) Don't count on them coming to church by themselves, go and pick them up!

5) Notify friendly churches, and give converts a list of friendly churches as well.

6) Keep a central card file, with a separate card for each convert, so that whenever the staff has something to record, others reading through the file regularly will be aware of any ministry and materials the convert has received.

7) Work out a systematic followup plan for YOUR outreach. Type it out, and Xerox copies so that new staff and volunteers can followup right!

8) Make up followup "packets" and have them prepared ahead of time to get into the hands of each person that receives Christ as Lord at the outreach, or through one of the witnessing teams. Get these in the converts' hands before they leave, or in the mail to them the next day.

57

Housing and Referrals

"I was a stranger, and ye took me in" Matthew 25:44.

"... Be ye therefore wise as serpents but harmless as doves" Matthew 10:16.

Seek out volunteer overnight housing from outreach regulars, staff, friendly churches, and believers you know. Keep the names and particulars on their accommodations, and restrictions, on file in the staff office at the Outreach. Here are several different housing needs and ideas.

1) **A Gospel trio ministering at the Outreach needs room and board overnight:** In this instance, an older church person's home would be fine. There would be no risk, as these would obviously be God's family members.

2) **A hitchhiker drops in at 11:30 p.m., needs a place to "crash" (stay):** This type of need should be met by "street-wise" Christian *young* people. He SHOULD NEVER be sent to an older church person's home, because:

   a) Younger street-people would probably better relate Jesus to him and

   b) He might be a 'Wolf' (two-legged species), and take valuables when he goes. When the host leaves for work, if no one else is going to be there, make sure the guest leaves too! Don't learn Matthew 10:16 (quoted above) the hard way!

3) **A young man and woman show up, ask for lodging, claiming to be married:** To many street people, living-together (in a shady way) represents the legal equivalent of marriage. It is not in God's eyes. Let God's love control your conversation when you ask if they have a marriage license, and they'll usually tell the truth. If they don't, gently explain that you'll be glad to find them separate bedding, take them for breakfast together and they can be on their way again. Love doesn't compromise the truth!

Referral Hints

Besides the many churches in your area that you should be working with, there are many other organizations, some not even Christian, that may offer services the Outreach staff should be aware of.

For example:

1) **Housing ministries:** Tulsa has an Emergency Shelter that gives free housing to the "needy" for two weeks, as long as they get a job. The Social Services (Welfare Dept.) may have a comprehensive housing referral list; check with them. Then there's the Salvation Army, YMCA's, etc.

2) **Other street-level ministries:** There may be a live-in discipleship house

in your town as there is in ours. Work with them!

3) **Social Services:** Your town may have a Welfare office that offers free dental, medical and/or employment services. They may have access to funds for severe needs. Call them and find out what type of help is available.

4) **National toll-free runaway service:** Call Runaways, Inc. 800-231-6946. Without charge an operator will telephone a runaway's parents anywhere in the U.S.A. and convey a message from them. "I'm alive; don't worry about me" is typical.

5) **Regional Teen Challenge Centers:** These centers are for wayward youth, who need a 24-hour Christian environment to fully shake off the chains of their past life in sin. You will encounter young people wanting and needing to stay with them!

6) **Professional and Ministerial Service Directories:** The Tulsa Metropolitan Ministry publishes an annual book compiling all types of services. Perhaps there is a similar publication in your city.

7) **Long-range Christian live-in and discipleship facilities:** Below are names of a few nationally known live-in homes:

a) **Mid-West Challenge,** 612/825-2466, 3049 Columbus Avenue, South Minneapolis, Minnesota 55407. They will help prostitutes who want to live for God by wiring a one-way ticket to any airport in the USA to help a prostitute escape her pimp and fly directly to Mid-West Challenge.

b) **New Life For Girls,** R.D. 3, Dover, Pa. 717/266-5614. Founded by ex-prostitute and ex-junkie, Cookie Rodriguez. New Life has centers in various parts of the country.

c) **Walter Hoving Homes,** Box 194, Garrison, N.Y. 10524.

d) **Lester Roloff Homes,** Box 1177, Corpus Christi, Texas 78403, 512/882-4211 or 883-8265. They care for several hundred wayward young people. They teach them a trade as well.

e) **Teen Challenge National Headquarters** will send you a list of their U.S. ministries and their address is 444 Clinton Ave., Brooklyn, N.Y.

8) **Order the author's N.S.D. (National Street Directory)** listing over 300 live-in facilities across the entire U.S.A. Cost $8.95. 1445 Boonville Ave., Springfield, MO 65082. (417) 862-2781.

58

Gospel Materials: Bibles! Tracts! Books! Tapes!

"The Scriptures tell us that bread won't feed men's souls: obedience to every Word of God is what we need" Matthew 4:4 (Living Bible).
"Peter, do you love Me? . . . feed my lambs . . . feed my sheep, feed my sheep" John 21:15-17.

Fishermen use different types of bait to catch different types of fish. Some fish like flies, others delight in worms, while others are turned on by lures, oils, minnows or cut bait! That point is clear: WHATEVER WORKS . . . USE IT! The Outreach should always have materials available for two main categories of people, 1) The unsaved, and 2) the newly converted. Below are several categories of printed Gospel materials to stock in **your** outreach!

Tracts

Tracts are pocketsized Gospel messages or sermonettes. See the Outreach chapter on tract evangelism.

Jesus papers

These are an excellent tool for spreading the Good News with the "anti-establishment" or "anti-Church" younger set! *Cornerstone* is the best. Theirs is published monthly, and costs $8 per hundred. Their address is 4431 N. Paulina, Chicago, IL 60640. Also write: The Love Inn, Freeville, New York. A free street-paper designed for prisoners is *The Crack In The Wall*, Box 191, Plainfield, NJ 07061.

Bibles

You should have several dozen copies of the Bible on hand at the Outreach, scattered on each spool table, and readily accessible. New Testaments in modern translations are more popular with the young, and can be purchased for under $1 a piece in bulk.

Contact your nearest Gideon chapter, they may supply you with free Bibles and New Testaments. Also contact The American Bible Society, Dept. S, Box 3575, Grand Central Station, N.Y., N.Y. 10017; or the New York International Bible Society, 144 Tice Lane, East Brunswick, N.J. 08816.

Christian comics

Unreligious as these sound, Christian comics can interest a junkie when a Bible may leave him cold. If it works use it!

Changed life Christian testimony books

This type of book is a matchless tool to use with young people. A list of over thirty books of this type ends this chapter. KIDS WILL READ THESE BOOKS! These books take their readers "to hell and back," stripping the glamour off of drugs, lust, alcohol, money, fame, exposing sin as the monster it is.

Send them anonymously to young people you know who need them. Don't use a return address or tell the parents. Thus, when the kids ask their parents if they know who sent it, they can honestly answer "No!" Kids will read it if they think their parents aren't up to something!

Things to avoid in using Gospel materials

First, never allow anything to be passed out that hasn't been approved by the staff. Secondly, watch out for "moldy-oldies," religious material that will turn the kids off before the Holy Spirit can turn them on! Thirdly, your give-away materials should be for newcomers and new converts. Older Christians should be taught to pay if they want them.

Gospel materials possibilities

1) Set up a "Materials" supply center in the staff office.
2) Assign one responsible regular to be in charge of all materials.
3) Set a minimum inventory level for much-used items, and have the materials director re-order whatever is running low, at that level.

4) Order a rubber stamp (or two) with the Outreach name and address on it. Stamp the back or inside book cover of all materials. It makes no sense fishing with great bait if there's no line attached!

5) Start a lending library of cassette tapes and paperback books. Ask friendly churches and Outreach partners for unused religious books and cassettes!

6) Sell selected materials from a sales case, or have a "for sale" table or bookrack. Very few Christian kids are without money these days.

7) Write, print, and distribute your own tracts.

8) Set up literature racks to distribute Christian paperbacks, etc. in your area's Methadone centers, VD clinics, YMCA's, bus and train stations, airports, jails, detention centers, etc.

9) Challenge each Christian bookstore in your area to make a donation of $10 or $20 each month in the form of changed-life Christian testimony paperbacks, to be placed in above locations. Bookstores might pledge five, ten, or more paperbacks each month, as part of their tithes to the Lord. Keep them informed with progress reports from this book ministry!

10) Write or call Dave Wilkerson Youth Crusades, Rt. 1 Box 80, Lindale, Texas 76771 for a free list of their materials. (214) 882-6691.

List of changed-life Christian testimony books

Bought and Paid For, By Dan Larson (ex-teenage prostitute), New Leaf Press, Harrison, Ark., $2.95.

Carmen, by John Benson (girl's life on the streets), Fleming Revell, $1.95.

Child of Satan, Child of God, by Bob Slosser & Susan Atkins (former Manson gang member), Logos, $1.95.

Cindy, by John Benton (girl's street-life), Fleming Revell, $1.95.

Coming Out, as told to Pat Boone (converted former lesbian), Bible Voice Publishers.

Cross and the Switchblade, by David Wilkerson (evangelizing New York's gangs), Spire, $1.50 or $.39 for comic book.

Escape from Witchcraft, by Robert Blankenship (former teenage witch), Zondervan, $.95.

God's Junkie, by Sonnie Arguinzoni, c/o Victory Temple Outreach, Logos.

Holiday in Hell, by Chico Holiday (former Las Vegas singer), Whitaker House, $1.75.

Home Where I Belong, by B.J. Thomas (rock superstar conquers drugs), Word, $6.95.

Hooked on a Good Thing, Sammy Hall (former junkie), Fleming Revell, $2.50.

I'm Gonna Bury You, by Gene Neil (ex-murderer), Voice of Triumph, Box 70, Glendale, CA 91209.

Just Off Chicken Street, Floyd McClung, Fleming Revell.

The Minnesota Connection, by Al Palmquist (freeing prostitutes), Bible Voice, $1.95.

Once a Junkie, by Sonny Arguinzoni, Logos (cassette only) $4.95.

Lulu, by Lulu Roman (Hee-Haw star saved off drugs), Fleming Revell $5.95.

Please Make Me Cry, by Cookie Rodriguez (former junkie and prostitute), Whitaker Press, Springdale, PA 14144, $1.95.

Prison to Praise, Merlin Carothers (prisoners' rebirth), Logos, $2.95.

Run Baby Run, by Nicky Cruz (New York gangleader gets saved), Logos, $1.95.

The Satan Seller, by Mike Warnecke (former satanist/high priest), Logos, $1.95.

Something for Nothing, by Sid Roth (former scientologist/con-man), Logos, $1.50.

Soul on Fire, by Eldridge Cleaver (former Black-Panther leader), Word Publishers.

Street Cop Who Cared, by Barrett (work helping 'street-people'), Fleming Revell.

Suicide, by David Wilkerson, Spire, $1.95.

Tell It to the Mafia, by Joe Donato (former Mafia member), Logos, $1.95.

The Challenge Can Be Fatal, by Luis Torres (ex-junkie), c/o 300 S. Fourth St., Fairfax, OK 74637.

The Third Sex, by Kent Philpott (stories of ex-'gays'), Logos.

Too Tough For God, by Jerry Golden (former thief and convict) Word Books, Waco, TX.

Twelve Angels from Hell, David Wilkerson (story of 12 street people coming to Jesus), Spire, $1.25.

Where Flies Don't Land, by Jerry Graham (armed robber and convict), Logos, $2.95.

Will You Die for Me? by Tex Watson, as told to Chaplain Ray (former Manson gang member and killer), Fleming Revell, $7.95.

Young Lions of Judah, by Mike Evans (stories of completed Jews), Logos, $1.25.

59

A Sample Nightly Ministry Report

"... Declare among the people His doing" Psalm 9:11.

Why use one?

A nightly ministry report sheet like the one below helps the Outreach both present and future. In the present, it gives the director 20 eyes and ears instead of only two of each. It also helps in assembling materials to share what God is doing throught your monthly newsletter . In the future, re-reading reports from six months or a year ago gives great encouragement and perspective. Keep the sample reports in a 3 ring 8"x11" binder.

Nightly Ministry Report

Date _____ Reporter _____
Name of person giving teaching _____
Topic _____
Name of music group ministering_____
Opinion of the message _____
Approximate attendance_____
Persons receiving Jesus as Saviour and Lord_____
Persons receiving prayer, counseling, healing, deliverance:
  Name _____
Nature of prayer or counseling _____
Approximate number of witnesses out to the streets_____
Designation of witnessing teams _____
What could have been improved on ministry-wise at the Outreach?
_____

60

Discipline

"Winking at sin leads to worry, bold reproof leads to peace" Proverbs 10:10.

"Anyone willing to be corrected is on the pathway to life. Anyone refusing has lost his chance" Proverbs 10:17.

"Punishment that hurts chases evil from the heart" Proverbs 20:30.

"Those who continue to sin, rebuke before all, so that the rest may be warned and stand in wholesome awe and fear" I Timothy 5:20.

"For the Lord disciplines the person He loves, and He lays the rod on every person He acknowledges as His . . . If you are without discipline, in which all true sons share, it means you aren't really God's son at all — that you don't really belong in His family" Hebrews 12:6, 8.

Jesus' Great Commission and commandment to His Church was to go and make disciplined students and followers out of all the nations. Discipline is vital to effectiveness in fulfilling any ministry on the street!

Visitors' Discipline

The entire staff has to have a united understanding of what is and isn't allowed, regarding the discipline of visitors at the Outreach. Below are common problems and solutions we've used.

1) **What about smoking?** You can get the point across with a sign or two saying, "Thank you for not smoking." If they must smoke and go outside, have a regular go with them.

2) **What about drugs and pills?** A first-time reprimand is usually enough. A second offense should mean expulsion for a time before re-entry.

3) **What about cursing?** Take them aside and tell them they'll either have to change their language or leave. Don't tolerate blasphemy or filthy language from a drunk or stoned person.

4) **What about alcohol?** Have them leave it outside the door, with the doorgreeter for safe keeping, or pour it down the stool. Have your staff know Proverbs 3:29 and 31:6, 7, 20.

5) What about freeloaders? Believers that come by too often to "lounge" without getting involved in the ministry will eventually drag down unsaved people or new converts.

Discipline for Christians:
staff and regulars

The first letter to the Corinthians in many ways relates to a street outreach. The epistle's first eight chapters deal with the discipline of believers. Some were sueing each other, others living in incest, getting drunk at the Lord's supper, dividing the church into cliques, etc. Be familiar with Paul's disciplinary recommendations to Corinth's "wild ones."

Discipline may mean a demotion (loss of position), suspension, exclusion from the Outreach for a period of time, public reproof or rebuke, or other means. In I Corinthians 5:11 Paul compares Christians' sinning to gangrene, and gangrene must be amputated before it spreads! However, keep in mind the eventual restitution of "wanderers" (II Corinthians 2:6-11).

Don't be too timid about correcting brothers who give every sister a big "bear-hug" or romancing staff members holding hands while "ministering." At different times we had to temporarily suspend girls who were picking up guys, a homosexual "brother" trying to "score" on new converts, and a brother who insisted on pushing his "pet" doctrine to the point of upsetting other people's faith.

One final word on discipline: DON'T BE AFRAID TO CALL THE POLICE if the situation warrants it! Locking the doors at certain times can help in explosive situations. The Bible says that the law IS for the "lawless," (I Timothy 1:8-10), and you owe it to the Lord, your partners, and to those that frequent the Outreach to keep the place run "decently and in order" (I Corinthians 14:40).

61

Refreshments

"I was hungry and you gave me food to eat, I was thirsty, and you gave me something to quench my thirst" Matthew 25:35.

"If a brother or sister be naked, and destitute of daily food, and one of you say unto them, 'Depart in peace, be warmed and filled ... notwithstanding, you give them not those things needful to the body, ... what does it profit?" James 2:15-16.

Free refreshments

There are many ways to feed the multitudes with a few loaves and fishes, while teaching them to feast their souls on the Bread and Water of Life! Local bakeshops will give you "Saturday" donuts, volunteers will bake homemade goodies and coffee or tea doesn't cost that much. An ice water dispenser by the front door is convenient. Do check with the local health department to find out where they draw the line on food handouts, and who does or doesn't need a food handler's permit.

Refreshments for Sale!

Local soda companies rent soda-pop machines. You can offset the $15-$25 monthly charge by 5¢ or 10¢ profit from each drink. Popcorn, juice, and candy machines can also be rented or bought. Coffee and tea may be brewed on a Mr. Coffee apparatus, a 30-50 cup percolater, or a $.35 per cup vending machine.

Refreshment possibilities

1) The rare case of true hunger can be met by using ministry money to take the person out or to a home for a wholesome yet inexpensive meal.
2) In warm weather a baptism cookout at a nearby lake is effective.
3) Weekly or monthly pot-luck dinners for staff and/or regulars.
4) A good neighbor pantry of canned goods for needy families or transients can be started.
5) On weekend nights keep communion elements in the office, or the prayer room for "whosoever will."

Things to avoid in refreshments

1) Avoid an icebox with free food that either ends up spoiling, or mysteriously disappearing all at once.
2) Avoid too many hands, cooks, mixers, pourers, servers ... confusion!

62

Training Staff

"And the teachings which you have learned from me among many listeners, the same hand on to other faithful men, who shall be able to teach others also" II Timothy 2:2.

"No student is above his master, but every one when he is fully trained shall be even as his master" Luke 6:40.

"And He Himself appointed some to be apostles, some prophets, some evangelists, some pastors and teachers ...

... to fully equip His people for the work of serving (Weymouth)

... to get His holy people ready to serve as workers (Beck's translation)

... that Christians might be properly equipped for their service ..." Ephesians 4:11-12.

"Allow your mind to be trained, and listen to intelligent words" Proverbs 23:12, Beck.

Ephesians 4:12 as quoted above defines the Lord's intent for the ministers He has placed over His Church. It is sad that some ministers see equipping others as a threat to their own position. Today millions of Christian "laymen" need training; the question is, who will do it? Fulfilling The Great Commission to minister in Ephesians 4:12 is the success secret of programs like "Evangelism Explosion."

The Outreach will need people trained in all three major ministry areas, Inreach, Outreach, and Backup. These must be taught to train others if the ministry is to succeed.

Motivation is the key to successful training. As people are ministered to and spiritually fed, they will respond by wanting to minister to others, passing on God's reality and victory. Your Outreach will grow into an effective ministry and layman's training center for personal one-on-one ministry.

You need a definite commitment from your staff for a set length of time (for example, four or eight weeks for two nights a week, one for training, the other a specific weekend night for ministry). You'll also want to pair off the older, more experienced Christians with younger believers to spend their weekend ministry times working together as a team.

Training Possibilities

a) Assign study books to read, for group discussion, **or** assign different books on different cults, having staff each prepare a 10 minute verbal book report and typed summary to xerox off and hand out to regulars.
b) Practice "Romans-roading" each other.
c) Try role-playing and role-switching in classical counseling situations.
d) During a two or three months span, cover a different aspect of the Outreach ministry each week.
e) If "training" begins at seven, lock the doors at 7:05. Habitual latecomers will start arriving early.
f) Invite neighborhood ministers to teach chosen topics.
g) Record the topic of each training session in a book, for future reference.

63

Twenty Classic Inreach Emergencies And Solutions

"The Kingdom of heaven is like a large fishing net, that was cast into the sea, and gathered every kind: which when it was full, they drew it to shore . . . and gathered the good into vessels, but cast the bad away!" Matthew 13:47-48.

"God is faithful to His promises, and will not let you be tested more than you can stand, but when you are tested He will make a way out, that you can not only hold out, but come through it victoriously" I Corinthians 10:13.

When you run a deep-sea "fishing boat" like a street-Outreach, deep in "enemy territory" (II Corinthians 4:4), you may occasionally drag sharks on board, or have a barracuda or swordfish leap on deck! Being prepared for such happenings will help insure victory in such an event. David must have heard of Goliath while he tended sheep far away. Surely David practiced slinging stones many times, dreaming . . . someday he'd get his chance!

The Inreach staff needs to be ready not just for trout and salmon, but for these occasional, spiritual "shark, barracuda, and swordfish" as well. This is one more reason why staff should arrive an hour early on **their** weekend night to pray before opening!

Picture **all** of the following walking through **your** Outreach door, one after another, withing five minutes:

1) A manic-depressive asking for a gun to commit suicide.
2) A backslid Christian drinking from an open can of beer.
3) A violent, cursing drunk looking for a fight.
4) A recruiting homosexual looking for an easy pickup.
5) A scantily-clad prostitute chased by her pimp.
6) A pot-smoking drug dealer, giving away samples.
7) A "moonie" selling flowers who "used to be a believer."
8) Three starchy-looking church board members.
9) Two irate parents.
10) Three bikers wearing their "colors" coming in on a dare.
11) An arguing young couple carrying their baby who has a 106° fever.
12) A young guy from a car accident out front, blood streaming down his face.
13) Two girls in "band-aid size" bikinis coming in to "blow some minds!"
14) A young man chased by the police for throwing a rock at their squad car.
15) A curious topless dancer (clothed) from the bar next door.
16) A Mafia member who's ready to trade the godfather for God the Father!
17) A $1000 donor asking "Who do I make the check out to?"
18) Another drunk, boasting black belt karate, threatening to burn the house down.
19) A new convert and the wife of a regular, who insist that God wants her to divorce and re-marry this new convert.
20) A one week old Christian feeling "the call" to Red China, stopping to say good-bye.

What Should You Do?

Quick! Lock the door! Don't let anyone else in until you sort the "fish" you've already got on board. One rule to keep in mind is that the Outreach is more of an "emergency-room" than a spiritual "out-patient" center. Jugular veins rank in priority over ingrown toenails, no matter how loud "toenails yell!

Let's say you have six workers available besides yourself when "the flood" hits. Below are some solutions we've worked out, which you may be able to improve upon.

1) Assign one counselor to go in the back with **the suicide case.**

2) Tell **the backslider** to dump out his beer, or leave.

3) Politely ask **the violent drunk** to step outside, while you call the two or three eldest believers there. Tell him this is God's house, and if he can't treat it as such, it's also private property, and the police may have already been called. Spike all you say with love! Let him know, if he behaves he's welcome, if not, then he's not!

4) **The recruiting homosexual** must take a quiet corner, and listen, or leave.

5) **The prositiute** should be welcomed and protected; tell **the pimp** to go.

6) **The potsmokers** must be taken out, and told no dope inside or out front is tolerated, but if they're tired of coming down, they can receive Jesus!

7) **The moonie selling flowers** should be told no peddling is allowed, but invite her to sit and listen to the music (and its Gospel lyrics).

8) **The three church board members** should be recognized, thanked for coming, explain the "flood conditions" and ask them to help you counsel!

9) **The irate parents** must be welcomed, but told it'll probably be a while!

10) **The three bikers** should be offered a free soda, and invited to listen to the music.

11) **The arguing couple and their sick baby** should be asked to wait in the back.

12) **The bloody faced car accident victim** should be a priority one-on-one case, take him to wash up; call the police or an ambulance if necessary.

13) **The bikini-clad girls** must be brought out and asked to return when dressed.

14) **The guy fleeing the police** should be taken to the back to wait, but if the police come in, don't lie; if they don't see him, do as God leads you.

15) **The topless dancer** should be welcomed and counseled later by a sister.

16) **The Mafia man** should be taken in the back and prayed with.

17) **The $1000 donor** should go to a back office or minister help if he/she is able.

18) **The black-belt karate "burn-the-place-down" character** should be offered a soda, but firmly given the choice of respecting God's house and

private property or leaving. Advise him that the police may have already been called. This, with a sincere "I love you and Jesus loves you too" will break the devil's back! Darkness flees God's love light!

19) **The mismatched romantics need** to not be condemned, but welcomed and scripturally counseled to let them see their error.

20) **The new convert headed for Red China** needs to be welcomed and counseled.

Of course it doesn't get THIS fast and furious, but by studying the above you'll be ready to handle any and all "fish!"

64

The Music Ministry

"And it came to pass, when the evil was upon Saul, that David took an harp, and played with his hand . . . So Saul was refreshed and was well, and the evil spirit departed from him" I Samuel 16:23.

"He (Jehosaphat) determined that there should be a choir leading the march, singing the song, 'His Mercy (Loving-Kindness) Endureth Forever,' praising and thanking the Lord! And at the moment they began to sing and to praise, the Lord caused the enemy armies to destroy each other" II Chronicles 20:21-22.

"After singing the Passover Hymn, they went up to the Mount of Olives" Matthew 26:30, Mark 14:26.

The primary thing to remember in the area of music and the Outreach, is that it must be ministry first, and entertainment second. Music is another means to God's goal of touching lost souls with His Love. The goal must be converts, not crowds. Music provides an atmosphere to minister in, but the ultimate question is: "Does God receive glory from it?"

Your Director of Musical Activities

You will need one person in charge of the many different facets of the music ministry. He will appoint worship leaders, schedule Gospel groups, help form musical outreach teams, and more.

Booking Groups

Music is an unparalleled relational tool in establishing common ground with young people, especially the unsaved. Your music director will need to book Gospel groups, so that each weekend night your Outreach can feature live music. He can start rounding up information on what groups and individuals are available in several ways. Signs can be put up in local music stores and local Christian book stores, especially near Gospel music ranks. Calls should be made to area churches, where church music ministers will usually have a few suggestions, names, and phone numbers to help out with. Bookings should be made in an organized manner; the music director will need a special calendar to keep track of groups and booking dates several months in advance.

In the area of finances, be honest and thoughtful. If there are no finances to pay the group a set fee, an offering can be taken up, or a local church may cover the group's expenses. If not, there are plenty of local area musicians and groups that need practice and exposure. They will gladly play for free, especially to help the Outreach get on its feet. Even if all you can provide is a tank of gas, or a meal afterwards, they will appreciate it. Ask what equipment they will need. Have two or three people there to help them carry in their equipment. Pray with them before they start ministering, and be sure you thank them. A RECOMMENDATION LETTER FROM THE OUTREACH DIRECTOR COSTS NOTHING, BUT WILL HELP ANY GROUP OR INDIVIDUAL'S MUSIC MINISTRY. When possible, sending $10 or $20 to a scheduled group after the booking date is arranged, will help insure their appearance on the evening they agreed upon.

The music ministry inside

1) Do start beginning musicians in the non-hostile environment inside.

2) Do "screen" musicians, making sure they will lift up Jesus and not begin "grinding an ax," pushing their pet doctrine, and stumble baby Christians.

3) Christian radio stations are good to use as background, but appeals for money, though necessary, often stumble sinners. Pre-recording an unbroken

string of Gospel-rock favorites on a cassette, or an endless repeating cassette works much better. Remember that instrumentals provide better background for counseling work than do vocals.

4) The Outreach can borrow sound equipment to start out. Pawn shops sell amplifiers, speakers and microphones very reasonably. PA systems can also be bought inexpensively in kit form if you have an electronically-minded person to assemble it.

5) A "house-band" comprised of regulars at the Outreach is a great help.

6) Compile and xerox or mimeo off your own songbook and favorite songs. If you make these three-hole notebook style, you can add new songs as desired. (Be careful, however, of copyright restrictions).

7) Take popular song-melodies and Christianize the words. Both John Wesley and Martin Luther did this with great results.

8) When your song or worship leaders are teaching new songs, have them "feed" the listeners the next words in the breathing spaces in between lines.

9) Use as many "scripture" songs as possible. God's Word changes lives!

10) Have believers to share their own compositions.

11) Send each group a thank you and a brief summary of ministry (e.g. souls won) results to bring them back again.

12) A ceiling-to-floor wall with a see-through window and door separating entrance and refreshment area noise from the main music area will greatly enhance your music ministry.

The music ministry outside

Music impresses young people, and is effective outside the Outreach as well as within. An outdoor speaker high out of reach above the front door can spread the inreach music ministry outdoors and often snares passersby. This, however, is only a start of the possibilities of taking the music ministry to the streets!

Outdoor concerts

Using a parking lot adjacent to the Outreach facility, either in front, alongside, or the parking lot of a Church down the "strip" for an outdoor concert, can be very effective. Below are a few "do's" and "don't":

1) Do be aware of city ordinances, concert cut-off times, permit needs, etc.

2) Do aim your music paralleled into the traffic flow, instead of across the street when it will carry into residential areas.

3) Do keep public sidewalks and city streets clear of people and equipment.

4) Do make clear to the band that they must start at almost an unreasonably low volume level, and work their way up, instead of vice-versa.

5) Don't wait until the song ends if the band is too loud, and they refuse to turn down. Pull the plug before a police confrontation develops.

Outdoor music possibilities

1) Send outreach music teams out to play in parks and down the streets where kids hang out. A good rule of thumb in letting others use your guitar is that daytimes, in a park, letting them play their favorite song and gather their friends around is alright. Once they are gathered, you can minister Jesus Christ through song to them. But at night, on the "strip," the action is too fast and wild to let others control the guitar. They'll still listen to you sing.

2) Use a pickup truck or flatbed truck (with or without a portable generator) and have Jesus groups or bands play outside after large rock concerts to the exiting crowds.

65

Staff Fellowship Meetings

"Behold how good and how pleasant it is, for brethren to worship together in unity" Psalm 133:1.

"By this will all men recognize you as My disciples; it will be because you have such love one for another" John 13:35.

"And now faith, hope and love continue on ... but the greatest of these is Love" I Corinthians 13:13.

"One new command I give you, that you love one another as I have loved you" John 13:34.

The Scriptures tell us in Galatians 6:2 . . . "Bear ye one another's burdens and so fulfil the law of Christ." John 13:35 (quoted above) tells us what this law of Christ is. But how can you bear one another's deep, intimate problems and burdens, when you don't even know each other's names?

We found that even mature staff members can eventually get the "used" or drained feeling. The entire staff needs a time of fellowship every so often, a time of relaxing, and refilling. Whether you hold these meetings regularly once a week, once a month, or as the need arises, it is up to you.

This should be not so much a time of training, but rather a very personal time of appreciating and getting to know and love one another more deeply, a time of learning about each other. You might have one or two staff members give their testimony in 5 or 10 minutes each.

66

Inreach Possibilities

"Jesus said unto him, If you can believe, all things are possible" Mark 9:23.

1) **A Guest book** by the front door for newcomers to sign.

2) **A house guitar and piano** as funds develop; they always come in handy.

3) **A testimony file** of regulars and converts is good for making up tracts.

4) **A brother-sister list** with name, address, and phone numbers of "family."

5) **Monthly or bi-monthly communion** services binding the Outreach team into One!

6) **A cassette or paperback lending library.**

7) **A table or roomful of special Gospel materials for sale,** (Gourmet soul-food!).

8) **An expanded summertime schedule,** be open every night.

9) **A live-in house** for new converts, hitchhikers, young brothers, run-aways.

10) **In-house skits, puppets, Christian poetry reading, etc.**

11) A monthly "open-house" for civic leaders, parents and partners, held before dark!

12) A monthly inter-coffeehouse and area youth-ministers' meeting.

13) An original "Best Gospel song contest" ($5 entry fee, $25 or $50 prize).

14) An afternoon "open" schedule to minister to Jr. and Sr. High's.

15) A weekly new converts class, at the Outreach or an open home.

16) A monthly Friendliness award: steak dinner prize or certificate, etc.

17) A back cry-room, or nursery area for babies and toddlers.

18) A suggestion box will be very helpful and revealing. Keep blank slips of paper and some pencils in supply near it. Encourage anonymous constructive criticism from all those involved.

19) Inexpensive movie rental on appropriate subjects are available not only from national Christian contacts, but from local libraries as well.

III: BACKUP (The Ministry Behind the Scenes)

67

What is Backup?

"The children of this world are wiser in their generation than the children of light" Luke 16:8.

The above verse puzzled me for a long time, but as I grew in the Lord, the meaning became clearer. Worldly people know if they don't, "take care of business," business will "take care of them!" In the same breath Jesus was saying that God's people often forget this fact. He was reproving them for their slack attitudes.

"Back-up," is the backbone, the skeleton of the entire ministry, the vital, indispensable foundation Inreach and Outreach must be built upon. It includes everything done behind the scenes, all the unseen reinforcing that countless volunteers do but often only God knows about. It is taking care of a thousand and one details that will eventually cripple the Outreach director and ministry if not taken care of.

"Back-up" is the least glamorous ministry, yet it was from a "back-up" role bringing bread and cheese to his brothers, that David became a national hero by killing Goliath (I Samuel 17:17-18). Proverbs 18:12 says: "Before honor comes humility." Zechariah wrote: "Despise not the day of small things" (Zechariah 4:10). For every soldier on the front lines during World War II, at least ten people were working on the homefront, producing, shipping, and keeping the front-line supplied so that together they could win the war. This is what "back-up" is all about!

68

Administration

"Any enterprise is built by wise planning" Proverbs 24:3.

"In the multitude of counselors, there is safety" Proverbs 11:14.

"Behold also the ships, even though so great, and are driven by fierce winds, yet even they are turned about with a very small rudder wherever the pilot steers it" James 3:4.

"And God hath set some in the church, first apostles, secondarily prophets, thirdly teachers, after that miracles, then gifts of healing, helps, governments, diversities of tongues" I Corinthians 12:28.

"A sensible man watches for problems ahead, and prepares to meet them" Proverbs 27:12.

The Greek word used above in I Corinthians 12 for "governments" and for "counselors" in Proverbs 11:14 is *kubernesis* which also translates as "steering." As the newborn Outreach gains size, shape, and momentum, administrative or "steering" responsiblitities will too. The steering on a rowboat doesn't match that on a large ocean liner. The ministry's growth will bring complications that will have to be handled properly by the right qualified persons.

Several areas that Outreach administration covers include:

1) Overseeing the entire Back-up operation, 2) overseeing major decisions affecting the ministry's forward progress; 3) inter-coffeehouse communications and inter-ministry brainstorming sessions; 4) making short, medium and long range goals and plans for the ministry, and seeing them become working realities; 5) proofing and/or okaying all printed materials that go out under the name of the ministry. This includes newsletters, tracts, brochures, news articles, soulwinner bulletins, etc.; 6) annual reports: putting together a quarterly and yearly report of the overall growth, accomplishments and needs of the ministry; 7) scheduling meetings for the ministry's Board of Directors, and Board of Advisors as well, throughout the year, especially when specific needs arise.

God will bring you the people you need. Keep an eye out for them, and their particular God-given ability to help STEER the Outreach ministry.

69

The Office

"The children of this world (and their operating procedures) are wiser in their generation, than are the children of light" Luke 16:8.

Location

Locating the office in a separate building, somewhere other than the Outreach, will not only cut down confusion that results from mixing business and ministry, but will also avoid exposing valuable equipment and irreplaceable records to unnecessary risks. You may be able to use a church office desk, or Sunday School room during the week as you first get started. They may let you use their phone number for preliminary contacts from those interested in the Outreach. You'll need a phone number written on your first round of business cards.

Minimum Office Needs

You'll need a desk, phone, access to a typewritter, and some peace and quiet. A "take-care-of-business" attitude must be maintained in the office, or the office will hold back the entire Outreach. Anyone who doesn't understand the importance of the office and its many functions MUST not be allowed to hang around the office, visiting, or joking, while dedicated "back up" personnel are concentrating on their tasks!

Inscribe all office machinery, as well as valuables left at the Outreach. Inscribing devices are usually available without charge from local police departments or civic organizations. This is a good theft deterrent.

70

The Secretary(s)

"Be not slothful in business: but be fervent in Spirit, serving the Lord" Romans 12:7.

"Take away the foxes, the little foxes that spoil the vines: for our vines have tender grapes" Song of Solomon 2:15.

The clerical office work can and will claw at and D–E–V–O–U–R the Outreach director UNLESS he has a competent, dedicated secretary to keep the "paper-tiger's claws" cut. Any director will soon find that the job in the office is too overwhelming to be tackled single-handedly!

Some of the secretary's jobs will be:

1) Typing letters (both correspondence and thank-you notes).

2) Bill paying, recording, receipting, depositing all donations, and keeping the petty cash box functioning.

3) Filing (invoices, letters, prayer requests, etc.).

4) Overseeing follow-up convert referrals to churches Monday mornings.

5) Recording all phone calls in a small ledger. She must distribute call information to the correct persons. Make up a "message board" or cubbyhole arrangement at the office and at the Outreach.

6) Keeping brother/sister lists updated.

7) Keeping a clear desk and the office looking business like and in order.

8) Running interference for the director, saving his time by answering the phone, taking messages, and sifting out the important from the trivial.

Qualifications of a good outreach secretary

A heart for the ministry: If the job isn't done as unto the Lord (Colossians 3:23), it might as well not be done at all.

Commitment to this specific ministry: Having to re-train a secretary every month is very time-consuming, unrewarding and unnecessary. Pray for and find a committed secretary who will commit herself to working with the ministry for a minimum of six months.

A good business sense: She must realize the importance of her work. She is not just dealing with paper, but with eternal souls.

Honesty and Integrity: The secretary should be allowed to sign checks up to $20 or $30, and also pay all bills by signing checks, saving the director's time.

Should know God's Word and know how to use it: Counseling situations and phone-in emergencies are unavoidable.

Should be responsible and mature: Too many younger people start out all ablaze, only to "turn-to-ashes" after a month of hard front-line work.

Should be able to delegate: Paper-work will increase, as will details, tasks, jobs, chores. One person will need to run errands, while one concentrates on paper-work.

Able to follow directions: The director must be obeyed, not asked "why?"

Concept of time on the phone: "Gabbing" with a friend might lose a phone-in suicide threat. The office is a place for ministry work, and private concerns must be taken care of at some other time and place.

71

Bookkeeping and Record-Keeping

"He that is faithful in that which is least, is faithful also in that which is great" Luke 16:10.

"And the books were opened . . ." Revelation 20:12.

"Submit yourselves to every ordinance of man, for the Lord's sake" I Peter 2:13.

Financial Bookkeeping

The Internal Revenue Service, (IRS), requires every religious non-profit organization to keep records, not only of yearly income, from whom, and when it comes in, but the filing of a yearly financial statement each spring summarizing all expenditures as well. To keep tax-exempt status, you must record all money transactions involving the ministry. This includes incoming and outgoing cash and checks. As the ministry grows, you'll soon see the need for the system as recorded below, or some other system you prefer. Quarterly tax reports and monthly withholding will also become a necessity.

Recording all ministry income

1) In a 3-hole notebook we record each day's donations, with the date, name and amount. This record will help you chart monthly and yearly income.

2) In a 3" x 5" file card box, record each donor-partner by name, each on a separate card, then file the cards alphabetically. For each future donation from the same partner, use the same card.

3) Send a receipt for each donation. The sooner the receipt is sent out, the better. Although most churches send out quarterly or yearly receipts, it is better for an Outreach ministry to be more frequent in receipting and sending of thank-you's. Because the Outreach is dealing with a wilder, unchurched element, and its methods are sometimes not as "traditional" as many mainline churches, the prompt return of a receipt, return-address envelope, and a personal thank-you note to partners when they send in a donation helps assure them that you do know what you're doing, and your office operation is as good as any other!

Recording all expenditures and outgoing cash

1) **Start a ministry checking account:** Open it in the name of the ministry as soon as a name has been agreed upon. Cash is harder to keep track of than checks. Every check comes back in your bank statement, and is its own receipt. The IRS does not require receipts under $20, but nothing beats the dependable return of a check as a record of your outgoing expenditures.

2) **Use a petty cash system in the office:** Buy a couple of petty cash voucher pads at a local office supply store, then designate one desk drawer for the petty cash to be kept in. Keep $20 or $30 on hand for the small daily

cash expenses not worth writing out a check for. The secretary and director should carry petty cash slips in their wallet. When they spend their own money on ministry items, they can fill it out, write R/B (for refreshment) with their initials on it, and reimburse themselves when next in the office. The IRS prefers larger reimbursement checks be made out to cash, and not to an individual's name. This helps bookkeeping. If a reimbursement is made out to an individual's name, proof that it was a reimbursement, not wages, lies on that person.

3) **Accounting in a ledger:** Office supply stores sell weekly Dome expense ledgers, or you can buy a fifteen column ledger, and record your daily expenses under different major ministry expense categories. If kept up, weekly or monthly, it will eliminate the huge task of sorting out and recording a whole year's expenses all at one time at the year's end. Categories we use include: Automotive, Building Improvements, Literature, Office Supplies, Payroll, Phone, Postage, Printing, Refreshments, Rent, Sound Equipment, Tithes, Travel, and Utilities.

A word about the IRS

Many people grimace whenever they hear these three initials. That is the wrong position to take. They are friends, not enemies. Use their free services and consult them when you have questions dealing with their area. Go into their office at the start and ask for suggestions to improve the way you are setting up your books, and records.

Personal Ministerial Record Keeping

I include in this the daily ministry reports, weekly staff forms, nightly soulwinner's sheets, and team captain reports. These records come in handy not just to keep key ministry people informed on the total picture of what God has been doing through the ministry, but are good for:

1) Public relations areas.
2) Newsletter "copy" and article sources.
3) Annual summations of ministry accomplishments.
4) Validation of the ministry to the IRS, local churches, and anyone who wants a deeper view of the work.

Keep track of the number of teams sent out, tracts printed and distributed, as well as the number of people counseled, prayed with, saved, filled, healed, and rededicated to God!

72

Coordinating Volunteers

"And God hath set some in the church . . . helps (helpers, those who can help others)" I Corinthians 12:28.

"But as his part is that goeth down to the battle, so shall his part be that tarries by the stuff; they shall part alike" I Samuel 30:24.

"We share and share alike in the rewards: those who go to battle and those who guard the equipment" I Samuel 30:24 (Living Bible).

Once you've opened the Outreach, simple jobs you thought one person could handle will expand quickly. Without many volunteers, the Outreach directors and secretary will soon be overloaded. Without a systematic method of interviewing, classifying, and putting volunteers to work in their separtate areas, you'll lose your volunteers!

How to use the volunteer "talent-finder" forms

1) Every "first-visit" Christian at the Outreach should be given one of these forms to fill in, if they wish to become more involved.

2) These blue forms are then relayed to the volunteer coordinator, who makes 3" x 5" cards up from each sheet, with the ordered preference number of each area chosen to work in. These cards are given to area leaders.

3) The director of preference area number one either uses the volunteer after contacting him, or contacts the volunteer coordinator telling him that this applicant really desires preference area number 2, whose leader is then connected to the applicant.

4) The volunteer coordinator also writes on a separate sheet reserved for *each* area in a letter-size file box their name, address, phone number, the areas they chose and preference numbers given, as well as final area chosen by the volunteer to work in. (See Chapter 87 for actual "VTP" format).

Things to remember when working with volunteers

1) Everyone likes to feel appreciated and needed, especially if donating their time and hard work. A little "thank-you so much" goes a long, long

way. If not put to work, a volunteer will find someone else to work with.

2) Make sure volunteers know what is expected of them, by when, how to do it, and who to report problems to.

3) **Don't let zealous volunteers "burn out."** Some zealous people join volunteer work with the ministry who let their other daily obligations get totally out of control. Volunteers shouldn't be allowed to work for the ministry for no pay while their rent is overdue, their car is broken down, and they are going hungry for lack of funds. *First*, they should find themselves a job. **Secondly,** they should offer their **SPARE** time to help out.

4) Set one "work-day" a month, preferably a Saturday, when all volunteers can be invited to the Outreach to accomplish larger tasks.

5) Even with volunteers, some things cannot be tolerated. Phones must not be tied up, directions must not be improvised upon, and a job half-done is better not begun at all (see Proverbs 10:26).

6) Volunteers must operate in the Spirit of God, and not be allowed to badmouth leaders or others while doing their "job" (see Proverbs 6:16, 19).

73

Your Monthly Newsletter

"Good news from a far country is like cold water to a thirsty soul" Proverbs 25:25.

"Where there is no vision, the people (and their interest) perish(es)" Proverbs 29:18.

Some may say: "The apostle Paul never sent out newsletters from his ministry, why should I?" Let me answer with four other questions: "Did Paul send out letters, or epistles?" "Did Paul command them read aloud, not just privately, but to all the saints present there, and in other cities as well?" "If he had the means, would he have sent a hundred copies at one time instead of having to wait for six months to have one letter circulated to various churches?" And fourth: "Did Paul's letters contain news? Were they newsletters, containing the Good News of God's Gospel, and specifically the Good News of what God was doing in and through Paul's ministry as well?" I answer "Yes" to all four of these questions from my resource book:

the Bible!

Why send out a newsletter?

1) It is God's command. "Proclaim His doings throughout the land" Psalm 9:11.

2) Good seed brings good harvest: As you proclaim God's deeds and challenge other people's Christianity, God will bless yours as well.

3) God supports His ministry through His people's tithes and giving. "Where there is no vision the people perish." Not only the people perish, financial support for a ministry perishes as well.

Why send it monthly?

Professional Development Associations for Christian Institutions and secular businesses as well have statistically proven that a good one page monthly news-bulletin is more productive than a slick paper six-page typeset edition sent out only four times a year.

To get it written: assign a Newsletter Editor

You will need a newsletter editor assigned to head the whole newsletter department, set deadlines, choose and edit "copy," get pictures taken and developed, and to see the newsletter through each month from a few rough starting ideas, through the printing and addressing to the bulk mailing department at the Post Office downtown. This is not as big a job as it seems at first, IF the newsletter editor does the following things:

1) Train key people, the Outreach director and other department heads, to watch out for newsworthy ministry occurrences, such as souls won, dramatic answers to prayer, interesting letters, intriguing comments, etc. They must write them down and get them to the newsletter editor as soon after they happen as possible.

2) Set deadlines, and plan backwards from these deadlines to prevent a last minute rush.

3) Set a definite desk drawer, or box in the Outreach and/or office for news articles to be deposited in.

4) Work on each newsletter during the entire month, week by week, as stories develop. This will simplify meeting the final deadline to cutting and choosing materials, not having to hunt it out, write it up, edit it, and lay it all

out in "camera-ready" format in a week or less!

Keep your newsletter simple

Remember, typesetting, expensive glossy paper, even pictures aren't necessary in a monthly bulletin. But you will find out that regular monthly communication with Christian friends, prayer partners and financial supporters is vital to a healthy, expanding ministry.

Simplest format: A self-mailer

A self-mailer is made form an 8" x 11" sheet of paper, folded either into fourths, thirds or halves. It has the masthead of the ministry across the top of one side, and then news filling the rest of that side. The back of the newsletter has either one-half or one-third left blank, so that when it is folded for mailing, the blank side faces out, for addressing and mailing. This blank half or third should have the organization's name and address in the upper left corner and its post office bulk permit number in the upper right hand corner.

It is best to include a small #6 (six inch) return envelope with the ministry's address on it. This fits perfectly within a 8" x 11" three-fold self-mailer, with either a staple, small white label, or scotch tape to keep it closed.

Newsletter and envelope costs

Return envelopes should cost you less than $30 per thousand printed on one side, while priniting 1,000 two-side 8" x 11" newsletters should cost you less than $40.00 Folding should cost less than $10/thousand.

Mailing a bulk mailing

If you have been collecting names, addresses, and zip codes of interested people, friends, relatives, right from the start, it won't take long to collect the minimum 200 names that permit you to mail newsletters for a bulk price of only 4.5¢ a piece, instead of the normal $.20 first class mailing rate. You can send 200 newsletters cheaper than 50 pieces at the first class rate. The post office will show you how to separate, bundle, and label your bulk mailing according to zip codes.

Obtaining a non-profit bulk mailing permit

Apply at your local post office for a third class bulk mailing permit for a religious, non-profit organization. If you have filed for your State and Federal incorporation papers, and bring xerox copies of these applications with you, you should have no trouble. If they question your application, bring recommendation letters until they are assured that you are as legitimate as any other church in town, just newer.

Newsletter possibilities

1) Look at the newsletters sent out by larger Christian organizations, and you'll find dozens of ideas. Ask your minister; he'll gladly give you some.

2) If the postmaster delays your bulk permit, your church or another will let you mail under their bulk permit.

3) Art supply stores sell "Chartpak" and "Presstype" which is professional lettering that can add so much to the layout.

4) Print extra newsletters each month to leave at friendly churches!

5) Include a calendar of upcoming Outreach events and musical groups.

74

Your Mailing List

"The sheep hear his voice, and He calls His own sheep by name" John 10:3.

"Even so has the Lord ordained that these who preach the Gospel should live on (or out of) the Gospel" I Corinthians 9:14.

Every time you meet persons interested in the ministry, ask for their business card or address, and tell them you'd like to send them the Outreach's monthly newsletter.

These addresses need to kept in alphabetical and zip-code order. Within and only within each five-digit zip code that is exactly the same, you will want to alphabetize the names for easier access. Across the bottom left corner of each newsletter's mailing front should be printed the words: "Return postage guaranteed: address correction requested." This notifies the Post Office that you want to forward these third class pieces to the new address. Without these words, the newsletter gets thrown away if the addressee has moved. There is a charge for each piece returned or forwarded, but it is well worth it to keep your mailing list current.

Mailing companies will keypunch your mailing list onto their computers, and address your newsletters each month automatically, after you bring the folded newsletter to them. Of course, there is a charge involved which varies from city to city. Less expensive but more involved is addressing your envelopes using volunteer help. One alternative to this is typing your mailing address names onto sheets of 8" x 11" labels available by the box at office supply stores or they can be ordered; Dennison Paper Company puts them out. When newsletter time comes around each month, simply xerox off the 8"x11" blank labeled sheets that you have fed into the xerox copiers' paper tray. This must, however, be done on a plain paper copier.

In using this xerox-label system, make sure all *new* mailing list names are recorded on a special *new-names sheet* so that they can be typed onto a new-names label list, and inserted in the zip-code order. Every couple of months you may want to retype the whole list on xerox-label sheets and integrate all new names into their proper zip code-alphabetical order sequence.

One Christian company that handles mailing lists economically by computer and invites mail-in service is Mission Center International, Cross Computer Service, Box 13026, St. Louis 63119 (314/692-1373).

75

Public Relations

"A good name is rather to be chosen than silver" Proverbs 22:1.

"After these things, the Lord appointed other seventy also, and sent them two and two before His face into every city and place, whither He Himself would come" Luke 10:1.

"Don't praise yourself; let others do it!" Proverbs 27:2.

What did Jesus send out the seventy ahead of Him to accomplish? Whether it was actual preaching, healing, casting out devils and cleansing lepers as Luke implies, the disciples were nonetheless out doing PR or Public Relations for the Kingdom of Heaven and its King, Jesus Christ.

To be properly carried out, public relations must be viewed as a ministry, not as a worldly, shadowy area of gimmicks. Public relations is promoting the Outreach, and this in reality is preaching what the Outreach is preaching, the Gospel of Jesus Christ. Below are some different areas that public relations covers:

Public Relations in the Church World

1) Initiating and developing working relations, and a growing mutual understanding and respect with other area churches and Christian ministries.

2) Seeking help from the churches. The Church is the storehouse. An Outreach must either make its connections with the rest of the Body of Christ, or die. The Church has the vast supply of volunteer helpers, contacts, services, referral agencies, financial support, and wisdom. Churches must be contacted, not only by the Holy Spirit through prayer, but by a living representative of this new work as well.

Public Relations with the community:

What is the image you want the public to have of the Outreach ministry? How will it get that image? Here are some ideas:

1) **The opening night press release:** See Section on this under "26 Steps to Opening Night."

2) **Articles in local newspaper:** They expect you to contact them. If you don't believe in your ministry enough to want others to know about it (through the newspaper), why should they? Invite a reporter to come by the Outreach on a specific night for a tour, or arrange a newspaper interview for the Outreach director if the ministry if just starting, or with a few of the people whose lives the ministry has helped to change. Using the anti-drug approach can often open doors with media people who would otherwise be closed to a hard-line "turn-or-burn" gospel approach. As Jesus said in Matthew 11:19 . . . "Wisdom is proven right by its results" (not its critics!).

3) **Contact local civic groups:** The local Rotary, Lions Club, Kiwanis,

etc., Clubs are always on the lookout for interesting speakers and/or worthy organizations to support. They may not invite you to come preach to them, but if the team comes sharing the way their past lives have been changed from drugs, alcohol, crime, etc., and the Answer just happens to unanimously be Jesus Christ, what can they say?

4) Make use of the media: Contact local TV and radio for free public service announcements (and/or ads) that follow anti-drug suicide prevention lines.

Contact the same above, specifically this time for a spot on nearby radio or TV talk shows that have interesting guests or musical groups on. You'll be surprised at how many doors open for the Gospel if God's people will only knock.

Contact local TV station managers, visit them, and check the possibility of producing one late Saturday night changed life/Jesus music TV program. One trial show (donated free of course, by the station) may be all you need to be donated a regular weekly TV spot, since all TV stations are required by the FCC to provide so many hours of free TV time per month. If you come up with a good "pilot" program, and ask to be aired after the station's regular operating hours, it costs them next to nothing, and gives them more of their required free time accounted for, thus allowing them to sell more normal times and increase their monthly budget, as well as reaching young people that would never watch a television church program on Sunday morning.

5) Contact local advertising companies. Ask them to donate a free billboard on the "strip" or near a youth hangout — a billboard to fight drugs (and to lift up Jesus Christ as the Answer).

6) Posters on telephone poles are useful, but make sure the posters don't become litter; take them down when they're dated.

7) Get testimonies of all converts. These testimonies will not just be useful in newsletters and tracts, but will cheer up converts during rough times.

76

Development: What, Why, Where, Who, and How

"Be diligent to know the state of your flocks, and look well to your herds" Proverbs 27:23.

"Give and it shall be given unto you, good measure, pressed down, shaken together, and running over" Luke 6:38.

"Development" means raising funds. Many people, particularly Christians, stumble spiritually at this part of the ministry, but without it, none of our larger Christian colleges, seminaries, or international organizations would exist or grow!

As the apostle Paul wrote in I Corinthians 9:7, "Who plants a vineyard and doesn't eat its fruit? Or who feeds a flock, and doesn't drink its milk?" Flocks don't pasture themselves, vineyards don't prune or harvest themselves, and neither does money for ministries grow on trees in the backyard of the minister's parsonage.

Why do people give to a ministry? Primarily, because God tells them to give, and are shown that it is a worthy, necessary cause which is investing their money in God's work, producing desirable results.

What do you give to your financial partners?

You give them an opportunity to be co-workers together with you, reaping eternal and temporal rewards God promises His partners. You must show them your faithfulness and fruitfulness, and remind them of God's promises. Make it easy as possible for them to give, by including return envelopes in newsletters and in thank-you notes, so they can avoid having to address them themselves.

Giving gifts to donors

Some ministries believe in offering their financial partners different gifts for specific financial donations. Some ministries do — others don't. Pray and consult your Advisory Board, as to what "premiums" (as this type of gift is called) to offer, or not to offer.

Offer to pray for your partners, and then DO IT!

Leave a place on your newsletter, or an enclosed "response-device," for partners to share prayer burdens or needs they have. From time to time schedule special partner prayer-breakfasts or Saturday afternoon "Open-House" at the Outreach where you specifically set time aside to get to know your partners in a way that once a year contracts will never provide.

Development possibilities

1) Have an annual radio care-a-thon on a local Christian radio station.
2) Have occasional "ministry-report" suppers where partners invite an interested friend (or several) for dinner to learn more about the ministry and hopefully to become an involved partner themselves.

77

A Ministry Slide Presentation And Sample Script

"Where there is no vision, the people perish" Proverbs 29:18.

The old saying goes: "A picture is worth a thousand words." A slide-presentation of the Outreach ministry will open doors into many churches that would otherwise be closed to a street ministry "preaching at" them. The slide show should work along with pre-recorded cassette script for maximum effect!

How to put a slide-presentation together

1) Start jotting down important items you think should be included.

2) Write a rough outline, refine it, having it flow from: a) introductory pictures; b) to the need for the ministry; c) to the ministry itself (including Inreach, Outreach and Backup); d) then on to the conclusion and; e) the final challenge to the viewer to get involved!

3) Keep it under twelve minutes.

4) One by one, make a list of the pictures you will need. Send out a Christian photographer friend with a good 35 mm camera to take color slide shots. Get the slides developed. Either buy, or borrow a carousel slide projector and start putting the slides into a rough order following your outline. Leaving spaces between the slides will help in shifting the order of different slides. Each time you "flick" through the sequence, the proper order will become more apparent. You'll see what slides to delete, and which additional slides to get. Write them down, and get them!

5) Wait to write the script until after you have the majority of your slides chosen, developed, and in approximate order.

6) Use a cassette while developing your script. Speak aloud whatever comments come to you. Then replay the tape while watching the slides again. Start putting into writing the exact words, scriptures and comments that God quickens to your spirit as the right ones to use.

7) You may order an inexpensive cassette copy of our ministry slide presentation by writing Worldshakers For Christ, P.O. Box P-1, Felton, CA 95018.

8) After the script is finalized, you may want to "dub" in music in the background, such as hard rock music behind street scenes, and instrumental Christian music behind slides relating to the mainline churches and how they can help bring in the harvest!

Avoid the "Slide-show 'side-show' side effect!"

Showing off new converts to church congregations can have disastrous side-effects on the new believer. Though not always the case, the new convert may start feeling inwardly that he's a "freak" or "ex-freak" in a spiritual "side-show" (similar to a carni side-show featuring the 600-pound lady or 8 foot tall man). Use older converts when possible, and keep a constant spiritual eye out to eliminate this disastrous side-effect.

Below is an abbreviated script from our Ultimate Trip/Eagle's Inn slide program. You may get some ideas about content and proper order to use in your own ministry's slide-presentation. Feel free to use any or all of it.

A Sample Slide Script

Peoria Street in Tulsa, Oklahoma has a Dr. Jekyll/Mr. Hyde character. Although it looks like any other business street during the day, at sundown it becomes ... "The Strip." Thousands of teenagers cruise in their cars, earning Peoria its nickname: "The Restless Ribbon." Young people meet their friends, practice drag-racing, deal and use illegal drugs, drink alcohol, and find someone to shack up with for the night. This picture shows how the "strip" looks to someone with drugs. There are a dozen bars on the "strip". This one specializes in mixing alcohol and young people!

During the day, youths hang out at Woodard Park, planning parties and discussing new ways of getting high. But at night they hang out at such places as this, which has been the largest drug-dealing place in South Tulsa for years. One dealer told us between $15 and $20,000 of drugs changed hands there weekly. He averaged up to $1,000 a night himself.

The ultimate social event each month are concerts held at Tulsa's Assembly Center where 9,000 young people see superstars like Eric Clapton. Tulsa has other concert spots, and several head shops where older hippies commercialize the "drug-counter/culture" into a profitable business.

Tulsa has six hundred churches offering every denomination and a variety of services. But as one pastor explained, his fellowship hall is adjacent to a bar, and his people don't know how to communicate God's love to those going in next door.

Solomon wrote in Proverbs 11:30, "He that is wise wins souls." In Luke 14:23 Jesus commanded His followers to "go out into the hedges and highways and compel them to come in."

This is the ministry that God has called the Rainbow's End: TO PUT GOD'S LOVE INTO ACTION OUT WHERE THE ACTION IS. When night falls and the "strip" comes to life, the Rainbow's End goes into action as well. There is live music, worship, praise, and Bible teaching starting off each weekend night's activities. Counseling is also an important ministry, especially inside. To help maintain a solid buisness foundation volunteers help in the office during the week. Every dedicated inreach staff member works hard to keep Jonathan and the Outreach teams sharing God's love out where the needs are.

One recent weekend, the National Hotrod Association's meeting here in Tulsa flooded Peoria with 7,000 young people. We decided to have a sidewalk parade, sharing Jesus. Four people gave their lives to the Lord that night, among them these two young men here with guitars. We go all over the city ministering as well as out on Peoria. This year at Tulsa's annual Raft Race, we distributed 10,000 specially written tracts, as well as preaching from our official raft entry via PA system to the thousands along the nine-mile Arkansas river course.

Few people know that Black Sabbath is a satanic rock group, but last year they had a 30' x 30' image of satan on stage, and 8,000 of Tulsa's young people chanting "Hail Lucifer." This year sixty Christians distributed specially written tracts there and shared the Gospel with the crowds afterwards. Several were prayed with to receive Jesus as their Lord. Over the last three years, we have ministered at three dozen of these concerts. One young man said, "I'm not a believer yet, but I keep seeing you, and I'm starting to believe."

We are currently visiting churches, sharing our ministry, this slide-presentation, and changed-life testimonies. In February 1978 Jonathan was a guest on the PTL Club. As a result of that, churches in Hinesville, Georgia asked us to hold a weeklong seminar on youth outreach there. The high point of the week there was a concert and Jesus rally where 52 prayed to receive Jesus.

In June of 1978, the 700 Club sent a video crew to Tulsa to film the ministry. During Jonathan's July appearance on the 700 Club, host Pat Robertson was moved by the young people's testimonies, and by the prospect of Jonathan's dream of helping other cities open youth street-Outreaches as well.

What are the results of this type of a coffeehouse/Outreach ministry?

"Steve" was a heroin addict at 16. At 24, he attempted suicide by taking thirty "reds," and was unconscious for two days. When he "came to," he found an Ultimate Trip card in his pocket from one of our witnessing teams. He called and was invited to our midweek Bible study, where he gave his heart to the Lord.

"Larry" became involved with drugs and organized crime. He spent time in the penitentiary, struggled through a divorce, and was looking for the way out. Instead on July 4th he found the way in . . . into eternal life . . . in Jesus Christ!

(There are other slides and testimonies on the full-length script.)

The most valuable resource a city has are its young people. Although the Church touches many in their youth, when they hit the rough teenage years, many rebel and wander far away into sin, drugs, alcohol and sex. Peoria is Tulsa's "teenage skid row." If not reached here, they may end up on skid row in a thousand cities and if not reached before it's too late there, they will (in Jesus' own words) end up in "eternal weeping and gnashing of teeth."

This summer Jonathan attended the funeral of an older hippie who put a bullet through his brain. He didn't let Jesus change his life. But "Maryanne" did. She started shooting drugs at the age of 13, and at 19 was contemplating a double suicide with her boyfriend. Out on Peoria in a car, she offered a "joint" to Jonathan who replied "no thanks, I've found something better." She said," Tell me about it!" He did, and she was born again that very evening.

Who cares about these thousands of unchurched, unreached young people? That's a good question, who cares? Woodlake Assembly and Asbury United Methodist care, Carbondale Assembly of God cares, Tulsa Christian Fellowship cares — does your church care?

There is a way to reach these young people, to bridge the gap between the world of the unconverted, and the many fine churches who do care to see these young people brought into the family of God.

Together we can bridge the gap . . . together we can bring them in!

IF THE JOB IS GOING TO GET DONE, WE'VE GOT TO DO IT . . . TOGETHER!

78

Presenting Programs in Churches

"I am made all things to all men, that by all means I might save some" I Corinthians 9:22.

It took us too long to realize that not only was our Outreach doing a job that the Church couldn't achieve otherwise, but that God had called us to go back into the churches, to challenge churchgoers to let God do more in their lives and congregations.

Just as army infantry troops in the front-lines dare not outrun their supply lines, even so the average street Outreach usually has one common, fatal flaw that sooner or later destroys it. If the supply line with the established churches is broken, or never established, the Outreach sooner or later will fail, and die.

How to get a church date to share your ministry

1) Read the chapter on "Working with the Church" under "26 Steps to Opening Night."
2) Call, set an appointment with the pastor and arrive early.
3) Present your slide-cassette presentation to the minister at his private viewing. Find out beforehand whether the church has a slide-screen, or a blank white wall that can be used.
4) Share with the minister what God is doing through your work on the streets, what your vision, goals, and needs are. Also emphasize that your coming will stir up his congregation to bring more lost souls in there, too.
5) Tell him you have such-and-such Sundays open and would he allow you to come and present the slide-presentation to his entire congregation.
6) All ministers you visit won't say yes, but some will. God will open the doors He wants you to go through.

79

Cleanup and Maintenance

"Man looks on the outward appearance . . ." I Samuel 16:7.

"The things which are seen are already passing away" II Corinthians 4:18.

I: CLEANUP

The word "cleanup" may bring to some minds unspiritual visions of Cinderella's mop, but "cleanup" is a nitty-gritty ministry area that can make or break people's opinions. First impressions are the longest lasting and hardest to change, and while the Outreach should NOT be sterile as a hospital or museum, it shouldn't have smelly trashcans greeting visitors just inside the front door!

One person needs to oversee all cleanup, and either do it himself, or be responsible to get it done properly. Cleanup includes:

a) Carpet vacuuming, linoleum mopping.

b) Trashcan emptying and relining with plastic bags.

c) Couch cushions being drycleaned.

d) Restrooms being disinfected, mopped, mirrors cleaned, and shined.

Give the head of the cleanup department a set budget per month for his supplies, say $20 so that he doesn't need to continually come by the office for $1 worth of tissue paper or cleaning fluid. This money should be accounted for at the end of each month before the next month's allotment is provided.

Buying larger quantities of whatever is needed at one time saves both time and money.

II: MAINTENANCE

At first glance, the term "maintenance" may appear to be the same thing as "cleanup." But cleanup's job is to keep things clean, while the job of maintenance is not just to keep things from falling apart, but to put back together those things which already have.

Maintenance responsibilities include such things as:

1) **Repair:** If some flood lights are hanging down halfway out of the ceiling, if an outdoor sign needs repainting, or if the piano ivories start coming up and need superglue, call maintenance.

2) **Construction:** If a new partition needs to be built dividing up existing space into counseling or tape-listening units, this is also maintenance.

Supplies

Buying, replacing, and seeing that a reserve supply of necessary Outreach items such as bathroom paper towels, tissue dispenser cups, etc. should also be the responsibility of the maintenance department. You will need one person to be in charge over the maintenance department. The person must be responsible and get the job done.

IV: TWENTY-SIX STEPS TO OPENING NIGHT

80

Twenty-five Habits to Develop

"Be ye therefore perfect, even as your Father which is in Heaven is perfect." Matthew 5:48.

"The disciple is not above his master (teacher): but every one that is mature, full-grown, and completely trained shall be as his master." Luke 6:40.

"Until we all come in the unity of the faith, and of the knowledge of the Son of God, unto a perfect man, unto the measure of the stature of the fulness of Christ . . . that we no longer be children . . . but speaking the truth in love, may grow up into Him in all things, Who is the Head, even Christ." Ephesians 4:13-15.

All right! So you want a weekend Jesus Outreach in your city! Praise God! If you're really going to see this Outreach dream become an ongoing reality, here are twenty-five scriptural habits to cultivate which will insure success!

1) **Check your motives daily:** Increase your prayer and Word time daily. Never get too busy for the Holy Spirit. Keep your spiritual fuel tank on full! (Ephesians 5:18; Psalm 139:13-14).

2) **Learn to be early for appointments:** If you plan on arriving right on time, you'll be consistently late. Plan to arrive at least five minutes early.

3) **Find a special #1 helper:** You'll soon be needing a committed volunteer to do anything needed to see the Outreach become a reality. Ecclesiastes 4:9 says:

> "Two are better than one; because they have a good reward for their labour. For if they fall, the one will lift up his fellow; but woe unto him that is alone when he falls; for he doesn't have another to help him back up."

4) Learn to delegate: Spurgeon said: "I'd rather put ten men to work, than do the work of ten men." You'll have to do the same to succeed. Jethro told Moses: "Find some helpers, or you'll burn out" (Exodus 18:18).

5) Start making and keeping lists: Keep a three-hole ring notebook. You'll be needing lists of different groups of people such as:

a) interested people

b) soulwinners

c) pastors and church workers

d) volunteer helpers, and their specific individual skills

e) converts, their names, addresses, miscellaneous information

f) music groups and individual music ministers

6) Start and keep up a daily diary: Every night briefly jot down daily obstacles, and victories. Years from now you'll be blessed as you look back.

7) Write it down: Great ideas may fly away and never return. IF IT'S WORTH REMEMBERING, IT'S WORTH WRITING DOWN!

8) Establish definite, written goals: Think and pray out short-range, intermediate, and long-range goals, for the ministry and your life in Christ as well. As someone put is so well: "FAILING TO PLAN IS PLANNING TO FAIL!"

9) Start looking for your Outreach location: See the chapter in this section on "Location."

10) Locate and visit a local Christian lawyer and accountant: People will start handing money to you for "the Outreach," and you will need some sort of system to show where it has gone.

11) Write down ministry expenses: Start asking for receipts for every ministry related expense. Start a central record book of expenses.

12) Prepare a personal resume and start using it: Include past employment, ministry experiences, testimony, credits, honors, talents, dreams and vision.

13) Get key recommendation letters: Ask your pastor, or other pastors who know you to write you a personal recommendation letter. These will help the Outreach get off the ground! Letters from your university chaplain, youth minister, former employers, or Christian professionals will help new pastors realize you are neither Elmer Gantry nor Marjoe!

14) Learn to be a good, regular tither and giver: If you're not tithing regularly, you should be!

15) Learn to be a good receiver as well as a good giver: Learn to say "thank-you" when others "dig deep" to help. Learn to write warm, brief thank-you notes to donors.

16) **Broadcast the vision:** Start sharing your burden and Outreach vision with anyone you can get to listen to you (Romans 10:17)!

17) **Offer up "Isaac" daily:** Keep Genesis 22 in your spirit. This is ultimately God's ministry, not yours!

18) **Reading books:**
   a) Don Wilkerson's *Coffeehouse Manual*
   b) Dave Wilkerson's *Untapped Generation*

19) **Send for whatever Outreach materials you can locate:**
   a) Visit your largest library and read whatever they have under the subjects of Coffeehouse(s), Street Outreaches and Street Evangelism. b) Write to (or telephone) other coffeehouse/street-Outreaches, asking them for whatever materials they might be able to send you to help get started. A list of several hundred Outreaches is located in WFC's directory ($8.95).

20) **Establish elder guidance:** Find men of God you respect and ask their advice on key decisions and issues facing you. Remember Proverbs 11:14 and 24:6 ... "In the multitude of counselors there is wisdom and safety."

21) **Collect relevant materials:** Keep an eye out for statistics and newspaper articles dealing with the drug, counter-culture scene locally and nationally. Jot down and file these things. Also jot down occasional memorable comments people make that you will want to use later on.

22) **Learn to love and keep loving people that neither love, nor agree with you:** Write Matthew 5:44 and Proverbs 9:8 on your heart.

23) **Visit several other operating coffeehouses:** Tell them you're coming and why. Ask them to share with you how they started and how they operate, mistakes to avoid, etc.

24) **Get business cards printed:** If the Outreach as yet has no name, just call it, "French Quarter Outreach" or use your own name, but have something neat looking to hand to people with an address, name and phone number for future contact. You may also want a brief description of the proposed Outreach ministry vision and location typeset on the card. Don't let the printer or typesetter tell you it can't be done, it can! (Perhaps on the back) For example, you might say! "Please contact us if you'd like to see a Coffeehouse open on weekend nights featuring live music in the Red-Fork area!" Carry extra business cards with you to not only give to other interested people, but "spares" for them to take and give out as well.

25) **Learn to operate on faith, not feelings each day:** Keep Hebrews 11:6 in mind:

"Without faith it is impossible to please God: for He that comes to God must believe that He is, and that He is a rewarder of those that diligently seek Him."

Put God's Word first and avoid the roller coaster that feelings will take you on.

81

Twenty-Five Stumbling Blocks to Avoid

1) Watch your prayer life: don't let it slide: Jesus prayed all night (Luke 6:12). Never trade your unction for your function. The anointing breaks the yoke (Isaiah 10:27). Esau traded his birthright blessing for beans and Martha was too busy cooking to feed on Christ's words. Be wise and be "Israels" and "Marys" instead!

2) Don't let criticism offend you: THEY MIGHT BE RIGHT! Proverbs 9:8 reads: "Rebuke a wise man and he'll love you." Proverbs 15:22 (Living) says "If you profit from constructive criticism, you'll be elected to the wise man's hall of fame."

3) Avoid "camel-swallowing" religious contests: (see Matthew 23:23). Major in minor, not vice-versa. Christians can disagree with you and still be saved!

4) Beware of "Lone-Ranger-itis": Elijah single-handedly defeated 850 false prophets on Mt. Carmel and called down the fire. The next day he cried out to God to let him die. He had an advanced case of "Lone-Ranger-itis." God cured him quickly by telling him that there were 7,000 that still hadn't bowed to Baal. Don't make the same mistake — believing you're the only one!

5) Beware of "anti-churchism:" Remember the ideal Outreach is *only* a stepping stone. Don't allow converts or believers to camp out in midstream! You are there to function with the communtiy churches, never to try to replace them.

6) Watch your keys! Keep your "key-people" accountable for their keys not being handed to others, or reproduced. Keep as few copies as possible.

7) Keep your personal touch in your correspondence: Direct mail (newsletters, mimeoed announcements, etc.) will never replace personal visits, phone calls, handwritten notes, especially in first time contacts. Don't learn this the hard way like we did. We bulk-mailed form letters to 500 churches and not one replied!

8) **Don't be bitter!** Some people will say "We're behind you brother," but you'll need a telescope to find them. Set a worthy example for them to follow later on as God may lead them (Job 42:10).

9) **Don't incorporate too late.**

10) **Use checks and balances in authority and responsibility assignments.** Don't give any one person enough rope to hang himself, and drag down all the others as well! Jesus never gave Judas Iscariot enough power to ruin God's redemption of mankind, even though he did ruin his own salvation.

11) **Don't expect anyone to be God, but God Himself!** Learn to forgive others their shortcomings, and learn to ask for forgiveness for your own faults as well! The healing promised in James 5:16 requires that we confess our faults, not other people's!

12) **Don't let your director burn out:** once the ministry gets rolling a flood of details will appear out of nowhere. Make sure people ask the director regularly: "What can I do to help?"

13) **Don't get behind on your bookkeeping:** Daily or weekly record-keeping will eliminate a yearend "knock-down, drag-out!"

14) **Don't expect too much too fast:** What if 1,000 people actually did show up and get saved on your Opening Night?

15) **Don't overcommit yourself:** For example, don't start off by buying a building, or renting something for $1,000 a month. Learn to say "No" when that is what God is telling you to say!

16) **Don't let any one person be (or become) indispensable.**

17) **Keep bills current.** Don't allow overdue bills and collection threats to occur.

19) **Be sure to feed your co-ministers:** Sometimes we can get so busy feeding the lost that we forget feeding the "found." Keep the flock fed! (John 21:15-17).

20) **Set a good example:** have a home church you attend regularly.

21) **Don't look down on other "non-street" ministries.** Don't get proud because you are touching the "untouchables" on the street. There are "untouchables" in all fields that God has people sent out as harvesters to reach.

22) **Avoid radicalism just for the point of being or pleasing those who are radicals themselves.** Let God's love always be your motive and driving

force.

23) Don't exclude older Christians: If they love kids and have hearts aflame with God's Spirit and His love, older Christians are an invaluable steadying influence and source of wisdom. More and more we are finding older Christians are a necessity!

24) Don't let evangelism exclude or preclude holiness! In Acts 1:8 Jesus said His disciples would "BE" witnesses, not "do witnessing." Words spoken for Jesus Christ only have genuine Holy Ghost power when a clean, holy life is being lived behind the scenes.

25) Don't spread yourself or your staff too thin: An Outreach run superbly on weekend nights outshines an Outreach open seven nights a week where a spiritual "flophouse" "anything-goes" attitude prevails.

82

Seven Types of Outreaches

"I am made all things to all men, that I might by all means save some" I Corinthians 9:22.

It is apparent that a Christian Outreach in Weedpatch, Missouri population 207 will differ from one directly on the "strip" in Las Vegas, Reno, Miami Beach, Hollywood, Times Square or San Francisco's Haight Street or North Beach section. God will help you to plant just the right Outreach seed to meet your locality's needs. Different fish take different bait! But one thing remains constant: FISHERMEN MUST ALWAYS GO WHERE THE FISH ARE TO BE SUCCESSFUL!

Several type of Outreaches can be blended together. Below are several Outreach types and features to consider.

1) A re-creation (recreation) Christian youth center. Foozball tables, pool tables, food in the front room, Bibles, tracts, music teaching, counseling in the back.

2) Restaurant type Outreach: Sandwiches, chili, submarines, etc. either sold or food can be offered free. Check with the local health department to meet requirements on food-handling, etc.

3) Classical Coffeehouse type Outreach: Serve different types of drinks such as teas, coffees, hot chocolate, hot cider, etc. Use round spool tables, feature guitars, singing, casual wear, no admission charge usually.

4) Stepping Stone Soulwinning Outreach: Heavy emphasis here on a soulwinning ministry will limit the type of Christians and non-Christian that frequent the establishment.

5) Nightclub Style Outreach: A "Light-Club" full scale stage with lighting, the whole works. Bring in large name groups, charge admission, but perhaps only to Christians, not to their guests or unsaved people. This could be a combined effort of church groups from several towns, and could reach and accommodate 100-500 people or more.

6) Church cellar Outreach: Relaxed, informal, come as you are, subdued colored lighting, this type can meet some needs but it's not really out in mid-stream where an Outreach by definition ought to be.

7) Combination Outreach/Live-in Center: Something like this could be open all night, and use one or more buildings for later night traffic or ministering to hitchhikers that are brought in. It can have the double function of not only being an Outreach, but also being a discipleship/training center as well!

83

On Location

"What man of you, having a hundred sheep, if he has lost one of them, does not leave the ninety-nine and go after that one which is lost, until he finds it" Luke 15:4.

The Outreach should be highly visible, out in the open, and preferably on the "strip" or near a hub of the activity of the type of people that God is leading you to reach, where they either park, cruise, hang out or gather.

Street people . . . are found on the "strip," at parks or near favorite hangouts.

Businessmen . . . in downtown areas.

Alcoholics . . . Skid Row or between two bars.

Travelers . . . Near bus or train stations, or airports.

Jr. and Sr. High School kids . . . Near or across the street from schools.

Beach crowd . . . Close as possible to the beach front.

College kids. . . Amidst college nightspot hangouts, or near "frat row" or near campus or dorm areas.

Military . . . Near the base, or near their "hangouts"

In Matthew 4:19 Jesus promised to make His followers not only "fishers" but "catchers" of men for His Kingdom. To catch "filet of soul," fishermen must go where the "souls" are. This obviously should be the #1 ingredient in picking the location.

If you can find a good location that also has a parking lot out front, or beside it, areas like this can be used for outdoor concerts and outdoor meetings. In our case on the busy "strip," thousands of cars drive by and see the outdoor concerts, and whether they stopped or not, the Gospel was once more confronting their eternal souls and empty lives.

84

Winning the Name Game

"Behold I send you out as lambs in the midst of wolves: therefore be ye wise as serpents and harmless (or undiluted) as doves" Matthew 10:16.

"A good name is rather to be chosen than great riches" Proverbs 22:1.

The name you settle on will soon become known all over town. Television and radio crews will eventually do reports on the evening news about the new Outreach. Nearby news reporters and magazines will also do articles, some of which you won't hear about until weeks later, others you may never hear about. Winning the "Name Game" is important!

One thing is certain: A STEPPING STONE OUTREACH NEEDS A STEPPING STONE NAME! A church may call itself: "First Traditional United Cathedral," and at the other end of the name spectrum, a topless bar might call itself "The Pit." Between the two former name classifications, however, the Stepping Stone Outreach must draw its clientele to itself by the name it bears.

Below are some sample names, all of which either have been used or could be used to name a soulwinning Stepping Stone Outreach.

Adam's Apple
Agape House
All Things New!
The Answer
The Ark

The Back Door
The Balm Shelter
The Book of Life
The Branch
The Bread Box
The Bread of Life
The Bridge

The Carpenter's Shop
The Catacombs
The Crossfire
The Crossroads

The Dewdrop Inn
The Dock
The Door
The Dove

The Eagle's Inn
The Eagle's Nest
Eden
The Empty Tomb
The Exit
The Exodus

The Fire Place
The Fire Station
The Fish
The Fishhook
The Fishnet
The Flame
Freedom Center

Freedom House

Glory Barn
Gone With The Wind
Good Thief
Grace's Place
The Grace Place
Guiding Light

Headquarters
Heaven's Gate
Heaven Unlimited
His Place
House of the
    Rising Son

I Am

Jacob's Well

The Lamp
The Launching Pad
The Light
The Lighthouse
The Light Club
The Lion's Club
The Lion's Den
The Lion's Paw
The Lion of Judah
The Lost Coin
The Love Inn
The Love Song

The Mustard Seed
The New Breed
New Jerusalem Club

One Sweet Dream

One Way In(n)
The Open Hand

The Parable
The Powerhouse
The Prodigal's
The Re-creation Center

The Room
Rock of Ages

The Salt Cellar
The Salt Shaker
Second Chance
The Servant's Quarters
Quarters
The Shelter
The Son Room
The Stepping Stone
The Stone

THC House
    (Take Home Christ)
TLC House
    (Tender Loving Care)
The Tree of Life
The True Vine
The Turning Point

The Upper Room

The Way Inn
The Way Out
The Welcome Table
The Way
The Wheel

85

Getting the Interested People

"He that plants sparingly shall also reap sparingly, but he that plants generously shall also reap generously" II Corinthians 9:6.

The primary rule in gathering together people that are interested in this Outreach project, is to share your burden and vision with **EVERYONE** you can get to listen.

1) **Start making and adding to a list of friends,** and believers that might be interested. Include their names, addresses, phone numbers, particular talents. Start with the dry kindling, those you know are "on-fire" believers.

2) **Make a list of pastors and church youth leaders you know.** Contact them!

   a) Start with your own church and pastor. Get an appointment to see him.

   b) Visit each pastor personally. Those you can't visit, phone or write.

   c) Ask several pastors to be on an advisory board when the Outreach starts.

   d) Ask each one, particularly those that aren't quite convinced of the need, to come walk "the strip" with you some Saturday night.

3) **Call all church prayer and intercessory groups that you know of. Have them pray!**

4) **Use the Media: As your plans solidify, contact:**

   a) Nearby Christian radio stations:

If there is a Christian radio station in your area (or several) or one that isn't local but broadcasts into your area, **contact each one,** and speak with the disc jockey and/or station manager that relates closest to contemporary Jesus-music, or Gospel music and Outreach.

Tell them who you are, what church you go to, where you live, and what your vision and burden for your area is. If the station is not too local, share with them that the counter-culture "drug, teen alcohol, immorality, cult" problems abound in every city they broadcast into.

Ask them if they would allow you to record a 15 second "spot" public service announcement to be played a couple of times a day for several days. Tell them the message would sound similar to this:

"If you live in the (name of your area), and would like to see a Christian coffeehouse/street-Outreach open soon, featuring live-music on weekend nights to help reach unsaved young people, please contact: (give your name, c/o the radio station.) With practice you can read through this under 15 seconds.

Using the station's address and your name will help more people make contact! If they insist on your name, and your address or phone, use it!

Be prepared to "sell" the disc jockey or station manager on the idea! If they said they can't allow a "local" announcement because they broadcast into too many other areas, tell them **GOD CAN USE THAT FACT TO REACH MORE UNSAVED YOUTH AND INVOLVE MORE CONCERNED CHRISTIANS BY MERELY ADDING** to the announcement the following words directly after "young people":

"Or, if you live in a different area, and your area needs a Christian coffeehouse as well (then go on), please contact: . . .

If they seem skeptical or hesitant, tell them you have recommendation letters, news articles, and more information that you'd like to send them by mail, or bring by and show them. You will be wonderfully surprised at the many contacts that come in from this method of gathering the interested people!

b) Contact religion editors or feature writers in your city, and other city newspaper departments. Even if the Outreach isn't opened, they might be interested in your testimony, your plan, and vision for their area!

c) Local cable television might be willing to run a free public service announcement for the proposed Outreach, as they do for other churches.

5) **Make use of the volunteer "talent-finder" sheet: Give them to each interested** person on your list, and to those you run into. GIVE EXTRA BLANK VOLUNTEER "TALENT–FINDER SHEETS" to all those you know who would be willing to pass them out as well to their own interested friends, church acquaintances, etc.

6) **Use posters and other visual announcements:**

a) Put posters up on community bulletin boards in supermarkets, laundries, churches, Bible schools, colleges.

b) Run short, inexpensive ads in local bargain-posts, free-ad shoppers, etc. Also run short ads in the student newspapers of nearby colleges, etc.

86

Getting People Interested

"Where there is no VISION, the people (and interest) perish" Proverbs 29:18.

"My people perish (and their interest does too) for lack of knowledge" Hosea 4:6.

Mr. Richard Schulz, who spent many years as administrative director and "right-hand" man for David Wilkerson, founder of Teen Challenge and World Challenge, told us:

"Take pastors out on the street with you, one at a time. Let them see first-hand the foozball, "strips," rock concert crowds, parking lot hangouts you want to reach . . . GOD WILL GIVE THEM THE BURDEN IF YOU GIVE THEM THE VISION.

If a pastor won't come with you, perhaps a local youth pastor, or Christian business man will. Don't force them to get involved in actual street-witnessing. Just let them see the need, and the Holy Spirit will take over and do the rest!

87

Sample Volunteer "Talent-Finder" Sheet

"The kingdom of heaven is as a man traveling into a far country, who called his own servants, and delivered unto them his goods (or TALENTS)" Matthew 25:14.

"For as the body is one, and hath many members, and all the members of that one body, being many, are one body: so also is Christ . . . for the body is not one member, but many" I Corinthians 12:12-14.

The sample "talent-finding" form below can be rewritten, retyped, and personalized to exactly fit the Outreach God is leading you into starting. This form can be used from the very start. As you and others with you gather the names of interested people, either give or mail them a copy of the talent-finding sheet.

VOLUNTEER "TALENT–FINDER" SHEET FOR (Your area's name)'s
NEW STREET OUTREACH

Jesus Christ promised: "If any man serve Me, him shall My Father honor." John 12:26

Would you like to be used by God to make others happy, to help them find Jesus Christ as personal Lord, and to help them spend eternity in heaven? If you have a little extra time, and talents, and if you enjoy helping others, WE NEED YOUR HELP! **WOULD YOU LIKE TO HELP A CHRISTIAN COFFEEHOUSE/STREET OUTREACH OPEN IN** (area's name)?

Please fill out the form below, and return it to: Box   , (your city, and state).
PLEASE PRINT

Name   Address   City   Age
Phone number   (home)   (work) Best time to call
I drive: Car   Pickup   Van   (other) I am   years old in Christ
My home church is   My pastor's name is
Circle days you can help? M T W T F Sat. Sun.   Today's date
Number of hours you can help: Morning   Afternoon   Evening
I CAN HELP IN THE FOLLOWING AREAS: (Pick 4, and number them in order of preference)

INREACH	OUTREACH	BACKUP
(The Ministry Inside)	(The Ministry Outside)	(The Ministry Backbone)
Bible Studies	Bar Witnessing	Accounting
Booking Music Groups	Door-to-Door	Administration
Counseling	Drug-Abuse Program	Artwork
Door Greeting	Jail Ministry	Board of Advisors
Followup	Poster Distributing	Board of Directors
Housing	Soulwinning	Carpentry
Intercessory Prayer	Soulwinning Team	Church Relations
Leading Worship	Captain	Cleanup
Music Ministry	Street Drama	Electrical
PA System	Street Music	Financial Partner
Preaching	Street Preaching	Fund Raising
Refreshments	Street Witnessing	Lay-Out
Ride Giving	Teaching On	Legal Assistance
Sound Recording	Soulwinning	Maintenance
Teaching	Tract Distribution	Newsletter Editing
Telephone Prayer	Tract Writing	News Writing
Chain		Photography

Printing
Public Relations
Secretarial
Writing Up
Testimonies

PLEASE LIST BELOW ANY OTHER TALENTS:

Have you worked with a coffeehouse/outreach before

If it is still operating, what is its: (name)   (address)
Thank you so much for filling out this form. We will be getting back in touch with you soon to
help make this Outreach dream a successful reality, bringing young people to Jesus Christ.

If you would like more of these blank forms to pass out to friends that may also be interested in
helping, please write the number in the blank at right!

Thank you once again, and **GOD BLESS YOU!**

You will be amazed how God brings together people that have every talent
the new Outreach will need. After retyping and personalizing the sheet, you
may want to get it reduced at a local printer's and then printed on either a
more convenient 5"x7", 4"x6", or 3"x5" card size for filing in a box.

With permission from your pastor (and/or other pastors), these talent-
finder sheets can and should be left by the door of your or their church.

88

Choosing and Locating a Director

"There is neither Jew nor Greek (neither 'straight' nor 'hippie'), there
is neither bond nor free, there is neither male nor female: for you are all
one in Christ Jesus" Galatians 3:28.

"For He is our peace, Who has made both one, and has broken down
the middle wall of partition between us" Ephesians 2:14.

Your founding committee or group may not be developed yet to the point
of seeing the need for a full-time director . . . you will! You can operate for a

time without one, but when the time comes that you are needing one, reread this chapter. It will all quickly come into focus.

The Word of God warns in I Timothy 3:5: "Don't place a new convert in too high a place of authority; he might be proud of being chosen so soon, and pride comes before a fall like satan's."

Below are several qualities, the more of which you can find in your potential director, the better he (or she) will fulfill the intended ministry of your street Outreach.

1) Their minimum age should be 23.

2) Their minimum spiritual age should be three or four years not only in Christ, but serving Him as well.

3) They must possess a deep love, understanding, and concern for youth.

4) They must ba a "bridge" person that can relate to saints and to sinners with equal ease.

5) They should be self-starters, self-disciplined, self-motivated, and hard workers.

6) They should have mature depth, and yet have an ALIVE personality.

7) They should have an established relationship with their own home church minister.

8) They must be able to teach, preach, and inspire other believers.

9) They must be able not only to train soulwinners, but win themselves.

10) They must know their Bibles well.

11) They must know how to form, motivate, lead, and work with a team.

12) They must give and take criticism constructively.

13) They must not be shocked by any sin, but be confident in God's ability to save and forgive the chiefest of sinners.

14) Past street-experience either B.C. (Before Christ) or A.D. (in ministering on the street, door-to-door, etc.), should count heavily as qualifications.

Jesus said in Luke 5:39; "No man having tasted old wine asks immediately for the new . . . because the old is better." The best wine has been in a wine cellar for years. It takes time to develop spiritual depth.

A potential director must have some spiritual "time and grade" to effectively perform his job.

Experience, even experience in sin before Christ, can be an invaluable plus, as unreligious as that may sound. Even as missionary societies have found that training "Nationals" (missionaries that have grown up in the country, and know its language and customs) aids greatly in getting out

God's Word abroad, even so in our "street-jungles" at home the same principle can be effectively and fruitfully applied!

Locating a Director

Your Outreach may in fact be already open and operating, but the need for or ability to support a full-time salaried outreach director may not have surfaced as yet. In time, both will, and God will meet each of these needs.

Where will you find the right person?

Below are several ideas which may lead you directly to your Director, or spark other ideas which will get the right person for your specific community and its needs in touch with you.

Church contacts:

Perhaps your church has just the person already in it who will surface in the ministry and prove himself to be the one chosen by God to be director full-time.

Perhaps another pastor or layman in your church, in your city or area already has the training, experience, and desires to be director of such a work. How will he find out that your city's Outreach needs him? Contact other churches with letters, send them bulletins or annoucements to post, or even run an ad in your local newspaper (and/or other cities as well) on the church page, sharing your need and alerting the Body of Christ to this opportunity to enter into the ministry.

If not led to run ads, or simultaneous to your local search, you can contact the Christian Bible schools and organizations that are listed below, letting them know:

a) who you are
b) what your specific need is
c) what your vision for the new Outreach and for your area is
- d) personal qualifications applicants must have

Jesus Christ made us a promise that applies in this search for a director in Matthew 7:7-8: EVERYONE WHO ASKS, WILL EVENTUALLY BE GIVEN: EVERYONE THAT SEEKS AND KEEPS SEEKING WILL

EVENTUALLY FIND, AND EVERYONE THAT KNOCKS AND KEEPS KNOCKING, TO HIM THE DOOR SHALL BE OPENED.

Do your part and God will keep His promise by bringing the exact person He has chosen to be director of the Outreach your city needs!

List of potential places you might find a director

Agape Force Ministries, Box 386, Lindale, TX 75771

Arthur Blessit Evangelistic Assn. Box 69544, Hollywood, CA 90069 213/652-7170.

Calvary Chapel of Costa Mesa, 3800 S. Fairview, Santa Ana, CA, 714/979-4422

Campus Crusade For Christ, Arrowhead Springs, San Bernadino, CA 92414

Christ For The Nations Bible Institute, 3404 Conway, Dallas, TX 75224 214/376-1711

Christian Broadcasting Network School of Theology, c/o CBN, Virginia Beach, VA 23463, 804/499-8241

Christians in Action, 350 E. Market St., Long Beach, CA 213/428-2022

Christ Is The Answer, Box 24450, Dallas, TX 75224

Elim Bible School, Lima, NY 14485

Genesis Bible School, 50 Mark West Springs Rd., Santa Rosa, CA 707/524-7000

God's Army Bible School, Box 11971, Fresno, CA 93776, 209/846-7301

Ed Human, Evangelist, Box 4806, San Antonio, TX 512/341-8469

Insight Ministries, Gene Griffin, Dr., 9809 E. 37th Cr., Tulsa, OK 918/627-8179

Interchristo Ministry, Box 9323, Seattle, WA 98109, 206/623-0715

Jesus People U.S.A., 4431 N. Paulina, Chicago, IL 60640, 312/935-2120

Love Inn, 1768 Dryden Road, Freeville, NY 607/347-4411

Melodyland School of Theology, Box 6000, Anaheim, CA 92806, 714/635-6393

Morris Cerullo's Minister's School, 702 Ash, San Diego, CA 714/232-0161

ORU School of Theology, c/o ORU, Tulsa, OK 74171, 918/492-6161

PTL School of Evangelism, c/o Heritage University, Charlotte, NC 28279 704/742-6700

Resurrection City, 1600 Shadduck, Berkeley, CA, 415/548-2476

Rhema Bible Training Center, P.O. Box 50126, Tulsa, OK 74150, 918/258-1588

Lester Roloff Evangelistic Enterprises, Box 1177, Corpus Christi, TX 78403 512/882-4211, 512/883-8265

Shiloh Temple Bible School, 3136 13th Ave. Oakland, CA 415/458-7947

Southern Arizona Bible College, Box 2960, Phoenix, AZ 85062

Spiritual Counterfeits Project, Box 4308, Berkeley, CA 94704, 415/458-7947
Spring of Living Water, Richardson Springs, CA, 916/343-5565
Teen Challenge Center, Box 15001, Philadelphia, PA 19121, 215/232-4636
David Wilkerson Youth Crusades, Rt. 1, Box 80, Lindale, TX 75771, 214/882-5591
Worldshakers For Christ, Inc. (the author's evangelistic association), Box P-1, Felton, CA 95018, 408/425-7760
Youth With A Mission, Box Y.W.A.M., Solvang, CA 93463, 805/688-8467
All Assembly of God Bible Schools (call local AG church for addresses)

89

Working with
and Visiting Churches

"Now there are differences of gifts, but the same Spirit. And there are differences of administrations, but the same Lord. And there are diversities of operations, but it is the same God at work in them all" I Corinthians 12:4-6.

The stepping stone Outreach is to be a tool of the church, not an end of the means (the Church) but a means to an end, Eternal Life in Christ, and fellowship in a local church.

Before you even have your first meeting, you must decide several things:

1) Is it going to be a one church, or multi-church effort?

2) Will it be denominational, or trans-denominational?

3) Are you going to control it as director, or will others control it through a board of directors?

OVERCOMING CHURCH SKEPTICISM AND OBJECTIONS TO STREET OUTREACH MINISTRIES WILL BE A LOT EASIER IF YOU KEEP THE FIVE FOLLOWING OBJECTIONS AND ANSWERS IN MIND.

1) **They don't want to be involved in anything not 100% theirs.** This is an objection that is not usually verbalized, but often present. Make it clear to each pastor that every participating church will be offered the opportunity to

place a representative on the Outreach's Board of Directors, or Advisors.

2) They don't know the actual needs outside the sanctuary: This need can be remedied by inviting the pastors to come out personally some night with you to see for themselves (one at a time).

3) They wonder whatever becomes of the converts. Make it clear to the pastors and church boards that churches will be contacted with the names of converts after each weekend, and that all converts and young people frequenting the Outreach will be repeatedly encouraged to actively have a church home. Tell them a list of friendly churches will be posted by the Outreach's front door!

4) They wonder where their money will be spent. Assure them that there will be an official treasurer, that a budget will be set up and adhered to under the control of the Board of Directors, and that the "books" will be open for inspection by participating churches at any time.

5) They see the Outreach as a financial threat or drain. Right from the start make and keep it clear that people are being encouraged to maintain faithful tithing to their home churches, and that you are believing Church contributions, mission pledges, and donations individuals make (above their regular church tithes) will be the supporting financial element.

Advantages of an inter-church "Outreach" committee go far beyond the obvious benefits of greater wisdom, prayers, personnel, talents, finances, organization, contacts, etc. Having several churches involved gives the entire Outreach venture more credibility in the eyes of other churches looking on from a distance that may join in later on.

Jesus said: "I pray . . . that they may be made perfect in one; **that the world may BELIEVE** that Thou hast sent Me" (John 17:21, 23). The world only half-believes a divided, splintered Christendom.

One churchman told me at my first church committee meeting: "If we move slow, it's because of whom we represent." I replied: "If I move fast, it's also because of whom I represent — those speeding dumbly into an eternal hell." Yet, in time, we learned to understand and appreciate one another and to work together. YOU WILL HAVE TO LEARN TO DO THIS AS WELL!

Susan Atkins, an ex-Charles Manson gang member, now a born-again Christian told me: "Help get the street Christians to the street sinners, and help the street Christians and established church Christians work together." As Ephesians 2:14 puts it; "Break down the middle wall of partition."

You not only MUST but CAN work together with churches. The Outreach will eventually fail if you don't stress time and again that the Outreach is a church supplement, not substitute. The Church has the depth, the Outreach is its fingertips. But Fingertips are of little value by themselves, unless completely subservient to the hand, arm, shoulder, and the rest of the Body that is supporting and coordinating them with the Head's plan.

Visiting Churches

1) When calling each church, ask for an appointment with the pastor. If the secretary asks why you need the pastor, just answer that it's something personal (which it is). Otherwise, you may get cut off before you reach him. Asking "why" is part of her job; reaching the pastor is part of yours!

2) Take an appointment at their convenience. The earlier in the day, the better, because pastors have a long day of visiting the sick in hospitals, and other expected meetings.

3) Dress neatly: wear a coat and tie! The I Corinthians 9:22 principle applies here as well as on the street. Polish your shoes, brush your teeth, hair, etc. Don't go in wearing blue jeans, or acting too casual.

4) Arrive ten minutes early.

5) Watch your time (and the pastor's): Don't stay over half an hour. He won't be rude and throw you out of his office, but be assured he has plenty to do.

6) Go prayed up. God's Spirit can say more through ten anointed words, than we can with 10,000!

7) Present your vision and plan in an orderly, prepared manner. Share with him:

a) Who you are (give him a brief recommendation letter or two to read).

b) What you were saved from — a minute or two at most of your "B.C." testimony.

c) What the local need is. Perhaps mention a local youth hangout near his church where even church kids drop in.

d) What your vision and plan for making it into a reality is.

e) How he and his church could help out in reaching more youth for Jesus.

8) Have definite goals as to what this meeting should achieve.

9) Ask for a definite committment from the Pastor and/or his church. (This should vary according to how well you know the minister.)

a) Ask for a church representative to attend Outreach meetings.

b) Ask for his approval to leave a stack of volunteer "talent-finder" sheets.

c) Ask if he'll put a notice in his Sunday bulletin for those interested.

d) Ask for a specific monthly pledge or one-time gift to the Outreach.

10) Ask to pray before you leave. If he's a praying man and leads out, let him start and close the prayer. If not, then you do so, but in humility.

11) Leave something printed in his hands: Either leave him a business card with the name of the Outreach or the Outreach project, a recommendation letter, a newsletter or neatly typed xeroxed sheet explaining the Outreach vision, including proposed location, needs, budget, and names of involved people and churches.

12) Leave on friendly terms: The pastor may be deeply moved, but not seem so. He may not join the Outreach project right away, but may join later on.

13) Write a brief thank-you note within the next three days to the pastor. Thank him for his time, prayers, and interest. Let him know you are praying for his church and ministry.

90

A Sample Questionnaire for Pastors

"Everyone that asks receives, and everyone that seeks, finds" Matthew 7:7.

This letter is only a sample form, and can be improved upon and retyped. Attach a sample volunteer "talent-finder" sheet and a reference letter or two with this letter. Also enclose a handwritten, stamped, self-addressed envelope with each of these letters that you send out to pastors you feel should be interested in the Outreach project. Send it FIRST CLASS MAIL! Type each pastor's name and address fresh, DO NOT send a xerox or mimeo. At the least, get your sample printed at a local print shop.

Dear Pastor   (or Mr.   ): _____
    I feel there is a tremendous need in our community for establishing a
youth-oriented Outreach open on weekend nights (and every night hopefully
during the summers) to help bring the Good News of Jesus Christ to those
outside the Church and its normal weekly activities.
    The purpose of this Outreach will be threefold:
1) To reach the unreached and unchurched with God's Good News.
2) To be a stepping stone for Christians to use in bringing their unsaved
friends in to hear Christian music and changed-life testimonies in a non-
ecclesiastical setting.
3) To provide a training place for younger Christians wanting to learn to
better share their faith with others.
    Would you take just a few moments from your busy schedule by answer-
ing this questionnaire. Please share your advice, suggestions, and ideas.
    Once again, thank you for helping, for your time, prayers, and Christian
cooperation.

Sincerely yours in Christ Jesus,
(signature) (your name, typed) (your address)
(state & zip code) (your phone number(s)

*Please detach the section below when completed and return it in the
enclosed envelope. Thank you again for your time and concern.*

===

Pastor's Sample Questionnaire
From: Pastor _____
                        _____
                                          (church)

1) Do you feel there is a need for young people to have a Christian place
open on weekend nights in our area?
____Yes ____No
2) Have you ever worked with a coffeehouse/outreach before?
____Yes ____No
3) If you have, or would like to, may we meet sometime, at your convenience, to pursue together the possibilities of this youth outreach?
____Yes ____No
4) If not, could you refer me to someone, especially locally, who has had
some experience in this type of youth outreach?

Name_____ Address_____
Phone Number_____
5) May we send some 'volunteer' sheets for distribution in your church?
____Yes ____No

91

Sample "Stepping Stone" Brochure

"Where there is no vision . . . the people perish" Proverbs 29:18.

"And the Lord said . . . 'Write the vision and make it plain upon tablets, that he may run that read it" Habakkuk 2:2.

". . . for the children of this world are wiser in their generation, than the children of light" Luke 16:8.

Why a brochure?

Businessmen in the world use brochures to advertise anything! An attractively put together 3-fold 8x11 inch brochure is a neat effective information package to "sell" their product to potential customers or users. Jesus wasn't complimenting His disciples when He told them what He did Luke 16:8 (quoted above).

It will be well worth your time and money to eventually put together a brochure for your Outreach. It will not only open doors for you and inform others inside the church world of what you are doing, but doors into prisons, youth homes and colleges can also be better opened with the help of an attractively put together brochure.

92

Sample First Organizational Meeting Letter

"And let us consider one another to provoke unto love and unto good works" Hebrews 10:24.

Wait at least two weeks, or until you have several dozen interested people and a minimum of two or three interested churches, before setting a date and sending this out. Remember, you can adapt or change any part of this format.

Dear Brother/Pastor/Sister/Mr./Mrs. _____

The Lord Jesus is raising up workers together to bring in the harvest of precious souls among the youth of (name of your Outreach's proposed area).

Many have expressed an interest in seeing a Christian youth Coffee-house/Street-Outreach featuring live music and living Christianity open on weekend nights in our area.

The first organizational meeting for our new local Christian youth Outreach in (name of your city) will be held:

    date:
    time:
    location:**

We are looking forward to seeing you there! If for any reason you can't make it to this first meeting, please send a representative of your church, or a friend. Please also feel free to:

1) Post this letter on your church or community bullentin board.
2) Have this meeting announced in your church bulletin or Sunday School class, or from the pulpit.
3) Let everyone interested know that they are warmly invited and welcome.

"The harvest is great, but the harvesters are few: pray therefore to the

Lord of the harvest, that He will cast out laborers into His harvest"
Matthew 9:38.

> Trusting to see you there,
> In our Saviour's service,

(your name)

**You may want to avoid a church meeting place, to prevent anyone from
claiming denominational preferences. You can acquire either a conference
room, free small dining room in a local cafeteria, or the clubhouse at a local
apartment complex.

93

First Organizational Meeting Preparations

"Be thou prepared, and prepare for thyself thou, and all the company
that are assembled unto thee" Ezekiel 38:7.

"With the right strategy, you can fight and war, and plenty of advisers
mean victory" Proverbs 24:6, Beck.

"Plans go wrong without advice, but with many advisers they succeed" Proverbs 15:22, Beck.

1) Prepare yourself:
   a) Pray an extra hour or two. It will work wonders!
   b) Leave NO last minute details for the last minute, plenty will
   arise.
   c) Remember: Jesus is there with 2 or 3, not just 2 or 3,000! (Matthew
   18:20).
   In other words, don't fall apart if the whole town doesn't show up for
   the first meeting.
2) Prepare the meetings agenda:
   a) Plan first on welcoming, recognizing and introducing all those

present.

b) Discuss the Outreach's possible name(s), location(s), nights open, hours.

c) Discuss what night and time is best for the next (or regular) organizational meetings: weekly, bi-monthly, or monthly.

3) Research beforehand all details you may need to know at the meeting:

a) Possible location(s) — (if there's a choice)

b) Rents, leases available or required (on each possibility).

c) Utility deposits (Call and find out approximate amounts.) It's surprising.

4) Xerox copies of the combined proposed first budget and a list of things to do (see first organizational meeting material in the next chapter).

5) Compile the completed volunteer "talent-finder" sheets that have been handed or mailed in to you. Doing this beforehand will let you know at the meeting's beginning what people and talents you have available to form committees and pick committee leaders from. Also plan on mimeoing or printing 250-500 "talent-finder" sheets to distribute at the first organizational meeting.

6) You must learn to delegate. Your job will be sort of matchmaker to divide the necessary primary tasks with the available, willing people.

7) Buy stick-on or pin-on name tag labels for this meeting and future use. These will help a large number of strangers or first timers to feel more at home, and also to learn each other's names quicker. This is to add to the comfortable feeling you want this and every meeting to have. These stick-on labels read: "Hello! My name is _____," and are available inexpensively from local office supplies, or department stores.

8) Work on a tentative "statement of purpose" for the Outreach. Rough it out, type it up double-spaced, and xerox sufficient copies for others to work over and refine with you at the first organizational meeting.

9) If you can, arrange for coffee to be available.

94

Your First
Organizational Meeting

"The ants are a people not strong, yet they PREPARE their meat in summer" Proverbs 30:25.

"Plans go wrong with too few counselors: many advisors bring success" Proverbs 15:22.

1) Get there at least half an hour early.

2) Give name tags to everyone attending.

3) Open the meeting with a prayer of faith concerning the Outreach vision.

4) Welcome and introduce each person you know. Welcome each new person and have them say a few words about themselves, their vision, and church.

5) Pass a notepad around the table and have each PRINT their name, address, phone number, and church affiliation.

6) Pass another pad for each to write names and addresses of friends and contacts of theirs that would be interested in attending the next meeting. People know people!

7) Distribute copies of the proposed Outreach budget and list of things to do to take it through opening night. Ask for volunteers — divide tasks with the available people.

8) Discuss the Outreach name, nights and hours to be open.

9) Discuss the next organizational meeting; should it be weekly, bi-weekly?

10) Set a tentative date for opening night; 2 or 3 months away.

11) Below are definite things that must be done for opening night. Who will volunteer to take care of which area?

   a) Raising money for rent, and utility deposits. Who will be the treasurer? What bank will be used? Who will sign checks?

   b) Secure building, sign lease, get keys and key copies.

   c) Remodeling/decoration (Carpentry, painting, electric, carpet, furniture — see preliminary budget sheet).

   d) Prayer — who will contact prayer groups, and who will be in charge of the prayer room at the Outreach?

e) Music — live bands or soloists are best; use record player and instrumental Christian records for background.

f) Who'll head up advertising (posters, church bulletins, bulletin boards, paid ads, and free public service announcements on the radio, and in city papers, etc?)

12) Handout a stack of volunteer "talent-finder" sheet blanks to each person present, to keep "the ball rolling" toward spreading the word about the new Outreach in their home church among their personal Christian friends, and with those they meet day to day.

13) **Work on a STATEMENT OF PURPOSE** for the proposed Outreach. Take xerox copies of a tentative statement of purpose ready for those present at the first organizational meeting to comment on and revise. A sample follows:

STATEMENT OF PURPOSE
FOR A STEPPING STONE STREET MINISTRY

The (name of ministry) is designed to be both an Inreach and Outreach Christian Coffeehouse street ministry.

Inreach

1) To provide a place for early training, Bible teaching, counseling and musical entertainment on weekends for new converts.

2) To provide an outlet for training young ministers and counselors in on-the-job situations.

Outreach

1) To reach out to young street people otherwise shunned or not related to by the Church. To present Jesus through tracts, witnessing and street preaching on the street, in hangouts (bar, foozball halls) and at public gatherings (rock concerts, football games, etc.).

2) To train street ministers in on-the-job situations. This ministry is to bring unsaved men, women, boys and girls to the saving knowledge of Jesus Christ and to help establish them in the faith, with the goal of building a bridge between the street people and the established Church.

95

Incorportation: Why and How

"Submit yourselves to every ordinance of man for the Lord's sake..."
I Peter 2:13.
"Let every soul be subject to the higher powers and authorities... Do that which is good, and thou shalt have praise of the same: for he is the minister of God to thee for good" Romans 13:1, 4.

One of the two major benefits to incorporating the Outreach as the nucleus of committed believers solidifies unity of direction and purpose, is the limitation of personal liability. This means that if the Outreach was ever sued, only the assets of the corporation itself would be subject to the suit. None of the people involved in the corporation, even the president himself, would be personally liable to lose his car, home or property.

The second major benefit of incorporation is that doing so not only adds respectability to the whole Outreach project in the eyes of the world and other Christians and churches, but it provides the basis for receiving official tax-exempt status from the IRS which helps donor-partners give more of God's money to the work of the Gospel.

It must be kept in mind that both the limitation of personal liability and the offering of tax-exempt receipts for financial gifts is contingent on the proper forms being used, filled out, and returned to the proper agencies, etc.

A Sample Declaration of Purpose of Incorporation

"To evidence the establishment of a Christian church (or Outreach) for the propagation of the Gospel of Jesus Christ to the ends of the earth, the maintenance of Christian fellowship and worship with those of like faith, and the promotion of a spiritual and social ministry to the community.

"The church (Outreach) shall be limited exclusively to religious, charitable pursuits; shall render general assistance, including the furnishing of housing, meals, and counseling services to persons who are alcoholics, drug-addicts, transients, and similarly distressed people.

"In the fashion to distribute assistance as well as evangelical equipment, such as but not limited to recordings, loudspeaking equipment, printed

Gospel messages, Christian books, Bibles, etc. and to support by means of television, radio, and newspaper the propagation of the Gospel of our Lord and Saviour Jesus Christ. To undertake such other activities as may be determined to be consistent with the principal objectives of the organization."

There are Christian lawyers in your area who would be glad to help you take care of the necessary paperwork, form-filling and filing. Ask your pastor, or other pastors and God will lead you to the proper lawyer. Some will do the work as a tithe, others may give you a discount rate, but *make sure* you have a clear understanding of the fee expected by your lawyer BEFORE he begins the job.

The How

The first step in receiving offical IRS tax-exempt religious non-profit status is Incorporation with your state. Call your city hall for the proper form, or for the address of the Secretary of State in your state's capital. Write them and they will return the proper forms to fill out to you.

96

Budget Planning

"For which of you, intending to build a tower, doesn't sit down first, and count the cost to see whether he has sufficient to finish it?" Luke 14:28.

How much money will you need to open?

How much money will you need to keep operating?

"God WILL supply all your needs according to His riches in glory by Christ" Now, just what are your needs?

There are three types of financial needs you will run into:
1) Primary (these are indispensable for opening)
2) Secondary (desirable and needed, as money allows)
3) Future (eventually these come in handy)

Primary (indispensable) expenses	**I will need**

Rent (you may need to put up first and last month's rent in advance; avoid a long lease when possible) $ _____

Utility deposits _____

Telephone _____

Lumber (sheetrock, paneling, studs, paint, etc.) _____

Lighting (spotlights, fixtures, wiring, inside, out) _____

Furniture (churches may loan you one or two dozen folding chairs . . . old couches) office desk, several tables, local electric or cable TV companies have spools good to use for tables _____

Outreach director's salary (importance will vary) _____

An insurance policy for Outreach contents _____
   A policy can be obtained for $75 yearly covering $3,000 worth of contents. This is especially important and a wise investment if someone else's equipment is involved at the Outreach.

Refreshments (per week/per month) _____
   Local soda company will rent you a machine for under $20 per month. Same with popcorn and candy machines.

PA System (live music is a big draw to the young). Pawn shops have PA systems $200-$300 for a start. _____

Printing (you'll need letters, envelopes, to start. A local church may let you use its mimeo to copy invitations and loan you an unused typewriter as well). _____

Secondary expenses
A window sign with interchangeable letters _____

Better couches   _____

File cabinets   _____

A lighted marquee with changeable 8" letters   _____
  4'x6' is a good size — $400-$600
Carpet (primary unless you use chairs, couches and
tables)   _____

Mailing equipment (as you develop a regular newsletter)   _____

Future Expenses
An Answer-mate (to take calls when nobody is there)
A van
A multiphone telephone line
Typewriter
Addressing machines
Printing Press, etc.

97

Fund Raising

"Surely there is a vein for the silver, and a place for gold where they
fine it" Job 28:1.
"My God shall supply all your need according to His riches in glory in
Christ Jesus" Philippians 4:19.
"He that gathers in summer is a wise son" Proverbs 10:5.
"You have not . . . because you ask not" James 4:2.

Many today wrongly believe that "Money is the root of all evil." Of
course this is not what I Timothy 6:10 says. The love of money, the lust for
money, is the root of all evil.
On the other hand, we as believers needn't worry about provision.

Provision, indeed, is one of God's very own redemptive names, Jehovah-Jireh, meaning The Lord will provide. (Genesis 22:8).

God has promised to supply all our needs as we first seek his kingdom, His will, and His righteousness in every part of our lives. Although payday with God is not every Saturday night, God has His own mysterious, wonderful ways of providing for His children's needs. Included in this provision plan is His promise to provide for His ministers and ministries as well.

God used many different delivery systems in the Bible:
1) He used the riches of the Egyptians to enrich Israel before their exodus out of the land of slavery.
2) He used ravens (or blackbirds) to bring daily bread and meat to His "Outreach director" Elijah!
3) He used a fish with a coin in its mouth to pay taxes for Peter and Jesus. (Matthew 17:27).
4) He also used widow's mites (Luke 21:2), the sale of believers' lands (Acts 4:36-37), pledges and gifts from other churches (II Corinthians 8:14, and Philippians 4:10).

Faith pledge promises

Oswald J. Smith, pastor of the People's Church in Toronto, Ontario, Canada raised multiplied millions of dollars for overseas missionary work through the use of FAITH PROMISE PLEDGES, for specific projects, worded similarly to the pledge typed in below:

"As God provides and enables me, I will endeavor to give $100 $50 $25 $10 _____each month to the ministry of _____ _____." It seems very simple but it will work for you.

Oral Roberts' successful fund raising comes in part from giving his partners a specific project to become a partner of, helping a worthwhile idea become a reality.

You will find a monthly partner faith pledge of $20/mo. much more valuable than a one time $100 gift for more than merely arithmetic and financial reasons. It is a dependable inflow that can help you plan and expand the Outreach budget.

Several ideas for raising opening funds

1) Plant a seed to meet your need (be a tither and give yourself).
2) Have a telethon or radio-thon on a local Christian radio station.

a) Share your vision with the station; the manager may donate free time.

b) Bring in several saved street people to share the need and their testimonies.

c) Ask people to give above their regular church tithe; this way you avoid church hassles.

d) Have people call in over the air with their pledges, and set two definite amounts:

    1) Immediate cash needed to open the Outreach, and projected opening night date.

    2) The amount of monthly pledges needed to keep at least the minimal Outreach budget going.

A radio fund-raising is the way the Ultimate Trip was opened and it did the job!

3) Contact local pastors and Bible schools, and ask to speak to their mission boards. Share the need and seek their active help. (Would they allow a designated funds offering to be collected or mentioned in their Sunday church bulletin? Ask them.)

4) A newsletter sent to your friends detailing the Outreach specifics will also help raise opening funds.

Where will your main support come from?

You'll find, that as most of a stepping stone's ministry is done outside the church, so most of its support will come from outside the church as well, especially for its first year.

Currently we have three or four churches out of 600 in Tulsa that support us regularly. The great majority of our finances comes from individuals that attend scores of different churches in the Greater Tulsa area.

Support from secular groups

Civic Groups like Kiwanis, Lions Club, Sertoma, Optimists, Jaycee's, etc. are not out to see the world won to Jesus Christ, but they might allow you to present a program that is anti-drug abuse, and having results in rehabilitating young people off of alcohol, drugs, immorality, and crime!

98

Common Sense about Money

"If therefore, you have not been faithful in the unrighteous mammon, who will commit to your trust the true riches? And if you have not been faithful in that which is another man's, who shall give you that which is your own?

"Owe no many anything, but to love one another" Romans 13:8.

Common sense covers a lot of things that are learned the hard way, like keeping forks and fingers out of electric sockets. There are a number of financial electric sockets to steer clear of, and it's worth repeating. Number one is to avoid financial competition with the churches by stressing that the Outreach should be supported by gifts above the Outreach regulars' normal church tithes, which should go to their church!

Churches have all suffered because of the rip-offs like "Elmer Gantry" and "Marjoe." If they are suspicious of who you are, and where the money will go, perhaps they have their reason. The more open the Outreach committee can be in financial matters, the better.

Don't beg! Confess Psalms 35:27 and 37:25 daily, as well as Philippians 4:19 and other prosperity scriptures. God will pay His own way, as long as you let Him lead you His way! He doesn't want us begging from others. WHERE GOD GUIDES, GOD PROVIDES!

Contact a local accountant, preferably a Christian, and ask him to help you set up a bookkeeping, cash-in and cash-out recording system.

Keep an attitude of gratitude. Get in the habit of writing thank-you notes to every donor-partner who contributes.

Pay some if you can't pay it all. If you get behind, don't stay silent and let creditors think you're skipping out. Write them, tell them that you've gotten behind, that you fully intend on paying them, and you'll be sending so much a month until the bill is paid in full. They'll appreciate it and this will not only save your credit rating, but will keep the reputation of the Outreach, the Gospel, and the Lord from being smudged as well. If you "play the cash flow," it will end up "playing" you!

Remember: "The borrower is slave to the lender" (Proverbs 22:7), so the less you stay in debt, the freer you and the Outreach will be! One other word of caution, Proverbs 6:1-3 warns against counter-signing notes for others.

99

A Sample Floor Plan

"Surely in vain is the net spread in the sight of any bird" Proverbs 1:17.
"Wisdom is justified by all its results" Matthew 11:19.

We have found that a rectangular floor plan, going back from the front door towards the platform, far surpasses an even larger square room. In back of the platform, space is left for a back area divided into offices, prayer and counseling rooms. Once again, feel free to adapt the ideas to your specific needs.

You'll notice that the way the room is set up, all eyes are on the platform, away from the front door, allowing sinners, backsliders, and nervous first-timers to come in unnoticed, except for the door-greeter and refreshment-area folks.

Given enough space, personnel, and money, many other "extras" can be built into this basic design, including:

1) Individual soundproofed counseling rooms or booths in the back area.
2) A cassette-tape listening room and cassette library with individual listening earphones.
3) A room where specially chosen youth-oriented Gospel materials can be purchased (such as paperbacks, bumperstickers, Christian T-shirts, etc.).

100

Decorations

"... man looks on the outward appearance" I Samuel 16:7.

Just as different fish take to different bait, so it is in the area of decorating. You will want a contemporary, friendly, down-to-earth style that makes people feel at home. Many little creative, loving "touches" here and there will achieve the decor your "fish" require.

The Ultimate Interior Decorator, the same Holy Spirit who decorates our souls to please God Himself, will direct your decorating. Usually, for young people, informality is a great plus; formality is a hinderance and a barrier.

A local cable TV or electric company should have some free spool tables 18" or 24" high that will look great and work well as you will have most people sitting on your carpeted floor. These can be cut down to 12" high.

K-Mart sells red, glass, fishnet-covered candles for well under a dollar, these will also help set the mood. We dislike the institutional image most storefronts come with; colored, subdued lighting is much more desirable than sterile Fluorescent light.

Posters on the walls, even in the restrooms, can add a lot. They're available from Christain bookstores.

If at all possible, visit one or two other coffee-house Outreaches during their regular open hours, even if it means traveling 100 or 200 miles. It'll be worth it. Let them know you're coming, especially if you need overnight accommodations.

All three of our Outreaches were in a rough, hostile neighborhood, and we boarded over the windows with 1"x8" boards. This not only saved the glass but provided a large area for a beautiful mural as well. Most Outreaches don't need the boards, however.

101

Turning Your Staff
into a T-E-A-M!

"By this shall all men know that ye are My disciples, if ye have love one to another" John 13:35.

A stepping-stone Outreach is not and cannot be a "one-man" show or ministry. Dozens of people with varying backgrounds working together, contributing their different, individual talents will be the only successful path. God will supply the needs you have with not just funds, but much more importantly, with people. His people!

Using a vacuum cleaner to cut the grass will be as fruitless as milking a horse, or using a cow to pull a plow! Each of God's people has his proper work and talent. (Matthew 25:15).

Working with Volunteers

Your staff will be 100% volunteers to start with. Four basic needs of volunteers are:
1) They must know they're wanted, and needed.
2) They must know they are appreciated.
3) They must believe they're doing a worthwhile job.
4) They must know just what is expected of them.

Weekly Organization/Staff Meeting

Your first organization meeting should become a weekly or bi-weekly meeting until opening night. It should then become a weekly staff meeting.

We tried Sunday afternoons at 2 p.m., but found that Saturday nights at 6 p.m. were better. This brought the people to the Outreach 2 hours before opening (at 8 p.m.); one hour before "Happy Hour" (Intercession). It didn't bring them out without a ministry opportunity immediately following the meeting.

Staff should be at the Outreach at least one hour before opening time on "open" nights, prayed up, ready to minister the Word of God and Love of Jesus to a lost and dying world.

102

Planning Opening Night

"According to the grace of God which is given unto me, as a wise masterbuilder, I have laid the foundation . . . " I Corinthians 3:10.

Opening Night Checklist:
1. Utilities turned on?
2. Decorations finished?
3. Chairs and/or carpet?
4. Tracts, Bibles, Jesus papers?
5. Sign out front?
6. Music arranged for?
7. Is the word out?
8. Preliminary staff set up?
9. Phone installed?
10. Refreshments provided?
11. PA system worked out?
12. Staff arrives one hour early?

Your meetings should be bringing a sense of organization and unity in purpose and a family feeling to all those involved. As you work in the Gospel harvest fields together, an increasing spiritual "family feeling" will develop. If it is ever lacking, something is wrong, and that one ultimate spiritual vitamin, God's love, must be supplemented. (See I Corinthians 13 for the full prescription and the Great Physician's recommended dosage.)

103

A Sample Press Release

"For there is no man that does any thing in secret, and he himself seeks to be known openly. If you do these things, show yourself to the world" John 7:4.

(To be sent to local newspapers 10 days before your opening night, along with a good, clear 8 x 10 glossy black and white photo of the Outreach).

A new type of night spot in the _____ area will be opening it's doors _____ , _____ , 19___. It will be a "watering-hole" and meeting place for the young. It will feature live Gospel bands, soloists, and a place for many to find the answers to the hard questions facing young people these days.

Admission will be free, and so will all the refreshments on opening night. The (name of Outreach) will be regularly open weekly on (days of week) from 8-12 p.m. See you at the (name of Outreach) soon.

For more information call or contact

Name

Phone Number (Office)   Phone Number (Home)

104

Opening Night at Last!

"First the blade, then the ear, then the full wheat kernel in the ear" Mark 4:28.

Jesus is there tonight and He is Lord!

He promised in Matthew 18:20 to always be right there in your midst, even where two or three are gathered together in His Name!

This is the big night; official declaration of invasion into satan's fishing pond (or what used to be his!). Bigger nights are ahead, be assured! That's what's great about a "stepping stone" Outreach. It's not just a weekend or week-long evangelistic crusade or revival meeting. It's a year-round continuous on-going soul-winning evangelistic ministry! It will grow! The Outreach will crawl before it walks, and walk before it runs. Be patient! Faith mustard seed (Matthew 17:20) doesn't become a large mustard tree overnight (at least — over one night alone)!

If you have Outreach teams prepared for Opening Night, as well as your Inreach activities, hold them in until 9 p.m. and follow your problems that may arise. Hebrews 12:2 tells us that Jesus used this principle to see beyond the cross to "the joy that was set before Him!" It worked for us as well.

It's up to us to do our best, and God will take over from there and do the rest. You've lit the Outreach fire with what kindling you could find. God has promised to bless your fire, reinforcing your kindling with His logs! Hallelujah . . . just watch and be faithful . . . abide in Him and in His Word . . . He WILL!

105

Yes, You Qualify

"In all truth I tell you, among them that are born of women there has not risen a greater than John the Baptist: notwithstanding he that is least in the kingdom of heaven is greater than he" Matthew 11:11.

Of course, all believers aren't called to be Outreach directors, but many who are called, are stuck in the swampland of not feeling qualified to start such a venture.

Do you remember Moses? The Bible tells us he was, "learned in all the wisdom of Egypt and mighty in word and in deed" (Acts 7:22). He was confident that he was "the one" and killed the Egyptian. He felt "qualified" and fled in fear to take 40 laps around Mt. Sinai! Forty years later when God called him at the burning bush, Moses said: "Lord, I can't talk, I'm unknown, I've no miracle powers, Lord . . . I'M NOT QUA-

LIFIED!" PRAISE GOD, AT THAT POINT GOD KNEW THAT MOSES WAS READY! Moses no longer was relying on his limited self, but rather on God's unlimited resources!

Fulfill God's call for you . . . that's all He asks!

It may just be to help someone else be director . . .

It may be just to assist in Inreach, Backup, or Officework. Whatever God has called you to do know this, IN HIM, you are super-qualified to get the job done!

YOU MAY SAY	BUT	GOD'S WORD SAYS
I just can't do it		I can do all things through Christ . . . Philippians 4:13
I don't have the funds		God shall supply all your needs . . . Philippians 4:19
I'm just too young		Let no one despise your young age, but rather be an example . . . I Timothy 4:12
I'm not bold enough		The righteous (saved) are bold as a lion . . . Proverbs 28:1
I'm just plain afraid		God hasn't given us the spirit of fear but of power . . . II Timothy 1:7
I have no education		We have the mind of Christ . . . I Corinthians 2:16
I'm an unknown, a nobody		God chose what is nothing to make what is nothing something . . . I Corinthians 1:28
I'm too weak		God's strength is made perfect is our weakness . . . II Corinthians 12:9
There'd be too many battles		The battle's not yours, but mine, saith the Lord . . . II Chronicles 20:15

REMEMBER . . .

You can never walk on water until you get out of the boat!

What I am saying is that YOU do qualify, if God is calling you in your heart, to AT LEAST get the project started, and to break the ice!

Outreaches may begin with one person who not only starts the whole idea in motion, but eventually becomes the director, or, they may be born out of one person's concern spreading to others who take over from there. Then again, an Outreach may be born from already existing inter-church committee or church mission board's concern about reaching unreached areas in their "own front yard." There are more ways Outreaches begin than these three. All God asks of each of us is that we're willing to do OUR part! When we do He in turn will do His!

Leviticus 26:8 reads:
   "And five of you shall chose a hundred, and a hundred of you shall put ten thousand to flight: and your enemies shall fall before you by the sword."

It took just One perfect Saviour to bring salvation to all men. (Hebrews 10:12).
It took just one Samaritan woman to bring revival to her entire town.
It took just one Peter (plus God) to preach Pentecost and win 3,000 souls!
It took just one Paul to write ⅓ of the New Testament and reach his world!
It took just one "good Samaritan" to save the traveler's life from sure death!
It took just one Edison to bring electric light to the entire world.
It took just one Hitler to overrun all Europe.
It took just one Churchill to stand up and say: "NO FURTHER!"
It took just one woman to strip prayer and the Bible from USA's Public Schools.
It took just one Anita Bryant to defeat homosexual teachers in all Florida.
   You may not be a multitude, but indeed, you also, are just ONE. One plus God is a majority. One plus God is always enough. You alone can't win, but God and you cannot fail! In your city it may take just one and you just may be the one!

> *"Let others have a quiet chapel*
> *Beneath an ivy-covered bell;*
> *But let me run a rescue ship,*
> *One foot away from Hell."*

"I must work the works of Him that sent me, while it is day: the night is coming, when no man can work" John 9:4.

Additional
National Ministry Contacts

Ron Delagdo, Young World Outreach, Box 4085, Birmingham, AL 35206

James R. Summers, Outreach Ministries of Alabama, Inc., P.O. Box 3194, Huntsville, AL 35810, 205/536-4786

Souls for Christ Outreach, 501 Daisy St., Bakersfield, CAL 93306, Bill Cowles, 805/366-2905 (2 homes for girls — juvenile and over 18)

Agape Incorporated, Box 408, Pinole, CA 94564 organizer: S.O.S. San Francisco, 1980

New Life for Girls, 16250 Juniper, Hesperia, CA 92345, 714/244-9047, Bruce LeDoux

Youth Awakening, 13562 Jackson St., Westminister, CA 92683, Paul Lindbold

Kathy Boone Girls' Home, 1155 Locust, Long Beach, CA 90813, Rev. Frank Miller (Lime Ave. Baptist Church) 213/437-4963

Centrum of Hollywood, 1730 North Sycamore, Hollywood, CA 90028, Kleg Seth, Director, 213/874-2951

Nicky Cruz, P. O. Box 1330, Colorado Springs, CO 80901

Simon Castillo, Helping Hands, 555 Maplewood Ave., Bridgeport, CT 06604

Raul Gonzalez, Youth Challenge, P.O. Box 763, Hartford, CT 06101, 203/728-5199

PIVOT, Alonzo J. Smalls, 17 Quintard Ave., S. Norwalk, CT 06854, 203/838-7685

TLC-A Sanctuary, 854 Conniston Rd., West Palm Beach, FL 33405, Greg and Mary Finegham, 305/833-2390

Somebody Cares (Runaways) 15ew NE 62nd St., Ft. Lauderdale, FL, Jean Hanse, Director, 305/491-4663

Mark House, Haven House, 3012 Chebette Ave., Lakeland, FL 33801

Steppin Stone Farm, Inc., Rt. 2, Box 261B, Lithia, FL 33547, Mrs. Lois Keiser, Director

House of Hope, 456 Pine Holl Rd., Port Richey, FL 33568, Albert Keller, Director

Dan Nawara, Youth Services Program, Box 549, 317 W. Tompkins St., Inverness, FL 32650

John Koth, New Life City Ministry, P.O. Box 42346, Atlanta, GA 30316, Phase I Male and Female

Midwest Christian Training Center, Box 354, Potomac, IL 61865, Directors: Jerry Jones, 217/987-6186

Prevention, Inc., 1336 N. Hoyne St., Chicago, IL 60622

Ron Williams, Hephzibah House, 508 School St., Winona Lake, IN 46590

Three Crosses Ranch, Strawberry Point, IA 52076 Ed Lafgren, Director, 319/933-2278, 12-18 yr. olds.

Helen Martin, New Life Center, Box U, Des Moines, IA 50311

Fellowship Mission, Box 3311, 907 Louisiana, Shreveport, LA 71103

Cornerstone Coffeehouse, 407 Waverly St., Framingham, MA 01701

Rev. Julio Rogue, Youth Pastor, 7008 Belclare Rd. Baltimore, MD 21222

Detroit Challenge, Rev. Julius Dodson, 4540 Scotten, Detroit, MI 48210

Hopehouse, P.O. Box 175, Iron Mountain, MI 49801

The Fish House, 2629 Broadway Ave., Slayton, MN 56172, 507/836-6067, A.J. Larson, Director

New Life for Girls, RD 1, Box 428, Pass Christian, MS 3957a, 601/255-7778

Marketplace Ministry, 337 Pine St., Manchester, NH 03104

Youth Challenge of New Jersey, P.O. Box 703, Perth Amboy, NJ 08862, Director Frank
Collazo

Goodwill Home and Rescue Mission, 79 University Ave., Newark, NJ 07102

Keith Newton, Mission Teens, Inc., P.O. Box 52, Norma, NJ 08347

Don Compton, Shalom Ministries, P.O. Box 668, Santa Fe, NM 87501, 505/988-5591

Russell Resnik, D.A.R.E., P.O. Box 25387, Albuquerque, NM 87125

Better Life for Girls, 150 Genesee, Skaneateles, NY 13152, Rev. Gene Dillard, Director,
315/685-7366 or 475-3992

Faith Christian Academy, Calvary A/G, Stottville, NY 12534, 518/828-6021, Frank Flores,
Pastor

His Farm Fellowship, Box 233A, Berne, NY 12023, Rev. Jay Francis, Director,
518/872-0426 (2505)

Jack and Pat Roberts, Hope Christian Center, Box 189 Boulevard Station, Bronx, NY 10859

Staten Island Girls' Home, 1117 Woodrow Rd., Staten Island, NY 10312

Way Out, Mrs. Anna Villafane, 520 E. 148th St., Bronx, NY 10455

Eckert Youth Home, Bob Derheim, Dir., 1102 7th Ave. East, P.O. Box 223, Williston, ND
58801

Outreach for Youth, Victor Maldonado, 3862 Palmer Rd., Rt. 3, Pataskala, OH 43062

Jose Reyes, Tri-County Girls' Home, 12185 Princeton Pike, Springdale, OH 45256,
513/671-0404

Larry Stitt, 690 Home Ave., Xenia, OH 45385

John Kenzy, Teen Challenge Institute, RD 2, Box 33, Sunbury, PA 17801, 717/286-6442

Lazarus' Tomb, Main St. and 14th Sts., Parnassus Station, New Kensington, PA 15608

New Life Children's Home, RD 2, Box 37, Glen Rock, PA 17327

Demi and Cookie Rodriquez, New Life for Girls, RD 3, Dover, PA 17315, 717/266-5614

Rev. and Mrs. Tom Taylor, Youth Challenge, P.O. Box 411, Travelers Rest, SC 29690

Harold Witmer, Youth Challenge, P.O. Box 149, Clarksville, TN 37040

Edgar Ackerman, Manna House, 535 Stadium Rd., Port Arthur, TX 77640

Catacomb's Ministries, 2300 Benrus Blvd., San Antonio, TX 78228, Fred Fleming, Director,
512/434-4477

Freddie Garcia, Victory Outreach, P.O. Box 37387, San Antonio, TX 78237

The Bridge, 2709 Cherry Lane, Pasadena, TX 77502, Bob and Carolyn Russell,
713/946-3571

Hope Ministries, Box 973, Fredericksburg, TX 78624, Jim Sheppard, Director,
512/699-2258

David Wilkerson, World Challenge, Inc., Rt. 1 Box 80, Lindale, TX 75771

Trinity Ministry Center, 7002 Canton, Lubbock, TX 79413, Cynthia Wynn, Director,
806/792-3363

Michael Hirsch, New Life for Youth, P.O. Box 8209, Richmond, VA 23226

Southeast New Life for Girls, Rt. 1 Box H 41A, Purcellville, VA 22130

Victor Torres, New Life for Youth, P.O. Box 8209, Richmond, VA 23226

Betty Tyson, Emmaus, P.O. Box 77, King George, VA 22485

The Overflowing Cup, 512 Public Ave., Beloit, WI 53511, Dave Fogderud, Director,
608/365-0365

Rev. Maury Blair, Toronto Teen Challenge, 650 Broadview Ave., Toronto, Ontario,

M4K 2P1 Canada

George T. Glover, Hamilton Teen Challenge, 97 John St., Hamilton, Ontario, L8N 3H8 Canada, 526-1414

Mark Moody, Vancouver Challenge, P.O. Box 24777, Station C, Vancouver, B.C., V5T 4E9 Canada

Dwayne Trelenberg (Resident Supervisor), Vancouver Challenge, 982 Granville St., Vancouver, B.C. V5T 4E9 Canada

Rev. John Swank, Apartado 85-I, Ciudad Satelite, Mexico

Dennis Caughy, Teen Challenge, P.O. Box 386, Matamata, North Island, New Zealand

Reto Ala Juventud, Box 3351, Aguadilla, Puerto Rico 00603

Irvin Rutherford, Teen Challenge Tanglin, P.O. Box 424, Republic of Singapore 10

John Ortiz, Teen Challenge, P.O. Box 1337, Fredericksted, St. Croix, U.S. Virgin Islands

Howard Foltz, Eurasia Challenge, 6200 Wiesbaden, Mainzer Strasse 27, West Germany 06121/303435 — telephone

Jim Patton, Teen Challenge Okinawa, P.O. Box 279, Okinawa City, Okinawa, Ken 904 Japan, 098937 — 1330 — telephone

ADDITIONAL TRACT SOURCES

Last Days Evangelical Association, Box 40, Lindale, TX 75771

Evangelism Literature in America C.E.L.A.

Why Suicide? $.50 for 100, ELA, 1445 Boonville, Springfield, MO 65802

Osterhus Tract Society, 4500 W. Broadway, Minneapolis, MN 55422 (send for free catalogue)

Street Church Intl., 352 E. 18th St., Erie, PA 16503

Tract Evangelistic Crusade, Apache Junction, AZ 85220

Under ground Gospel Handouts, Box 1301, Orange, CA 92669

Victory Outreach, P.O. Box 33285, Los Angeles, CA 90033, Sonny Arguinzoni, Director, 213/268-2916

Victory Outreach, 1030 W.W. 39th Street, San Antonio, TX 78237, Freddie Garcia, Director, 512/433-1198

Also write all ministries listed in Chapter 88 for sample tracts and materials.

ADDITIONAL CHANGED LIFE
TESTIMONY BOOKS

BEN ISRAEL, by Arthur Katz with Jamie Buckingham (Born Again Jew), Logos International, $1.95

COME INTO MY PARLOR, by Avril Flinn (former medium and spiritualist), Logos International, $1.95

DEATH OF A GURU, by Ragindranath R. Maharaj with Dave Hunt (former yogi and Eastern Religion Guru), A.J. Holman Company, $3.95

ESCAPE, by Rachel Martin (young woman caught in robe-wearing Jim Roberts cult), Accent Books, $3.95

ELDRIDGE CLEAVER: ICE AND FIRE!, by George Otis (former Black Panther Leader),

Bible Voice, Inc., $1.95

HELLBENT KID, by McClean, $1.95, Whittaker House

KICKED OUT OF THE KINGDOM, by Charles Trombley (former Jehovah's Witness), Whittaker House, $2.95

LOCO, by Ron Depriest with Cecil Hall (former Hells Angels rider), Ft. Worth, TX, $3.00

MARJI, by John Benton (heiress to ghetto), Spire, $1.95

MIRACLE ON DEATH ROW, by Bradford, Whittaker House

ONCE A JUNKIE, by Sonny Arguinzoni (junkie on the streets), Sonny Arguinzoni, $1.25, write Victory Outreach, Box 33285, Los Angeles, CA 90033

PEOPLE'S TEMPLE, People's Tomb — Keornes (story of Jim Jones cult and Guyana Massacre), Logos, $1.95

PERRY, by Perry Desmond (a transformed transexual), Metamorphosis Books, Ironton, MO, $2.95

REBORN, By John A. Oliver (reborn Black Panther), Logos $1.95

TEENAGE RUNAWAY, by John Benton (girl on the street), Spire, $1.50

THIRTY YEARS A WATCHTOWER SLAVE, by W.J. Schnell (converted Jehovah's Witness), Baker Book House, $1.45

THE OTHER WOMAN, by Judy Mamou (ten year stripper, dancer, and prostitute, now in Christ), $3.95, Vision House, Santa Anna, CA 92705

THEY FOLLOWED THE PIPER, by Lee Hultquist (former "Children of God") Logos, $2.95

These testimony books are excellent to place in both church, youth group, and public school libraries. Chaplain Ray, Box 63, Dallas, TX 75221, has over a dozen ex-convict testimony books. Write for names, catalogue, and prices.

CHANGED LIFE TESTIMONY CASSETTES

Ben Israel, by Arthur Katz (a completed modern intellectual Jew), Logos Tapes, 3103 Hwy. 35, Hazlet, NJ 07730, $4.95

Once A Junkie, by Sonnie Arguinzoni (former junkie, now pastor) Logos Tapes

LaDonna (girl in gay lesbian lifestyle 2 years), from Exodus Ministries, c/o Box 5439, Seattle, WA 98105, $3.00

Frank Reuben Testimony (was "gay" 20 years, now free in Christ), write: Love In Action, Box 2655, San Raphael, CA 94902, $4.00

Tell It To The Mafia, Joe Donato (converted former Mafia hit-man), $4.95, Logos Tapes

The Satan Seller, by Mike Warnke (former satanic high-priest), $4.95, Logos Tapes

Luis Torres, testimony (former junkie, now evangelist), $4.00 write: New Hope Ministries, Box 576, Jenks, OK 74037. Write for their free tape catalogue on drugs, witchcraft, etc. 918/299-6351 .

CASSETTES DEALING WITH ROCK AND ROLL:

"Facing the music" by Kelly Carner, 5748 N. Ave., Carmichael, CA 95608, or write us $5.00 per cassette. Cassette holds hundreds of revealing behind-the-scene facts, analyses of lyrics, very devastating to Rock & Roll worshippers.

"Pied Piper" cassette by Rev. Alton Garrison, $5.00 c/o P.O. Box 140331, Dallas, TX 75214
— dynamite expose and sermon on Rock & Roll vs. a Holy Walk.

MISCELLANEOUS ADDITIONAL TOOLS
FOR DRUG, ALCOHOL, AND LUST ABUSES

An Ounce of Prevention, by John King, a church based program of drug abuse prevention, for
each grade K-12, plus 13 adult units, 225 page manual, $27.95, from Christian Civic
Foundation, 3426 Bridgeland Drive, Bridgeton, MO 63044

Addiction Research Foundation, 33 Russell St., Toronto, Ontario, M5S-2S1, ph. 595-6000
(send for catalogue of materials)

Fast Track To Nowhere, Don Wilkerson, Spire Books, $1.95, shocking facts of teenage
alcoholism

How to Live with an Alcoholic and Win, by Hunt, Whitaker House, $1.95

How to Stop the Porno Plague, by Gallagher, Whitaker House, $3.50

Juvenile and Adult Correctional Depts., Institutions, and Parole Authorities Masterlist
(every "prison" in North America listed by state or province, name, phone number, etc.)
336 pages published annually by American Correctional Assoc., 4321 Hartwick Rd.,
Suite L-208, College Park, Md. 20740 (301/864-1070) $20.00

National Institute of Drug Abuse (N.I.D.A.), 11400 Rockville Pike, Rockville, MD 20852
(write for miscellaneous drug abuse materials – free)

Odyssey House, 30911 E. 6th St., NY, NY, top authority in nation on working with child
prostitutes, Dr. Judianne Densen-Gerber (write for information and materials)

Shocking New Facts About Marijuana, Don Wilkerson, Spire Books, $1.95

With Love From Dad, Malcolm E. Smith, 1000 news articles on "pot," 238 pp., Suffolk
House, 155 E. Main St., Smithtown, NY 11787, $9.95 (money back guarantee)

MOVIES/DRUGS
(Excellent ex-drug testimonies)

Jesus Factor Film, by Don Wilkerson, Write: Teen Challenge Headquarters, 1445 Boonville
Ave., Springfield, MO 65803, 417/862-2781

Angel Death, secular but potent film on horrors of Angel Dust (PcP) epidemic sweeping youth
nationally — 30 minutes, 16mm, color, sound, $425/purchase, rent $50/week from
Media Five, 1-800-421-4519

Free Forever, story of Anthony Zeoli, former teenage heroine addict considered incorrigible

Reading, Riting, and Reefers, good in drug prevention work, Films, Inc., 733 Greenbay Road,
Wilmette, IL 60091, 800/232-4222

TOP TEN TESTIMONY & YOUTH FILMS

Cult Explosion, New Liberty Enterprises
Deceived, Jim Jones Cult
Family Gone Wild, New Liberty
Mystics, guru gets saved

Set Free, born again San Quentin inmate testimonies
Eldridge Cleaver Story, ex-Black Panther leader's story
The Enemy, demon-possession, occult
The Occult, ECRF Productions, by Hal Lindsey
Youth Drug Scene, teen on opium, speed, LSD comes to Christ

Write Gospel Film Outreach for a total list of all Christian films in existence, distributors, etc., 1515 S. Denver, Tulsa, OK

Also contact: Christian Film Distributors Assoc., 1457 S. Broadway, Denver, CO, 80210, 303/744-3329 for their free annual membership directory

MATERIAL ON SETTING UP AND RUNNING TELEPHONE HOTLINES

Richard Fort c/o Box 1468, Orange, CA 92668 has access to written materials on Hotlines used by Teen Challenge there. Write him or us for copies.

Sherm Jenne c/o FCF, 700 N. 36th St., Tulsa, OK 74106 has run a hotline, and is putting how to's down into book form. Should be in print.

Melodyland Hotline (714/778-1000) is perhaps the nation's oldest hotline. Write them for written materials and tips.

Also write:
CBN, Virginia Beach, VA
PTL, Charlotte, NC
Trinity Broadcasting, Anaheim, CA, 100 Huntley St., Toronto, Ont. M4Y 2L1 Canada
Las Vegas Christian Center, 3900 Paradise Rd., Las Vegas, NV 81909 for information and telephone counseling aids they are using in their hotline/telephone counseling works.

MISCELLANEOUS MINISTRIES AND TOOLS TO REACH HOMOSEXUALS

Exit Ministries c/o Box 6000, Anaheim, CA 92806

Exodus Ministries c/o Box 5439, Seattle, WA 98105, a coalition of ministries dealing with "gay" problems. Write and ask for Exodus ministries referral list 205/524-8684.

Lifeline Ministries attn: Sharon Kuhn, Box 5439, Seattle, WA 98105

Love in Action Ministries, Box 2655, San Raphael, CA 94902, 415/454-0960, 3 tape series, $10.00. attn: Lori Thorkelson. They travel to churches and give 8-hour "gay ministry" workshops. Also have a live-in house for discipling "ex-gays"

The Outpost, Robbi Kenney & Ed Hurst, Box 4222, Minneapolis, MN 55414, Director, Ed Hurst, has an excellent printed "ex-gay" testimony tract. Also holds seminars & travels.

Theophilus Ministries, Ron Dennis, Director, 218 Warm Springs Rd., Las Vegas, NV 89119, 702/361-3022, have live-in ranch.

There are scores of ministries now dealing with the homosexual sin problem. The above are major ministries in that area. Write them for their monthly newsletter, catalogues of their tracts, cassettes, books and contacts closer to your area.

TOOLS TO REACH HOMOSEXUALS

Cassette tapes: All from Exodus ministries . . .
Help! My Loved One is Gay $3.00
Counseling the Homosexual $3.00
Pitfalls for Christians Dealing With a Gay Past $3.00

BOOKS TO REACH HOMOSEXUALS

The Gay Theology, Kent Philpott, Logos, $1.95
Healing for the Homosexual, The Communion, 2629 NW 39th Expressway
#2B, Oklahoma City, OK 73112, excellent little booklet containing testimonies of 4 ex-
   "gays" counseling tips. ($1.00)
The Homosexual Crisis in the Mainline Church, Jerry Kirk, $3.95 published by Thomas
   Nelson (ministry techniques)
Where Does a Mother Go To Resign, Barbara Johnson, Bethany Fellowship counsel for
   parents of gays, $3.50
Agony of Deception, Ron Rigsbee, Huntington House, 1200 N. Market, Shreveport, LA
   71107, $6.95

You Need The Church

"On this Rock I will build My Church" Matthew 16:18.

There are two classical flaws in Stepping-Stone Street Outreaches. They become either "stopping-stones" or "slapping-stones." "Stopping-stones" hinder street Christians from going deeper into Christ's Body. When Outreach becomes a substitute for the local church, it dies. As a "slapping-stone," the Outreach people develop a "holier-than-thou" attitude toward "church people." This prejudice kills the Outreach as well.

Winning (souls) is just the beginning! Men don't harvest wheat to let it rot in the field . . . harvested crops need a barn. Even so, the church has the manpower, wisdom, resources and maturity to love, protect, direct, and perfect "street-babies." The Church is God's delivery system for His Kingdom on earth.

Many street-people despise church people, and vice-versa. This pleases satan, and greatly displeases God. Ephesians 2:14 tells us Jesus came to break down the middle dividing wall between Jew and Gentile. This is comparable in our day to the common prejudicial wall between "straight" and "street" Christians.

Many say, "I'm still looking for the right church. I ask, "How right?" because if it's perfect when they join it, it will be immediately ruined by their joining. Only One is perfect, and He perfects His people IN and THROUGH His Church.

Many church people want to help reach lost youth but don't know how. All street ministries need what the Church has to offer them, but many feel unwanted and unappreciated. Such was I. I was saved, I loved Jesus, I wanted to reach the lost. But I had no use for the Church. As far as I was concerned, the Church was out to lunch, playing religious games while the world "burned." It took me seven years as a Christian to finally outgrow and discard this ignorant, spiritually immature, but all too common street prejudice. Finally, God showed me I related to street people in their way (levi's, informality), and I needed to relate to church people in their way. Bit by bit, we learned to respect each other for our respective talents.

YOU NEED THE CHURCH! Without the Church, not only the Street-Outreach will fail, but you yourself will fail as a Christian. I go to church now as well as to rock concerts and bars witnessing. I do it for Jesus Christ. He blesses me for it. It is the Church that made my ministry and this book possible. I PRAISE GOD FOR HIS CHURCH! THE SOONER THE BETTER . . . BUT SOONER OR LATER . . . YOU WILL TOO!

National Association of Street Ministries and Resources

"They overcame satan by the Blood of the Lamb . . . and their testimony" Revelation 12:11.

"Equipping (arming) the saints to accomplish THEIR work of ministry" Ephesians 4:12.

Christians across America are confronted daily with satan's end-time flood of filth. This flood is catching the saints without the proper tools they need to rescue multitudes going down around them. But God's promise in His Word stands true: "When the enemy shall come in like a flood, the Spirit of the Lord shall raise up a standard against him" (Isaiah 59:19)!

Several weeks ago a pastor called asking me for help with the cocaine problem in his town of 1500 people. Another pastor asked for materials to deal with a ten-year-old boy on the verge of homosexuality. Still another pastor asked for anything; a tract, testimony book, cassette, or contact with an actual "former exhibitionist" to deal with a man in his church who was caught in that same "sin-trap."

The truth is, people formerly into every sin that exists have been set free by Christ's blood and are new creations in Him. These people want to help liberate others from these "wolf-traps."

The problem is, millions of young people are being enslaved by cults, drugs, alcohol, and lust abuses. And **by-and-large, the unlimited power of a personal testimony** (past experience with, and current victory in Christ over these same "wolf-traps") **is not being used to even one percent of its potential!**

The solution is, hook up the saved "used-to-be's" with the lost "are now's" through a comprehensive stockpiling and listing of changed-life testimony books, tracts, cassettes, films, personal correspondence and counseling. For example, a saved "ex-exhibitionist" best understands a current exhibitionist's problems.

How to implement it: A computer, a 24 hour, 800 toll free national watts line, and advertising in national Christian publications, and over Christian radio and television to both alert and involve Christians.

God is moving us towards this. We are currently registering, collecting, and creating books, tracts, testimony cassettes, and an ever-growing file of personal contacts which will eventually cover every "sin-area" on the next page (and more).

When a Christian calls in someday asking for help, day or night, the phone counselor will press the computer button for the problem area, theosophy, cocaine, or whatever. The computer will then read out 1) whatever materials are available on that subject and 2) which persons living within either a 50-or 100-mile radius of the person (or Christian in need) have had experience with that particular sin area, with his phone number, address, etc.

One example: When the pastor here asked for help with an exhibitionist, I personally knew of no resources, tracts, cassettes, books or personal contacts or ministries dealing with exhibitionism. BUT I'M SURE THERE ARE SOME SOMEWHERE NATIONALLY IN THE BODY OF CHRIST . . . THEY JUST NEED TO BE LOCATED AND MADE AVAILABLE. Now when the National Resource Center is set up the pastor, you, or I could have called in. Not only would tracts, cassettes and at least one book have been on the computer readout under "exhibitionism," but someone's name (or several) would have shown up in the Tulsa area, someone who once was an "exhibitionist," but who now is a blood-washed, born again Christian, just dying to help someone . . . anyone out of the psychological torment and bondage of exhibitionism that he formerly was into himself . . . BEFORE CHRIST!

"Satan-Traps" — category sheets based on using Revelation 12:11 and computer technology

FALSE RELIGIONS, CULTS, & PHILOSOPHIES
atheism
agnosticism
astara
anthroposophical society
ananoa marga
ashrams
Baba ram das
Buddhist
Children of God (Moses David Berg)
Christian Science
Deism
Divine Light Mission (Guru Maharj Ji)
Encounter Groups
EST (Werner Erhard)
Evolution
Existentialism
The Farm (Steve Gasken)
Fatherhood of God/ Brotherhood of man
Gurus (misc.)
Guru Dev.
Hinduism
Hare Krishna
Holy Order of Mans
Humanism
Jesus Christ Lightning Amen
Jehovah's Witnesses
Judaism
Orthodox
Conservative
Reform
Hasidic
"Love Israel" Cult
Liberal Christianity
Metropolitan Community Church (homosexuals)

Meditation (misc.)
Meher Baba
Mormons
Reincarnation
Rosicrucians
Science of Midn (Rev. Ike)
Scientology
SDS (Students Democratic Soc)
Seventh Day Adventist
Shintoism
Swami's (misc.)
Sufi's
Telekenesis
Theosophy
Thanatology
Transcendental Meditation (Maharisi Mahesh Yogi)
UFO's
Unification Church (Moonies)
Unitarian
Unity
Way, The (Wierwille)
Walk, The (John Robert Stevens)
White-Robers
Witness Lee (The "local" church)
Yippies
Yoga
Yogi's (misc.)
Yogi Bajan
Yoga (Bajan)
Yoga (Kundalini)
zen
other.

DRUGS
user
dealer
manufacturer

grower
(Please fill in approximate amounts)
angel dust (PCP)
amphetamine (speed)
cocaine
dilaudid
freebase
GRASS (Marijuana)
HASHISH hash oil
heroine
LSD (acid)
mescaline
morphine
Peyote
Preludins
Quaaludes
reds
THC
injected drugs
junkie
on what
how long
injected # of times
other
busted for drugs

ALCOHOL
alcoholic
bartender
bouncer
beer
wine
wino
up & outer
skid-row
whiskey
nightclubs
discos

CRIME
ex-convict
years in jail
where
armed robbery
black market
counterfeiting
bribery
extortion
forgery
gambling
hijacker
hit-man
kidnapper
mafia
murder
numbers racket

SUICIDE
# of times
manner attempted?
smuggler
theft
vandalism
white slaver

LUST ABUSE
abortion
adultery
bi-sexual
child abuse
child molester
child pornography
child prostitution
drag queen
exhibitionist
female impersonator
fornication
groupie
incest
homosexual
lesbian

male prostitution
massage parlors
necrophilia
nymphomania
nude modeling
nudist camp
open marriage
"peeping tom"
pimp
Playboy
pornographer
prostitution
rapist
stripper
transexual (sex change)
topless dancer
S&M (Sado-masochist)
Transvestite
unwed mother
wife-beater
wife-swapper
other.

OCCULT & DEMONIC
animal sacrifice
Astral projector
astrology
black magic
black masses
blood-rites
chart-reader
ESP
demon possession
fortune-telling
hypnotism
I Ching
Illuminati (John Todd)
Kaballah
Masons

mind control
necromancy
orgies
palm reader
pyramids
rosicrucians
satan worship
satan priesthood
spiritualist
voodoo
warlock
white magic
witch

POLITICS
anarchist
communist
marxist

PREJUDICE
Black Muslim
Black Panther
Jewish
Defense League
John Birchers
KKK
Nazis
P.L.O.

LIFESTYLES
Biker
Communes
Gangs
Hobo
Jet Setter
Mental Asylum
Rock & Roll
Runaway
Vegetarian

You can help make this National Resource Ministry Dream Come True:

1) Whatever materials, cassettes, books, tracts, tract societies, and ministries dealing with the following problem areas that you know about, run across, or can locate, **PLEASE TAKE THE TIME AND EFFORT to send us that information** . . . and if possible, a sample of the tract, cassette, book or ministry catalog or literature.

2) Pray and intercede for this "resource" ministry to become a reality.

3) Become a partner with Worldshakers in your giving, so that we will have the national financial undergirding necessary to step out soon into launching this National Resource ministry.

4) Send us names of Christian friends you believe would be interested in knowing more about this project. Also send the names of coffeehouses, live-in houses, drug-abuse programs, and any and all specialty ministries in your area, or that you know of nationally or abroad.

Outreach — Planting Street Ministry Workshop

In the past eighteen months, I've received over 120 requests from Christians in almost all fifty states. They need and want a Street Outreach opened in their areas. God has led me to develop an Outreach planting workshop not only to supplement this book, but to personalize the workshop to a specific area's particular needs and problems.

We held our first National Outreach Workshop here in Tulsa June 21, 1980. Believers from street-needy areas came from eleven states, and from both coasts. We will be moving ahead into more Outreach Workshops across the nation. AND in specific churches to help God's people take Him to THEIR streets! Below is a response from one of our Outreach-planting Workshop participants:

"I came home ten feet above the ground. We're checking out buildings for our Outreach, and HAVE SO MUCH TO DO! Thank you for the workshop. I think if it had been any longer, my brain would have cried: 'Overload!'

"Again, thank you for the ideas, the instruction, the encouragement, the love, and for letting God use you mightily. And thanks for letting us learn from your mistakes . . . life's too short to make all the mistakes ourselves.

We need to take advantage of learning from others."

M.C., Wisconsin

If your area needs a Street-Outreach/Street Ministry begun, write us, pray about attending our next Tulsa workshop, a regional workshop in your area, or pray about arranging a workshop specifically held in your town or church to help your Street Outreach get launched.

ADDITIONAL OUTREACH IDEAS

1. **Additional soulwinning materials** (send for catalogues of materials)
Kenyon's personal evangelism course, Box 33067, Seattle, WA $2.00
Bold ones on Campus, by Deffner, Whitaker House, $2.50
Lay Evangelism, Inc., Box N. Rt. 718, Pleasant Hill, OH 45359
Personal survey evangelism: write us, we'll send you one.
Jail ministry brochure: write, Box 63, Dallas, TX 75221
2. **Training soulwinners and teams:**
a. **Make up sample soulwinning conversations on paper. Write for different** "category" types, "dopers," "moonies," etc.
b. **Have team members write their name down on several 3x5's with phone numbers** *before* hitting the streets. Saves interruptions later.
c. Buy books on evangelism. Have them available to buy at the Outreach.
3. **Tract Evangelism:** mail back-in tracts must now be at least 3"x5".
Put at bottom of tracts in 5 pt. type: Do not destroy; PASS ON TO another.
4. **Wholesale Bullhorn Supplier:** Ametron, Sound Co., 1200 N. Vine, Hollywood sells Fanon bullhorns (see p. 82) to the public at wholesale price.
5. **Servant business cards:** the title "servant" or servant of Christ is a lot more effective on the streets than evangelist, director, etc.
6. **Run spot evangelism ads** in "Thirty" type community papers. Run ads like "Needs a friend?, call   ". Have them "reverse" it is possible.
7. **Write** American Atheist Box 2117, Austin, TX and NORMAL (National Organization for Reform of Marijuana Laws) 2317 M. St. West, D.C., to keep aware of what their latest move is. They will add you to their mailing list.
8. **Annual Rose Parade Outreach:** America's largest annual crowd of 1.5 million. Write Sondra Berry, Box 3684, Pasadena, CA 91103. On Jan. 1, 1980, she led hundreds of Christians out soulwinning: scores were saved!
9. **Mardi Gras Outreach:** Each year JPUSA, Chicago, and Christ For The Nations, Dallas, sends outreach teams. Write them or us for information.
10. **National Smoke-In (Preach-In) Alert:** Yearly, since 1975, thousands of pro-dope forces have rallied July 4th in D.C. at the White House to force marijuana legalization. We preached there in 1979, and plan on '81, '82, til He comes! Write for more information.
11. **S.O.S. San Francisco and Summer Inst. of Evangelism.** Darrell Walker, Director of Crown of Life Inst. for Urban Evangelism held a 10 week training school the summer of 1980. This culminated in S.O.S., San Franciso August, 1980, where over 2,000 Christians from across the USA worked together sharing Christ on the streets of San "Sodom" Francisco. Write him for future ministry developments, or for help in

doing something similar in your city. Box 408, Pinole, CA 94564.

12. **Christian Prison Volunteers** get 400 new prisoners requesting Christian correspondence monthly. Write: Box 1949 E. Hollywood, CA 90028. **Also:** The back page of Rolling Stone magazine lists monthly 30 prisoners seeking mail. They state they have too many requests to list them all. Write and ask if they'll pass contacts to you if you supply them with stamped envelopes with your address!

ADDITIONAL INREACH IDEAS

1. Followup

a. Preaddress and stamp envelopes to new converts, hand out at weekly staff meetings.

b. Make up local Christian information and resource sheets for new converts. Include: lists of Bible studies (night, time, address, phone numbers, etc.) local Christian radio stations, upcoming concerts, Christian cinemas, coffeehouses, live-in houses, phone numbers of strong 'street' Christians, and names of 'street' loving local churches.

c. Read "*Dynamics of Personal Followup*" by Gary Kuhne, Zondervan

2. Staff: For $4.00 have made up staff badges: "Rainbow's End, Counselor." Helps newcomers perceive order amidst informality.

a. Implement a "most helpful volunteer" award each month.

b. Keep a "minutes" book of each staff meeting; Each week review.

3. Music:

a. Have new musicians fill out a fundamental Christian belief checklist sheet. Include basics: Christ's Deity, blood atonement, etc.

b. At the end of each "set," have musician or staff announce that people who care (have staff raise hands) are available to 'rap.'

4. Decorations:

a. India import tapestries cut into fours make handsome tablecloths for spool tables.

b. 12" square mirror stick-on tiles help make an intriguing mirror cross, 8' high, 6' wide.

c. Fire extinguishers are legally required.

d. Keep 2 emergency phone numbers inside front door, visible from outside.

5. Locating an Outreach Director: an addition to p. 195, also contact: Frank Reynolds, National Teen Challenge Coordinator, 1445 Boonville Ave., Springfield, MO 65802 (417/862-2781).

ADDITIONAL BACKUP IDEAS

1. Organization? Need help?

a. Global Sales, Box 15551, Santa Ana, CA 92705 puts out a wallet sized "Classic Diary System" that includes not only daily dated sheets, but monthly sheets for the next 16 months with each day spaced. It also contains an alphabetical section, credit card holder, penholder, stamp holder, etc. A portable desk in your pocket. Send for free price list. Costly but well worth every penny!

b. **Duplicate Checks**
Each check has an exact carbon replica, helps keep track of loose checks if you carry and use them.
c. **Books on Time Management**
1. *How to Get Control of Your Time and Your Life*
     by Alan Lakein, $1.95, Signet Books, Box 999, Bergenfield, NJ
2. *Time Trap* by Alex MacKenzie
3. *Managing Your Time* by Ted Engstrom
2. **Development (fundraising):**
a. Fotomat (1-800-325-1111, in Missouri: 1-800-392-1717) Put 400 feet of Super 8 sound film or 100 35mm slides onto a videocassette for approximately $10.00
b. Write D.A.C.I. (Development Association for Christian Institutions)
Box 4215 S. Columbia Pl., Tulsa, OK 74105 (915) 747-4141) Ask to receive monthly newsletter. Excellent fundraising ideas.
c. Write us — we'll send you our current ministry brochures.
d. Write: Foundation Center: 818 Lexington Ave. N.Y. N.Y. for fundraising ideas.

TEEN CHALLENGE

The ministry of Teen Challenge is varied and diverse. The services rendered are determined by human need in the city, region, or area served and the purpose of the individual center. The overall purpose of Teen Challenge has been stated. "Evangelize people who have life-controlling problems and initiate the discipleship process to the point where the student can function as a Christian in society applying spiritually motivated biblical principles to relationships in the family, local church, chosen vocation, and the community. Teen Challenge endeavors to help people become mentally sound, emotionally balanced, socially adjusted, physically well, and spiritually alive." Each Teen Challenge Center will have a vital part in achieving this objective.

Phase I — Basic confrontational evangelism. The purpose and method is to conduct evangelism outreach directly to the people i.e. street meetings, jail and prison services, helpline substance abuse prevention programs, and drop-in counseling, literature distribution, etc.

Phase II — Crisis Intervention, pre-induction, and referral. Persons with life-controlling problems are provided a place to stay long enough to meet the immediate crisis, to receive a clear witness of the gospel, and to evaluate whether they need or desire the long term discipleship training offered by Teen Challenge.

Phase III — Induction. This is the beginning of the discipleship process which involves 10-12 weeks of Bible study and character development.

Phase IV — Training Center. Long term residential program, 8-12 months involving Christian growth and development, academic, and vocational improvement.

Phase V — Re-entry. This process is commonly initiated by the induction centers and frequently provides one or more of the following: temporary housing, personal and family counseling, assistance in finding suitable employment and a vibrant church fellowship.

TEEN CHALLENGE, Division of Home Missions
1445 Boonville Ave., Springfield, Missouri 65802
417/862-2781 ext. 1367
Frank M. Reynolds, National Teen Challenge Representative

Teen Challenge Centers
and Outreaches

ALABAMA
Teen Challenge
of Birmingham, Inc.
P.O. Box 3626
542 15th St. S.W.
Birmingham, AL 35211
Director: Dan Delcamp
205/780-2094
(Phase I, II, Male Res.)

ALASKA
Teen Challenge
of Alaska, Inc.
236 West 10th St.
Anchorage, AK 99501
Executive Director:
Joe Filancia
Director: Duane Guisinger
(Phase I, II, III, IV, Male
and Female Res. Ages 16
and over)

Teen Challenge
Training Center
Star Rt. Box 6912
Palmer, AK 99645
Director: Duane Guisinger
Supervisor:
Mrs. Doris (Mark) Freeman
(Phase I, II, Female Res.)

ARIZONA
Main Administrative Office
Teen Challenge of Arizona
P.O. Box 5966   85703
729 N. Fourth Ave.
Tucson, AZ 85705
Executive Director:
Snow Peabody
602/792-1790

Teen Challenge
of Phoenix
P.O. Box 13444   85002
2810 N. 16th St.
Phoenix, AZ 85006
Director: Wayne Soemo
602/277-7469
(Phase I)

Teen Challenge
of Yuma
P.O. Box 123
1700 S. First Ave.,
Suite 112
Yuma, AZ 85364
Director: John Sanchez
602/783-1147
(Phase I)

Springboard Home
for Runaways
3644 Nufer
Tucson, AZ 85705
Supervisior:
Paul & Diane Tripp
602/792-1790

Teen Challenge of Tucson
729 N. Fourth Ave.
Tucson, AZ 85705
Director: Greg Brewer
602/792-1790
(Phase I)

Christian Growth Center
P.O. Box 593
Cave Creek, AZ 85331
Director: James Beach
602/465-7810
(Phase II, III Male Res.)

ARKANSAS
Teen Challenge
of Arkansas, Inc.
Rt. 10, Box 8155
Hot Springs, AR 71901
Executive Director:
Tim Culbreth
501/624-2446
(Phase I, II, III, IV,
Male Res., 18 and over)

King's Ranch
P.O. Box 11
Morrow, AR 72749
Director: Robert Stone
501/848-3105
Phase II, III, Male Res.
Ages: 13-17

CALIFORNIA (Northern)
Teen Challenge
Men's Center
San Francisco Center
P.O. Box 40100
1464 Valencia St.
San Francisco, CA 94140
Director: Tom Alexander
415/285-1353
(Phase I, II, III, V. Male Res.
Ages 18 and over)

Oakland Men's Crisis
Care Center
P.O. Box 5097
2222 89th Ave.
Oakland, CA 94605
Director: Cary Busk
415/562-1141 or 632-1928
(Phase I, II, III, V
Male and Female Res.
Ages: 18 and over)

Teen Challenge
Prison Team
P.O. Box 1755
San Jose, CA 95109
Director: Joe Sambrano
408/984-0876
or 241-0691-home
(Phase I)

The Bridge Outreach Center
506 W. Fourth St.
Antioch, CA 94509
Director: Glen White
415/757-0577
(Phase I, II)

New Life Coffee House
438 E. Market Street
Stockton, CA 95202
Director:
Bill Ross
209/463-4979
(Phase I, II)

Gwen Wilkerson
Home for Girls
P.O. Box 28464
204 Asbury St.
San Jose, CA 95159
Director: Conrad Cooper
408/275-8240
(Phase I, II, III, V
Female Res.
Ages: 18 and over)

Jacob's Ladder Coffeehouse
140 S. Second Street
San Jose, CA 95110
Director: Conrad Cooper
408/275-9617
(Phase I)

Sacramento Women's
Center
P.O. Box 160343
3030 "O" Street
Sacramento, CA 95816
Director: Efraim Diaz
916/456-3819
(Phase I, II, III, IV, V,
Female Res.
Ages: 18 and over)

CALIFORNIA (Southern)
Main Office
P.O. Box 5068
5445 Chicago
Riverside, CA 92517
District Director:
Glenn Timmons
District Administrator:
Richard Fort
714/683-4241
Director of Evangelism:
Dennis Griffeth

Bakersfield Teen Challenge
P.O. Box 1011   93302
326 S. "H" Street
Bakersfield, CA 93304
Director: Patrick Harrelson
805/832-4920
(Phase I, II, III, Male Res.
Ages: 18 and over)

Los Angeles Teen Challenge
P.O. Box 18946
2249-63 S. Hobart Blvd.
Los Angeles, CA 90018
Director: Byron Berwick
213/732-8141
(Phase I, II, III, Male Res.
Ages: 18 and over)

Christian Life School
P.O. Box 5068
5445 Chicago Ave.
Riverside, CA 92517
Director: Henry Luzano
714/683-4241
(Phase IV, Male Res.
Ages: 18 and over)

San Diego Teen Challenge
P.O.Box 8087   92102
1304 24th St.
San Diego, CA 92102
Director: Clando Brownly
714/239-4157
(Phase I,II)

Ventura Teen Challenge
P.O. Box 1064
27777 Ventura Blvd.
Director: Herb Davis
805/648-3295
(Phase I, II, III, IV,
Female Res.
Ages: 17 and over)

COLORADO
Administrative Office
Teen Challenge
of the Rocky Mtns, Inc.
Box 5000
Woodland Park, CO 80863
Executive Director:
Royce Nimmons
303/687-6550

Christian Growth Ranch
Box 5000
Woodland Park, CO 80863
Director: Royce Nimmons
(Phase IV,
Male and Female Res.)
303/687-6550

Denver Center
17467 Emerson Street
Denver, CO 80218
Director: Randy Rowe
303/839-1465
(Phase I, II, III, V
Male & Female Res.
Ages: 16 and over

Teen Challenge
Coffeehouse
212 E. Pikes Peak Ave.
Colorado Springs, CO
80903
Director: Jim Zilonka
303/635-3020

Salt Lake City
Teen Challenge is
temporarily closed.

FLORIDA
Haven House
Rt. 1, Box 1460
Avon Park, FL 33825
Executive Director:
Reg Yake
Director: Dale Weaver
813/453-4650
(Phase I, II, III,
Female Res.
Ages: 17 and over)

Jacksonville
Teen Challenge
1409 Cherry Street
Jacksonville, FL 32205
Executive Director:
Reg Yake
Director: Mark Goodman
904/384-6739
(Phase I, II, III, Male Res.
Ages: 17 and over)

Miami Teen Challenge
3516 N.W. 7th Ave.
Miami, FL 33127
Director: Bob Stultz
305/633-4157

HAWAII
Teen Challenge of Hawaii
Main Office:
66-470 Kam Highway
Haleiwa, HI 96712
Executive Director:
Dan Vargas
808/637-6215

Keola Hou Training Center
P.O. Box 1016
Waipahu, HI 96797
Director: Larry Reed
808/668-8330
(Phase I, II, III, IV
Male Res.
Ages: 18 and over)

Teen Challenge
Hawaii-Maui
Camp Olowalu
P.O. Box 250
Wailuku, HI 96793
District Director:
Billie Sexton
Business Adminstrator:
Joe Crowe
808/661-3914
(Phase I, II, III, IV,
Male & Female Res.
Ages: 14 and over)

ILLINOIS
Chicago Teen Challenge
315 S. Ashland Ave.
Chicago, IL 60607
Director: Ed Howe
312/421-0111
(Phase I, II, III
Male Res.
Ages: 17-29)

Rockford Teen Challenge
1304 W. State Street
Rockford, IL 61102
Director: Mike Lindquist
815/962-3790
(Phase I, II, III
Male Res.,
Ages: 18 and over)

INDIANA
Indianapolis
Teen Challenge
2542 N. Delaware St.
Indianapolis, IN 46205
Director: Kenneth Isom
317/924-5463
(Phase I, II, III, IV,
Male & Female Res.
Ages: under 17)

IOWA
Teen Challenge
3650 Cottage Grove
Des Moines, IA 50311
Executive Director:
Roger Helle
Supervisor: Don Dey
515/277-8864
(Phases I, II, III, Male Res.
Ages: 18 and over)

KENTUCKY
Teen Challenge
of Louisville, Inc.
P.O. Box 4382
1228 E. Broadway
Louisville, KY 40204
Director: James Franklin
502/583-3155
(Phase I, II, III,
Female Res.
Ages: 11-19)

Teen Challenge
of Lexington
P.O. Box 12193
Lexington, KY 40581
Director: Terry Collier
606/299-0489
(Phase I, II Crisis Center)

Teen Challenge
of Owensboro
P.O. Box 2542
Owensboro, KY 42302
Director: Richard Kennedy
502/926-7245

LOUISIANA
Louisiana Teen Challenge
P.O. Box 888
Folsom, LA 70434
Executive Director:
Rawson Carlin
504/796-3130
(Phase I, II, III, Male Res.
Ages: 18 and over)

Caring Place
431½ Dauphine St.
New Orleans, LA 70112
Ass't Director:
Keith Ruggles
504/524-6401

MARLYAND
WASHINGTON D.C.
Teen Challenge
P.O. Box 8591
6900 Central Ave.
Capitol Heights, MD
20027
Director: Michael Zello
301/350-6373
(Phase I, II, III, Male Res.
Ages: 17 and over)

MASSACHUSETTS
New England
Teen Challenge
P.O. Box 3265
1315 Main Street
Brockton MA 02403
Executive Director:
Robert Beuscher
Director: Ken Baum
617/586-1494
(Phase I, II, III, IV, V
Male Res.
Ages: 16 and over)

Girl's Home
1279 Main St.
Brockton, MA 02403
Director: Susie Beuscher
(Phase I, II, III,
Female Res.
Ages: 16 and over)

MICHIGAN
Detroit Teen Challenge
Main Office:
14600 Kentfield
Detroit, MI 48223
Men's Residence:
238 W. Hazelburst
Ferndale, MI 48220
Director: Sam Dobroiks
313/531-0111
(Phase I, II, III, IV
Male Res.
Ages: 18 and over)

Women's Resident Center
14600 Kentfield
Detroit, MI 48223
(Phase I, II, III, IV
Female Res.
Ages: 18 and over)

Teen Challenge
of Greater Muskegon
440 Pontaluna Rd.
Muskegon, MI 49444
Director: Phil McCain
616/798-3788 or 798-3786
(Phase I, II, III, IV, V.
Male & Female Res.
Ages: 18 and over)

Teen Challenge of Saginaw
P.O. Box 1020
503 N. Jefferson
Saginaw, MI 48606
517/753-1103
Director: Salvador Flores
(Phase I, II, III, Male Res.
Ages: 18 and over)

MISSISSIPPI
Teen Challenge
of Mississippi
P.O. Box 1143
3219 Nathan Hale Ave.
Pascagoula, MS 39567
Director: Mark May
601/769-8332
(Phase I, II, III, IV
Female Res.
Ages: 17 and over)

MISSOURI
Mid-America
Teen Challenge
Training Center
P.O. Box 1089
Oriole Road, Route 1
Cape Girardeau, MO
63701
Director:
Herbert Meppelink
314/335-6508
(Phase I, III, IV. Male Res.
Ages: 17 and over)

Heart of America
Teen Challenge
Mail: P.O. Box 15326
Kansas City, MO 64106
Director: Merle Horning
House: 82 S. 13th St.
Kansas City, KS 66102
913/371-2234
Phase I, II, III

Teen Challenge of St. Louis
P.O. Box 213
High Ridge, MO 63049
Director: C.R. Kersten
314/667-1776 or 677-1778
(Phase I, II, III, Male Res.
Ages: 18-29)

Teen Challenge
of the Ozarks
P.O. Box 429
1641 E. St. Louis St.
Springfield, MO 65801
Director: Doug Dezotell
417/864-6305
(Phase I, II)

MONTANA
Teen Challenge of Montana
P.O. Box 31173
Billings, MT 59107
Director: Gary Clark
406/656-9997
(Phase I, II, III,
Female Res.
Ages: 18 and over)

NEBRASKA
Teen Challenge
of the Midlands
2916 N. 58th St.
Omaha, NE 68104
Executive Director:
Roger Helle
402/551-2322
(Phase I, II, III,
Female Res.
Ages: 18 and over)

NEW YORK
New York Teen Challenge
444 Clinton Ave.
Brooklyn, N.Y. 11238
Executive Director:
Don Wilkerson
Director: Randy Larson
212/789-1414
(Phase I, II, Male Res.
Ages: 17 and over)

Camp Champion
Box 113,
Mohigan Lake Road
Glen Spey, NY 12737
914/856-3652
(Phase III, IV, Male Res.
Ages: 17 and over)

The Walter Hoving Home
Box 194
Philipsbrook
and Avery Road
Garrison, NY 10524
Director: John Benton
914/424-3674
(Phase III, IV,
Female Res.)

Empire State
Teen Challenge
P.O. Box 145
Rochester, NY 14601
(Phase I, II, III)
Executive Director:
Reg Yake
75 Alexander St.
Rochester, NY 14620
Director: Donald Boldt
716/325-7123
(Phase I, II, II Male Res.
Ages: 18 and over)

Syracuse . . .
(Phase I, II, III)
124 Furman Street
Syracuse, NY 13205
Director: Dave Pilch
315/478-4139
Male Res.
Ages: 18 and over

Buffalo . . . (Phase I, II)
500 Leroy Ave.
Box 25, Station F 14212
Buffalo, NY 14215
Director: Paul Edwards
716/832-5559

NORTH CAROLINA
Teen Challenge
of North Carolina
Rt. 2, Box 260
Harmony, NC 28634
Director:
Genevieve Wheeler
704/546-2531
(Phase I, II, III, Male Res.
Ages: 18 and over

Greater Piedmont
Challenge
Teen Challenge, Inc.
P.O. Box 7795
Greensboro, NC 27407
Director: Jim Sparks
919/292-7795
(Phase I, II, III, Male Res.
Ages: 18 and over)

OHIO
Teen Challenge Village
3032 Perry Park Rd.
Perry, OH 44084
Director: Robert Harman
216/951-2893
(Phase I, II, III, IV
Male Res.
Ages: 18 and over

Cincinnati
Teen Challenge, Inc.
Box 249
1466 US 50
Milford, OH 45150
Executive Director:
James Gray
Administrator: Larry Stitt
513/248-0452
(Phase I, II, III, IV, V
Male Res.
Ages: 18 and over)

Friendship Center
1410 Vine St.
Cincinnati, OH 45210
Executive Director:
James Gray
Administrator: Jeff Baker
513/721-5755
(Phase I, II, V)

Columbus Teen Challenge
47 E. 12th Ave.
Columbus, OH 43201
Director: Carey Girgis
614/294-5331
(Phase I, III, IV, V,
Female Res.,
Ages: 18 and over)
(Phase II, III, Male Res.)

PENNSYLVANIA
Teen Challenge
of Western Pennsylvania
Box 55
LeFever Hill Rd.
Rural Ridge, PA 15075
Director: Richard Turgeon
412/265-4110
(Phase II, III, IV, Male
and Female Res.
Ages: 18 and over)

Teen Challenge
Training Center
Box 98
Rehrersburg, PA 19550
Director: Reg Yake
717/933-4181
(Phase IV, Male Res.
Ages: 18 and over)

Teen Challenge
Home for Boys
P.O. Box 4196
156 W.Schoolhouse Lane
Philadelphia, PA 19144
Executive Director:
Reg Yake
Director: Tim Bonarrigo
215/849-2054 or 849-9974
(Phase II, III, Male Res.)

Teen Challenge
Home for Girls
P.O. Box 4196
329 E. Wister St.
Philadelphia, PA 19144
Executive Director:
Reg Yake
Director: Dave Stewart
215/843-2887
(Phase II, III, Female Res.)

Harrisburg Teen Challenge
P.O. Box 3143   17105
1421 N. Front St.
Harrisburg, PA 17102
Executive Director:
Reg Yake
Director: Terry Whitmore
717/233-6549
(Phase I, II, III, Male Res.
Ages: 18 and over)

PUERTO RICO
Teen Challenge
de Puerto Rico
Box 4273
Bayamon Gardens Station
Bayamon, PR 00619
Director: Jaime Perez
809/783-0522
(Phase II, III, Male Res.
Ages: 18 and over)

SOUTH DAKOTA
New Life Educational
Foundation
(a division of Teen Challenge
Ministries)
317 Third Ave.
Brookings, SD 57006
Director: Mark Flaten
605/692-9753
(Phase I, II, III, IV
Ages: 12-30)

TENNESSEE
Teen Challenge
of Chattanooga
P.O. Box 3396
510 S. Willow St.
Chattanooga, TN 37404
Director: Wayne Keylon
Intake Supervisor:
Paul Montoya
615/698-3495
(Phase I, II, III, Male Res.
Ages: 16 and over)

Teen Challenge
of the Cumberlands
P.O. Box 1156
Cookeville, TN 38501
Director: Howard Eads
615/526-2103
(Phase I, II, Crisis Center)

Teen Challenge of Memphis
P.O. Box 22363
2114 Union Ave.
Memphis, TN 38122
Director: Jack Dennis
901/725-1769
(Phase I, II, Male Res.)

Teen Challenge of Nashville
P.O. Box 23281
Nashville, TN 37202
OFFICE: 121, 21st Ave. N.
Suite 404
Nashville, TN 37203
Executive Director:
David Finto
615/327-4357
(Phase I, II, III)

Girls' Residence
721 Old Hickory Blvd.
Madison, TN 37115
Director: Nancy Alcorn
615/868-0786

PROJECT 714
Box 8936
Chattanooga, TN 37411-9036
Director: Jimmy Lee
615/821-0385

Teen Challenge
of Cleveland
P.O. Box 3811
Cleveland, TN 37311
Director: Basil Adams
615/476-6627

TEXAS (North)
Dallas Teen Challenge
P.O. Box 26112
Dallas, TX 75226
Executive Director:
Paul Ecker
214/824-6181
(Phase I, II, III, IV
Male Res.)

Dallas Teen Challenge
Ranch
Rt. 4 Box 215-C-1
Winnsboro, TX 75494
Administrator: Jerry Holley
214/866-2463 or 866-2318
Ages: Juveniles 16-17

Teen Challenge
of Fort Worth
P.O. Box 731
747 Samuels Ave.
Fort Worth, TX 76101
Director: Larry Adley
817/336-8191
(Phase I, II, III, IV,
Female Res.
Ages: 18 and over)

TEXAS (South)
Houston Teen Challenge
Houston Intake Office
713/342-9505
Director: David Kirschke

Training Center
Box 134
Hungerford, TX 77448
(Phase I, II, III, IV,
Male and Female Res.
Ages: 18 and over)

Westwood Farms
Rt. 3 Box 61, Farm Rd. 536
Floresville, TX 78114
Executive Director:
James Terry
512/393-6762
(Phase I, II, III, IV,
Male Res.
Ages: Juveniles 14-17)

TEXAS (West)
Teen Challenge
of West Texas
P.O. Box 1738   79949
2200 San Jose
El Paso, TX 79930
Director: Gary Carnie
915/565-0300 or 566-8161
(Phase I, II, III, V,
Female Res.
Ages: 18 and over)

Teen Challenge of Amarillo
P.O. Box 508
(1718 S. Polk)
Amarillo, TX 79105
Director: Bob Dunstan
806/372-1953
(Phase I, II, III, IV,
Male Res.
Ages: 18 and over)

West Texas Teen Challenge
P.O. BOX 251
201 N. "C" Street
Midland, TX 79702
Director: Charles Redger
915/682-3244
(Phase I, II, III, Male Res.
Ages: 18 and over)

VIRGINIA
Teen Challenge of Tidewater
Mailing: P.O. Box 4619
Virginia Beach, VA 23454
925 Ingleside Road
Norfolk, VA 23502
Director: Emory DeBusk
804/461-6312

WASHINGTON
Northwest Teen Challenge
P.O. Box 9103   98109
1808 18th Ave.
Seattle, WA 98122
Director: Orville L. Danielson
206/324-3560
(Phase I, II, III, IV, V,
Male and Female Res.
Ages: 18 and over)

Teen Challenge
Box 1302
Weisgerber Bldg.
#410, Fifth & Main
Lewiston, ID 83501
Director: Tom White
208/746-3084
(Phase I, II)

WEST VIRGINIA
Teen Challenge
for New Life, Inc.
P.O. Box 6115
Wheeling, WV 26003
304/232-3777

A Final Challenge
From the Author

"**Provoke one another to agape love and to good works**" **Hebrews 10:24.**

I wholeheartedly invite you to write me and share your comments and criticisms with me. If you can add to the list of changed-life testimony books, tracts, films, cassettes, tract societies, or if there are areas this book fails to touch upon that it should have, please do write me. YOU CAN MAKE THE NEXT EDITION OF TAKE HIM TO THE STREETS better!

Our teams travel throughout the country helping local believers and churches take Him to their streets. We would like to help you open a Stret-Outreach in your area, if it needs one. If so, contact us. I would also like you to keep me informed as to whether this book helps you in your personal soulwinning, or in opening a street-outreach.

Isaiah wrote: "**The Spirit of the Lord is upon me, for He hath anointed me to preach the Good News, to bind up the broken**" **Isaiah 61:1.**

A house guest once asked the host's young daughter what her favorite doll was, out of the vast array of dolls decorating her room. The little girl replied: "This one," and then picked up a broken doll with a ragged dress half on, a broken leg, and one arm missing. The guest was very surprised, and asked her why. She quickly replied: "Sir . . . you see . . . if I don't love this broken doll, well . . . then . . . nobody will."

YOU CAN HELP US REACH THE BROKEN YOUTH OF OUR COUNTRY. Please help us locate and share with others the names of street ministries, Christian live-in communities, drug rehabilitation and drug abuse programs, Christian telephone "hotlines," tracts, cassettes, books, and specialized ministries. Working together as unified, coordinated God-glorifying Christians should be, we can help turn our generation back to the life-changing, sin-forgiving, satan-conquering, demon-dominating Gospel of our Father, and our Lord and Savior Jesus Christ!

Thank you for your prayers and assistance! My prayer is that God bless and use you more effectively with each passing day . . . for "the night is coming when no man can work" John 9:4.

I'm looking forward to hearing from and working with you in taking Him to the streets of our world.

Jonathan Gainsbrugh
P.O. Box P-1
Felton, CA 95018

Some ways you can help us take Jesus to every "strip," pool room, rock concert, bar, park and hangout in America:

☐ I will pray daily for WFC.
☐ I will ask local prayer intercession groups to pray for you.
☐ I've enclosed a love-gift of $ _____ to help you keep helping others!
☐ Count me in as a regular Worldshaker partner. As God enables me, I'll send $_____/mo. to help you in America.
☐ I'm interested in having you speak at our church. I have spoken to my pastor and shown him your book. He said to contact him:

_____ your name
_____ your address
_____ state & zip
_____ pastor's name
_____ church name
_____ mailing address
_____ state & zip
_____ phone number _____ church phone

☐ I would like to see our church's mission board include you in their giving. Please send me your packet of appropriate materials to give them.
☐ To help you with your book, "Take Him To The Bars" I have enclosed adventures and ideas for bar ministry that I've used or heard of others using.
☐ To help your "National Street-Ministry Directory," I've gathered and enclosed names and information on other coffeehouses, street ministries, live-in houses, hot-lines, street preachers, and Christian drug-abuse programs that I know of.
☐ I believe in your idea for the National Christian Resource Center on pages 220-223 in your book. I've enclosed name of materials, ministries and manpower (those who used to be into any of those specific sins) dealing with some of the specific sin areas mentioned in your list.

Additional WFC Tools To Help TAKE Jesus' Love To Your Streets:
FREE MATERIALS:
☐ Please add me to your monthly newsletter mailing list.
☐ Add the enclosed names of my concerned Christian friends to your mailing list.
☐ Please send me _____ copies of your newsletter to distribute to my Sunday school class, church mission board, friends, etc.

☐ Please send me free tract samples. I have enclosed a self-addressed, stamped envelope.

☐ Please send me tract-reprinting information sheet.

☐ Please send information on your "Anytown" slide program, to help interest my church and community in starting and supporting a local street Outreach here.

☐ Please send me information and application for your upcoming National Street Ministry Workshops.

☐ Please send information on WSU (Worldshaker Street University).

☐ Please send a copy of "The Rainbow's End" brochure.

☐ Please send a list and prices of cassette and videotape materials.

MISCELLANEOUS WFC STREET MINISTRY TOOLS AVAILABLE FOR PURCHASE

$_____ Please send _____ copies of your National Street Directory ($8.95 each), listing over 1800 street ministries across the USA by state and category within each state.

$_____ Please send _____ copies of your 400-pg. Street Ministry Workbook and 5 C-90 cassette series (availabe together only). $75.00 complete set.

$_____ Please send your complete "Anytown" slide program, script and cassette. $50.00

WFC TRACTS (Avail. in 100's)

_____ High Times (pot-leaf)

_____ The Dealer (pot-leaf)

_____ Backstage Pass

_____ Transformed

_____ The Rebel (pot-leaf)

_____ Just for Fun (occult, pot-leaf)

_____ Don't Read This (satanism)

_____ Dream that Wouldn't Die (JG's testimony)

_____ All-Star Rock 'n Roll Band

_____ Beat that Testimony

Amount enclosed for tracts: Total no. of 100's ordered X $3/100

$ _____   _____

SPECIAL BULK DISCOUNT FOR LARGE TRACT ORDERS:

100-900 $3/100   10,000-29,900 $1.50/100
1,000-4,900 $2.50/100   30,00 or more $1/100
5,000-9,900 $2/100

Write: WFC, Box P-1, Felton, CA 95018

MORE FAITH-BUILDING BOOKS
FROM HUNTINGTON HOUSE

The Agony of Deception, by Ron Rigsbee. This is the story of a young man who through surgery became a woman and now, through the grace of God, is a man again. Share this heartwarming story of a young man as he struggles through the deception of an altered life-style only to find hope and deliverance in the Grace of God.

America Betrayed, by Marlin Maddoux. This book presents stunning facts on how the people of the United States have been brainwashed. This hard-hitting new book exposes the forces in our country which seek to destroy the family, the schools and our values. Maddoux is a well-known radio journalist and host of "Point of View."

Backward Masking Unmasked — Backward Satanic Messages of Rock and Roll Exposed, by Jacob Aranza. Are rock and roll stars using the technique of backward masking to implant their own religious and moral values into the minds of young people? Are these messages satanic, drug-related and filled with sexual immorality? Jacob Aranza answers these and other questions.

Close Calls, by Don Garlits. Many times "Big Daddy" Don Garlits has escaped death — both on and off the drag racing track. This is the story of drag racing's most famous and popular driver in history. Share his trials and triumphs and the miracle of God's grace in his heart.

The Divine Connection, by Dr. Donald Whitaker. This is a Christian Guide to Life Extension. It specifies biblical principles for how to feel better and live longer.

Globalism: America's Demise, by William Bowen, Jr. A national best-seller, this book warns us about the globalists — some of the most powerful people on earth — and their plans to totally eliminate God, the family and the United States as we know it today. Globalism is the vehicle the humanists are using to implement their secular humanistic philosophy to bring about their one-world government.

God's Timetable for the 1980's, by Dr. David Webber. This book presents the end-time scenario as revealed in God's Word and carefully explained by Dr. Webber, the Radio Pastor of the highly acclaimed Southwest Radio Church. This timely book deals with a wide spectrum of subjects including the dangers of the New Age Movement, end-time weather changes, robots and biocomputers in prophecy.

The Hidden Dangers of the Rainbow, by Constance Cumbey. This #1 National Bestseller was the first book to fully expose the New Age Movement. The Movement's goal is to set up a one-world order under the leadership of a false messiah.

Murdered Heiress . . . Living Witness, by Dr. Petti Wagner. This is the story of Dr. Petti Wagner — heiress to a large fortune — who was kidnapped and murdered for her wealth, yet through a miracle of God lives today.

A Reasonable Reason to Wait, by Jacob Aranza. God speaks specifically about premarital sex, according to Aranza. The Bible also provides a healing message for those who have already been sexually involved before marriage.

Rest From the Quest, by Elissa Lindsey McClain. This is the candid account of a former New Ager who spent the first 29 years of her life in the New Age Movement, the occult and Eastern Mysticism. This is an incredible inside look at what really goes on in the New Age Movement.

The Twisted Cross, by Joseph Carr. One of the most important works of our decade, **The Twisted Cross** clearly documents the occult and demonic influence on Adolph Hitler and the Third Reich which led to the holocaust killing of more than six million Jews.

Who Will Rise UP? by Jed Smock. This is the incredible — and sometimes hilarious — story of Jed Smock who, with his wife Cindy, has preached the uncompromising Gospel in the malls and lawns of hundreds of university campuses throughout this land. They have been mocked, rocked, mobbed, beaten, jailed, cursed and ridiculed. Yet this former university professor and his wife have seen the miracle-working power of God transform thousands of lives on the university campuses.

Yes, send me the following books:

_____ copy (copies) of **The Agony Of Deception** @ $6.95   = _____
_____ copy (copies) of **America Betrayed** @ $5.95   = _____
_____ copy (copies) of **Backward Masking Unmasked** @ $4.95   = _____
_____ copy (copies) of **Backward Masking Unmasked Cassette Tape** @ $5.95   = _____
_____ copy (copies) of **Close Calls** @ $6.95   = _____
_____ copy (copies) of **The Divine Connection** @ $4.95   = _____
_____ copy (copies) of **Globalism: America's Demise** @ $6.95   = _____
_____ copy (copies) of **God's Timetable For The 1980's** @ $5.95   = _____
_____ copy (copies) of **The Hidden Dangers Of The Rainbow** @ $5.95   = _____
_____ copy (copies) of **Murdered Heiress Living Witness** @ $5.95   = _____
_____ copy (copies) of **A Reasonable Reason To Wait** @ $4.95   = _____
_____ copy (copies) of **Rest From The Quest** @ $5.95   = _____
_____ copy (copies) of **Take Him To The Streets** @ $5.95   = _____
_____ copy (copies) of **The Twisted Cross** @ $7.95   = _____
_____ copy (copies) of **Who Will Rise UP** @ $5.95   = _____

At bookstores everywhere or order direct from: Huntington House, Inc., P.O. Box 53788, Lafayette, LA 70505.

Send check/money order or for faster service VISA/Mastercard orders call toll-free 1-800-572-8213. Add: Freight and handling, $1.00 for the first book ordered, 50¢ for each additional book.
Enclosed is $ _____ including Postage.

Name _____

Address _____

City _____ State and Zip _____